The Spirit of Smithian Laws

The Spirit of Smithian Laws discusses Adam Smith's ethics. His impartial-spectator process is a dynamic call upward, enabling one to better sustain his or her locus of affirmation, to better cohere as a just human being. The puzzle is always: Wherein lies *better*? Which way is *up*? Smith's approach to the puzzle runs against foundationalism. His ethical thought is here called *beholderism*. It is organized by organons, chief of which is the notion of a beholder who is God or who is God-like in knowledge and universal benevolence (if not more). The chapters are:

About the author:
Daniel Klein is professor of economics and JIN Chair at the Mercatus Center at George Mason University, where, with Erik Matson and Don Boudreaux, he leads a program in Adam Smith. He is also research fellow at the Ratio Institute (Stockholm) and chief editor of *Econ Journal Watch*. With Matson, he is also codirector of CL Press and the monthly feature *Just Sentiments* at Libertarianism.org.

Eight testimonials for Dan Klein scholarship on Adam Smith

Richard Whatmore, Professor and Chair of Modern History, University of St. Andrews, editor of *History of European Ideas*, and Co-direct of St. Andrews Institute of Intellectual History:

> "In 2023 Adam Smith will be 300 years old. There will be a very large number of ill-informed books about him being published in this special year. Smith—now that we are recovering the actual historical Smith—still has a great deal to say to us. Dan Klein knows this, understands Smith as well as any scholar and has a gift for communicating (understatement). Everything he publishes is accessible and significant. It is also worth saying that his public presence is remarkable and remarkably wide-ranging. He reaches audiences fellow academics simply cannot reach."

Deirdre Nansen McCloskey, Distinguished Professor Emerita of Economics and of History, and Professor Emerita of English and of Communication, adjunct in classics and philosophy, at the University of Illinois at Chicago:

> "Klein is the rare economist who listens to what others say. In this he follows Smith, and with these volumes emerges as the sage's leading listener. He writes beautifully and with purpose, to bring us away from the Smith of left or right coercion and towards the Smith of what he calls "spiral," a vein of the Scottish enlightenment, and still therapeutic for our own troubled times."

Knud Haakonssen, Long-term Fellow at the Max Weber Centre for Advanced Cultural and Social Studies, University of Erfurt, Professor of Intellectual History, University of St. Andrews and Co-direct of St. Andrews Institute of Intellectual History, and General Editor of the Liberty Fund book series Natural Law and Enlightenment Classics.

> "Dan Klein's collection of papers represents an imposing body of work on Smith as an historical figure and as thinker of lasting relevance. The papers have an impressive range, which is

what Smith's many-sided work requires. At the same time, there is a keen engagement with the scholarly and critical literature. Klein's writing is clear and direct. It is a pleasure to recommend the collection."

Vernon Smith, Nobel laureate in Economics and Professor, Smith Institute for Political Economy and Philosophy, Chapman University:

"Three centuries after his birth, Adam Smith was never more relevant and inspiring. Dan Klein's essays convey that inspiration in an accessible style reinforcing the relevance of this greatest of 18th century scholars."

Thomas W. Merrill, Associate Professor, Department of Government, American University, Director of Special Programs at the Political Theory Institute, American University:

"Dan Klein has long been constructing a portrait of Adam Smith in his complexity—moving back and forth in a deepening spiral between Smith's policy recommendations, his rich phenomenology of ethical life, and even his reflections on our place in the cosmos. With this collection we can now see the richness of Klein's reading of Smith in synoptic view, both in the specificity of its parts and in the vision that animates the whole. Klein is a spirited and skilled advocate for liberalism in its original political sense. He sheds light on the presumption of liberty, the structure of justice, the spiraling complexity of ethical life, the subtlety of Smith's rhetoric, and Smith's religion. This work will be helpful to readers just coming to know Smith for the first time, and it certainly deserves the attention of scholars of Smith and of the history of liberalism. It enriches our sense of Smith even as we argue with it. It is an achievement worth celebrating."

Douglas Den Uyl, Vice President of Educational Programs, Liberty Fund:

> "Dan Klein is one of the most distinctive and thorough interpreters of Adam Smith working today. His insights into Smith are both instructive and compelling. It is of immense value to have many of these insights collected together, especially because so many of them are accessible to the scholar and general intelligent reader alike."

Peter Minowitz, Professor of Political Science, Santa Clara University and author of *Profits, Priests, and Princes: Adam Smith's Emancipation of Economics from Politics and Religion*:

> "An economist with abiding interests in public policy, Klein has developed an acute appreciation of how carefully Adam Smith wrote—and of how comprehensively he thought. Klein manifests a rare combination of virtues, and they are especially valuable in our world, which struggles to balance economic and non-economic goods. The precision and efficiency of Klein's prose, furthermore, provide a fitting tribute to Smith. More importantly, they should inspire—and even equip—us to counteract the literary degradations associated with tweeting and partisan hyperbole."

James Otteson, Professor of Business Ethics, University of Notre Dame, and author of *Adam Smith's Marketplace of Life* (Cambridge, 2002), *Actual Ethics* (Cambridge, 2006), *Adam Smith* (Bloomsbury, 2013), *The End of Socialism* (Cambridge, 2014), *Honorable Business: A Framework for Business in a Just and Humane Society* (Oxford, 2019):

> "Adam Smith is one of the most widely cited and least read great figures in the West. He is often pressed into the service of contemporary authors' ends without sufficient regard for the breadth, depth, subtlety, and sophistication of his work. Daniel Klein's essays provide an important corrective. Klein combines close reading of Smith with a critical yet charitable eye, helping us understand both the details in Smith's work and its larger

aims, and, in the process, showing why Smith deserves a place in the pantheon of great philosophers. Those new to Smith may be astonished at the range and penetration of Smith's insights revealed by Klein's essays. Even Smith scholars will find much that is new, enlightening, and challenging. This collection provides a rich resource for philosophers, economists, historians, and anyone else interested in one of the great observers of human behavior."

The Spirit of
Smithian Laws

Daniel B. Klein

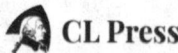
CL Press

Published by CL PRESS
A project of the Fraser Institute
1770 Burrard Street, 4th Floor
Vancouver, BC V6J 3G7 Canada
www.clpress.net

The Spirit of Smithian Laws
Daniel B. Klein

© 2025 by CL Press
Corrected, 23 August 2025 and again 23 September 2025 and again 25 October 2025

ISBN: 978-1-957698-04-5

Cover design by John Stephens
Interior layout by Joanna Andreasson

Contents

Contents

Preface

An author's motives for writing a book are nearly as mysterious to him as to the reader, maybe more so. My hope is that this book is, on the whole, useful or agreeable and thus a plus for beneficialness in the eyes of God/Joy. I don't claim any beneficence; the main motive "is not that feeble spark of benevolence which Nature has lighted up in the human heart" (TMS 137.4). I hope my wares are beneficial, like plain yogurt for sale at the grocery store, because I wish to avoid the disapproval of the man within the breast. As for you, I, like the good grocer, offer mere goodwill.

This book is one of three by me about Adam Smith:

1. *Central Notions of Smithian Liberalism*: I (and sometimes coauthors) treat Adam Smith and the liberalism he shared with David Hume and Edmund Burke. I explore notions jural, political, and economic, though others as well. I use Smith and others to develop classical liberalism.

2. *The Spirit of Smithian Laws*: I (and sometimes coauthors) treat notions central to Smith's allego-theistic moral approach—the dialectics of virtue, propriety, beneficialness, sentiment, sympathy, and "impartial spectator." I exposit the organons that organize Smith's thought.

   Poor Richard (Franklin 1914, 13) said, "An empty bag cannot stand upright." The remark helps explain a difference between the two books. *Central Notions of Smithian Liberalism* treats things that make Smithian thought stand upright. It treats things *inside the bag*—notably, the staples of Smith's conservative liberalism.

   The present book, however, *The Spirit of Smithian*

2 THE SPIRIT OF SMITHIAN LAWS

Laws, is more about the bag itself. Aspects of the bag—how we think—will affect how things inside the bag—what we think—sit together. There is the bag's fabric—it matters whether the bag is of silk, burlap, suede, or toughened leather, or some combination. And there is the design of the bag itself, which will affect the ordering it lends to things inside of it. Montaigne said that "ill-matched objects, put in a bag without order, find of themselves a way to unite and fall into place, often better than they could have been arranged by art" (1960, 730). But it depends on the bag—not all bags are alike. *The Spirit of Smithian Laws* delves into allegory, organonic formulations, nonfoundationalism, and Smith's esotericism. A motif is "spiral"—the emblem of nonfoundationalism. The main theme, which implies spirals, is beholderism.

To some extent, the distinction between the bag itself and the things within it corresponds to non-political and political. Our differences in politics pertain greatly to things within the bag. But the bag itself—how we think—is not wholly separable from politics. Again, the material and design of the bag matters. Not all bags are alike, and our political sensibilities play some role in determining which bag one sports. Still, bag-itself corresponds somewhat to non-political. The bag of choice will permit one to organize and carry considerably different sets of political staples. I personally find that the bag promoted here accommodates my conservative-liberal, anti-governmentalization sensibilities.

But the bag promoted here can serve other political outlooks. It might even be well-suited to doing so. Indeed, nonfoundationalism is often associated with 'postmodernism' and philosophical pragmatism, which are often associated with leftism. Of the three books, this one is least political.

3. *Smithian Morals* contains lighter pieces, deriving from essays in media such as Liberty Fund's Adam Smith Works. The book is shorter and contains 28 chapters.

The chapters of most of the three books were originally written in the style of the stand-alone essay.

In the present book, most of the chapters are long. Abstracts appear before Chapter 1. Chapter 1 provides an initiation to the main themes. In gathering material here, I have reduced repetitiveness and worked somewhat toward an integrated book, but the main style remains the stand-alone essay. I hope the reader can excuse the repetitiveness that remains.

The quotation-mark policy I've tried to maintain in the book: Double for genuine quotations (whether cited or merely citable) and single ('inverted commas') for air-quotes and for quotes within quotes.

Acknowledgments

I thank coauthors on three of the chapters, Erik Matson, Colin Doran, and Brandon Lucas. I am very grateful to Jane Shaw Stroup who copy-edited and formatted the final manuscript and to Jon Murphy for proof-reading. I thank Joanna Andreasson for layout and typesetting the interior, and John Stephens for designing the cover.

Of the eleven chapters here, nine derive from a piece in a scholarly journal or edited volume:

1. Chapter 1, "Major Themes and Ambling through a Few Spirals," is not based on something previously published.

2. Chapter 2, "Who Is Adam Smith's Impartial Spectator?," derives from "The Man within the Breast, the Supreme Impartial Spectator, and Other Impartial Spectators in Adam Smith's *The Theory of Moral Sentiments*," by Daniel B. Klein, Erik W. Matson, and Colin Doran. *History of European Ideas* 44(8), 2018: 1153–1168. That journal is published by Taylor & Francis.

3. Chapter 3, "Beholderism: In Praise of Adam Smith's Organon and Allegory," is not based on something previously published.

4. Chapter 4, "Hume and Smith on Utility, Agreeableness, Propriety, and Moral Approval," derives from a piece with the same title by Erik W. Matson, Colin Doran, and Daniel B. Klein, *History of European Ideas*, 45(5), 2019: 675–704. That journal is published by Taylor & Francis.

5. Chapter 5, "Adam Smith's Nonfoundationalism," derives from: "Adam Smith's Non-foundationalism." *Society* 183, 2021: 861–873. That journal is published by Springer.

6. Chapter 6, "Ought Is an Is regarding What Is Owed to God/ Joy: On the Positive-Normative Distinction," derives from: "Ought as an Is: On the Positive-Normative Distinction,"

Studies in Emergent Order 7, 2014: 56-73. That journal has evolved into *Cosmos + Taxis*, which holds copyright.

7. Chapter 7, "The Circumstantiality of Bivariate Relationships in TMS," derives from "The Circumstantiality of Bivariate Relationships in Adam Smith's *The Theory of Moral Sentiments*," *Research in the History of Economic Thought and Methodology* 41A, 2023: 59–78. That journal is published by Emerald Publishing Group.

8. Chapter 8, "In a Word or Two, Placed in the Middle" derives from "In a Word or Two, Placed in the Middle: The Invisible Hand in Adam Smith's Tomes," by Daniel B. Klein and Brandon Lucas, *Economic Affairs* 31(1), March 2011: 43–52. That journal is published by Wiley.

9. Chapter 9, "Smith's Attitude toward Rousseau," derives from a review essay (untitled) of a book by Dennis Rasmussen, published in *The Adam Smith Review* 7, 2014: 323-329. That journal is published by Routledge.

10. Chapter 10, "TMS's Appeal Moves with Openness to Non-foundationalism: 35 Critics, 1765–1949," derives loosely from "Dissing *The Theory of Moral Sentiments*: Twenty-Six Critics, from 1765 to 1949," *Econ Journal Watch* 15(2), 2018: 201-254. That journal is published by the Fraser Institute.

11. Chapter 11, "Circa 1800," derives very loosely from "Dissing *The Theory of Moral Sentiments*: Twenty-Six Critics, from 1765 to 1949," *Econ Journal Watch* 15(2), 2018: 201-254. That journal is published by the Fraser Institute.

I am grateful to the editors, referees, journals, and publishers listed above for their assistance is the development of these ideas by coauthors and myself. Many of the articles from which chapters here derive contain acknowledgments to individuals who aided with that article, and, without naming them here, I once again thank them.

Citing Works by Adam Smith and David Hume

Adam Smith's works:

TMS 263.5 means page 263, paragraph 5 of *The Theory of Moral Sentiments*. Citations to Smith's works are to the Glasgow Edition, published by Oxford University Press and republished by Liberty Fund. The abbreviations are as follows:

TMS—*The Theory of Moral Sentiments*
WN—*The Wealth of Nations*
EPS—*Essays on Philosophical Subjects*
LJ—*Lectures on Jurisprudence*
LRBL—*Lectures on Rhetoric and Belles Lettres*
Corr.—*The Correspondence of Adam Smith*

David Hume's works:

T—*A Treatise of Human Nature* (Hume 2007a [1739–1740]), followed by book, part, section, and paragraph number.

DP—*A Dissertation on the Passions* (Hume 2007b [1757]), followed by chapter and paragraph.

EHU—*An Enquiry Concerning Human Understanding* (Hume 2000 [1748]), followed by section, part, and paragraph number.

EPM—*An Enquiry Concerning the Principles of Morals* (Hume 1998 [1751]), followed by section, part, and paragraph number. Sections without parts in EHU and EPM are referred to by section and paragraph.

EMPL—*Essays, Moral, Political, and Literary* (Hume 1994), followed by page number.

H—*The History of England* (Hume 1983), followed by volume (in roman numerals) and page number.

Chapter Abstracts

Chapter 1:   Major Themes and Ambling through a Few Spirals

The Introduction has the following sections: (1) A Social Grammar; (2) The Three Justices: Commutative, Distributive, and Estimative; (3) The Liberal Program; (4) *The Theory of Moral Sentiments*; (5) Think Spiral; (6) The Correspondence between the Two Goods; (7) As Rivers Are Lost in the Sea; (8) An Empty Bag Does Not Stand Upright.

Chapter 2:   Who Is Adam Smith's Impartial Spectator?
Coauthors: Erik W. Matson, Colin Doran

In TMS, Adam Smith frequently uses the term "impartial spectator." It is infused with a plexus of related meanings, one of which is a super-being, which normally would aptly take the definite article *the*, and which bears parallels to ideas of a monotheistic God. As for any genuine, identified, human spectator of an incident, he can be deemed impartial only presumptively. Furthermore, his presumptive impartiality regarding the incident does not of itself carry extensive implications about his intelligence, nor about his being aligned with benevolence toward any larger whole. We may posit, however, a being who is impartial, and also posit that she holds higher levels of intelligence, and of benevolence, and then converse over what her sentiments would be about the matter under discussion. It is natural for people to conceive of a being who is unsurpassed and unsurpassable in such qualities, who is morally supreme, like monotheistic notions of God, and who naturally takes the definite article *the* without having been definitized by the writer (because unnecessary, just as we speak of "the world"). Signal passages in TMS, new to Ed. 6, suggest that Smith formulates the man within the breast as a *representative* of the always present and everywhere morally supreme impartial spectator. When Smith speaks of the man within the breast as "the supposed impartial spectator" (all new to Ed. 6), we interpret "supposed" as *sup-pos-ed* (purported), not *sup-pos'd* (posited). An Excel file collects all passages for key terms and codes all cases of "impartial spectator."

Chapter 3:   Beholderism: In Praise of Adam Smith's Organon and Allegory

I explain two features of Adam Smith's ethical thought, Smith's organon and Smithian allegory. Smith's organon is that every moral sentiment relates to a sympathy—that is, for any moral sentiment that a person has, there is another being who shares that sentiment as a 'fellow-feeling;' there is a sort of communion behind any moral sentiment. Smithian allegory is not singular, but it begins with a single master allegory, that good corresponds to pleasing to the supreme benevolent beholder of the whole. This paper argues that Smith's organon and Smithian allegory are good. Each feature deserves some praise in isolation but becomes praiseworthy especially for what it makes possible in combination with the other feature.

Chapter 4:   Hume and Smith on Utility, Agreeableness, Propriety, and Moral Approval
               Coauthors: Erik W. Matson, Colin Doran

We ambitiously reexamine Smith's moral theory in relation to Hume's. We regard Smith's developments as glorious and important. We also see them as quite fully agreeable to Hume, as enhancement, not departure. But Smith represents matters otherwise! Why would Smith *overstate* disagreement with his best friend?

One aspect of Smith's enhancement, an aspect he makes very conspicuous, is that between moral approval and beneficialness ("utility" in Smith) there is another phase, namely, the moral judge's *sense of propriety.* With that phase now finding formulation, Smith, if only implicitly, generates *a spiral* of beneficialness and propriety, a spiral shown in Figure 4.7. We consider Figure 4.7, illustrating the spiral, to be the most important arrival point in the chapter; it highlights the *nonfoundationalism* of Smith's ethics. But to arrive at the spiral, we must engage in extensive exegesis.

In Part IV of *The Theory of Moral Sentiments,* Smith presents a foil against which he develops his own theory, a foil supposedly representing Hume. According to the foil, moral approval derives from "utility." But, in multiple ways, the foil is misleading. We provide an interpretation of Hume, notably his four-factor account of moral approval, before examining Smith's representation of Hume.

One twist is that Smith used the words *utility* and *useful* differently than Hume did—Smith quietly stretched them to include species of agreeableness, thereby obscuring the importance of agreeableness in Hume's theory.

Another, more significant problem is that Smith allows the impression that in Hume moral approval derives quite determinately from beneficialness. In fact, Hume conveys the interpretive and sentimental spaciousness of the operations that generate moral approval; here, Hume even speaks repeatedly of "proper sentiments," thus almost using the term *propriety* himself.

But the propriety phase in Smith opens up to a key facet of Smith's development on Hume: He poeticizes a *locus of sympathy* not emphasized in Hume—namely, that between the moral judge and her own man within the breast; that locus enters the theory in addition to the sympathies emphasized in Hume, not in lieu of them. We distinguish lateral sympathy, which is important in Hume's thought, and vertical sympathy, which is especially characteristic of Smith's more inner-directed and allegorical thought. Smith embraces Hume's lateral sympathy and enhances moral theory by adding formulations ("the man within the breast," "the impartial spectator") that elaborate vertical sympathy.

Next, we come to something of a twist in the whole matter: We show that—as Smith well knew all along!—propriety is a species of agreeableness! Smith's propriety phase represents another dimension within which such agreeableness lives: Smith's vertical dimension thus gives rise to a spiral representing the diachronic development of the judge herself. It is a spiral of beneficialness and propriety: Each propriety phase in the next loop of the spiral engenders a species of agreeableness *now as a part of beneficialness.*

Smith's developments on Hume, then, involve the following three facets: (1) formulation of the propriety phase; (2) the poetic elaboration of vertical sympathy; (3) the diachronic spiral of propriety and beneficialness.

The three facets come together, especially in Ed. 6 of *The Theory of Moral Sentiments.* The whole development goes beyond Hume, but, really, is agreeable to Hume—though Smith himself portrays his developments as *disagreeing* with features of Hume's moral theory.

We speculate that Smith was more or less aware of all that that we say, including the absence of any really substantive disagreement. Why, in that case, would Smith have proceeded as he did? We address that question at the end of the piece. Our speculations suggest a method in the madness.

Chapter 5:   Adam Smith's Nonfoundationalism

The original version of this chapter was part of a symposium (in *Society*) on a target article by Amitai Etzioni. Using that article as a point of departure, I elaborate a reading of Adam Smith's moral philosophy that sees it as quite nonfoundationalist. Whereas foundationalism's metaphor is a block or pillar, as nonfoundationalism's metaphor I suggest a spiral. I claim that nonfoundationalism and Smithian liberalism dovetail.

Chapter 6:   Ought Is an Is regarding What Is Owed to God/Joy: On the Positive-Normative Distinction

It is common for those who affirm positive-normative talk to do so on the basis of a distinction between *is* and *ought*. But does distinguishing between *is* and *ought* make for an important, useful distinction? Are *ought* sentences, as a category, so different from *is* sentences? Here I suggest that: (1) it is easy to recast any *ought* sentence as an *is* sentence, and vice versa; (2) every *is* sentence can be understood as conveying tacit "oughts;" (3) every *ought* can be understood as an *is*—*ought* is a statement regarding what *is* owed. I invite the reader to consider whether positive-normative talk might be for her, as it is for me, an alternative that is always and everywhere dominated by some other alternative and hence something she ought to learn to expunge from her active vocabulary.

Chapter 7:   The Circumstantiality of Bivariate Relationships in TMS

In *Theory of Moral Sentiments*, Adam Smith reasons about how a change in one thing, *A*, is attended by a change in another thing, *B*. In expounding on such bivariate relationships, Smith sometimes seems to go out of his way to posit a state of the world in which the relationship would break down. That feature suggests an irony about knowing how a change in *B* attends a change in *A*. We might think we understand the bivariate relationship, but it holds only for certain states of the world. The relationship is circumstanced. The more one studies TMS, the more one realizes that circumstantiality suffuses its teachings. My discussion arrives at a place of doubt about the most important bivariate relationship—that between approval from our conscience and doing good. Smith seems to suggest, particularly at the end of his life, that a person can best know the relationship between his conscience's approval and his doing good under the circumstances of his having frank and open friendships. The implication for politics is that we want that kind of government that best conduces to frank and open friendships.

Chapter 8:   In a Word or Two, Placed in the Middle
            Coauthor: Brandon Lucas

We contemplate Adam Smith's intentionality in locating his famous phrase about intentionality, the 6-gram "led by an invisible hand to." The four most significant considerations are: (1) The physical evidence: The 6-gram occurs pretty much dead center of the 1st and 2nd editions of WN and of the final edition of TMS. The physical centrality in TMS has gone little noticed partly because the standard edition omits Smith's language-essay appendix. The expression in WN drifted only a bit from the center, only about 5 percent from the center in the final edition, and even less if the index is excluded. (2) The rhetoric lectures show that he not only was conscious of intentional placement of potent words at the center, but thought it significant enough to remark on to his pupils, noting that Thucydides "often expresses all that he labours so much in a word or two, sometimes placed in the middle of the narration." (3) In WN, "spectator" appears only twice: in the second paragraph of the first chapter and in the antepenultimate paragraph of the last chapter; that "spectator" bookending in WN suggests intentionality about the placement of key words in the entirety of the work. (4) The invisible hand paragraphs in TMS and WN both contend with Rousseau and hark back to the Rousseau passages that Smith had translated and provided in his 1756 article on literature. Furthermore, there are numerous and rich ways in which centrality and middle-ness hold special and positive significance in Smith's thought. It is natural to think that Smith might do something playful with his text, such as something that made posterity ponder whether the physical centrality of "invisible hand" was the art of an invisible hand.

Chapter 9:   Smith's Attitude toward Rousseau

The chapter is a review of Dennis C. Rasmussen's book, *The Problems and Promise of Commercial Society: Adam Smith's Response to Rousseau* (2008). The book superbly explains Rousseau's criticisms of commercial society and Smith's concern with and response to those criticisms. Rasmussen helps us appreciate that Smith took Rousseau seriously and implicitly used him as a foil, and that our understanding of Smith is greatly enriched by considering him in relation to Rousseau. My chief difference with Rasmussen is that I think he portrays Smith's attitude toward Rousseau as having been much more positive than it was. I contend, for example, that Smith's 1756 praise for Rousseau's dedication (of the *Discourse on Inequality*) to Geneva was satirical.

Chapter 10:   TMS's Appeal Moves with Openness to
               Nonfoundationalism: 35 Critics, 1765–1949

The appeal of *The Theory of Moral Sentiments* (TMS) has moved with openness to nonfoundationalism. That is, the more open people are to nonfoundationalism, the more they warm to TMS. This paper is devoted to providing evidence of that bivariate relationship. The paper stems from a 2018 article, "Dissing *The The-ory of Moral Sentiments*." I have pared down the quotations and added nine dissers. This paper evidences more pointedly that the appeal of TMS has moved with openness to nonfoundation-alism—though I do not mean to suggest that openness to non-foundationalism is the sole factor affecting TMS's appeal.

Chapter 11:   Circa 1800

What changed in culture and society circa 1800? The chapter quotes J.G.A. Pocock, Wayne C. Booth, Arthur Melzer, C.S. Lew-is and others on broad changes. They help us understand why TMS fell into oblivion circa 1800, why it long remained there, and how to recover the babies that were thrown out with the bathwater circa 1800.

CHAPTER 1

Major Themes and Ambling through a Few Spirals

In Europe, before the printing press, "the book" was the Bible. The author was God. The one true interpretation stemmed from the church and papal authority, in concert with the temporal powers. Jan Hus challenged that authority before the presses were ready to roll. Hus was burned at the stake in 1415. Religious deviance was like sedition or treason.

The printing press changed things dramatically. From about 1500 in the Christian West, one could try to distribute his or her interpretation of the world. Anyone could be an author, courting persecution, but persecutors could not always keep up with the presses, which often operated outside the realm. An author's interpretations could become a force, in a manner rather different than had been the case for Plato, Gratian (the 12th century author of the *Decretum*), Aquinas, Ockham, or Hus. Certain Christian moral intuitions about the individual soul and its dignity were going public in a new way (Siedentop 2014). Christendom was rocked by the printing press.

One important author was Hugo Grotius, who was sentenced to life imprisonment. After three years, he made his escape by hiding in a wooden chest.

Another, born 140 years after Grotius, in 1723, was Adam Smith, who never hid in a wooden chest but who kept some of his cards close to his vest. His interpretation of things wide and deep, concrete and abstract—his outlook—competes among other outlooks, offered by other authors. He built on the authors he loved most. We build on those we love most. Certain authors become for us authorities.

I presume that readers of this text have a budding or blooming love of Adam Smith. If we choose to let his interpretation guide us, it is good to sense its width and depth. We normally think of depth as an idea that extends downward into the ground. However, in sublime, profound, spiritual matters, depth is upward, in height. As Paul McCartney sang, "The deeper you go, the higher you fly. The higher you fly, the deeper you go." Deep thinkers are ones we look up to.

Today, in academia, pursuing a sense of reverence is unfashionable. But Michael Polanyi (1963) said: "We need reverence to perceive greatness, even as we need a telescope to observe spiral nebulae" (96). If greatness is what makes authorities and we need reverence to perceive greatness, then we need reverence as astronomers need telescopes. Reverence is a tool in the scientist's toolkit.

A Social Grammar

Once the printing press busted interpretation wide open, there were myriad blank pages to write on. With what shall one fill the page?

Previously, traditional life set a pretty clear plotline, and the church set the contours for the sublime and the beautiful. But now interpretations were becoming disjointed. Churches were multiple, and authors even more so. What church shall you be part of? What authors shall you take to heart? Whose program shall you get with? How shall you combine programs, to make your unique variation? What shall you fill your pages with?

Different programs competed. They even went to war, literally and literately. There was great upheaval, death, and destruction as people could not agree on how one ought to fill his or her page, including how to govern the filling of pages. Arthur Melzer tells what happened next:

> [E]arly modern thinkers...endeavored to find a form of politics that could do without such consensus. They deliberately set out to subvert traditional society and to replace it with a fundamentally new kind of social organization, one that would renounce the ever precarious attempt to define the truth about life's highest goods. Instead, it would unite men on the promise of preventing the most obvious and basic evils... Thus, by standing traditional society on its head, by openly switching the purpose and

moral basis of the state from our highest to our lowest end, they attempted to separate politics from the whole disputed sphere of morality and religion.... (2014, 171)

I would rephrase it thusly: As the Catholic Church increasingly declared its supremacy in spiritual matters, higher matters, the temporal powers increasingly worked to establish an integrated sovereignty in "lower" matters. There was a move among temporal rulers and the elites to ease up on leading, tending, and enforcing the higher things in life, and to focus more on defining and safeguarding the lower things. The refocusing on lower things expressed itself notably in jural theorizing, with Grotius a towering figure.

As the imagining of higher things was bust open by the printing press, and as the relations of the social world grew increasingly complex, the attitude of rulers and their advisors tended toward leaving the pursuit of higher things more to decentral action, including voluntary association, and, by implication, freer markets. For the proto-liberals like Grotius and Samuel Pufendorf, the point was not to abandon or forsake higher things, but rather to clarify, establish, and stabilize the lower things, so as to provide a good operating system for worthy human pursuits.

Jural theory and associated attitudes brought forward the conceptualization of a social grammar, and, as it were, textbooks in social grammar, such as Pufendorf's *The Whole Duty of Man according to the Law of Nature* (1673), the chief precept of the social grammar being: Don't mess with other people's stuff.

Grammar does not tell us how to fill the page. But the social grammar would tend to ensure that my filling of my page would not tangibly encroach on your filling of your page. We might agree and share fellowship and meaning in higher things. But, on the precept of not messing with one another's stuff, even if we do not agree on higher things, we could peacefully get on with our respective programs. If we wish to convert others to our understandings of higher things, we compete in the cultural market for higher things. You sell the pages you have written, and I sell the pages I have written. We compete freely and fairly in the marketplace of ideas.

A great paradox of liberal political theory is that the social grammar does not apply in the same way to the ruler, the governor. Indeed, what is distinctive to government is its institutionalizing of contraventions of a fundamental social grammar. An issue in liberal political theory is (or ought to be) how we establish and maintain other kinds of grammar in such contravenings of that most fundamental social grammar.

Three Justices: Commutative, Distributive, and Estimative

The justice which libertarians, classical liberals, and Adam Smith propound and flip around to formulate liberty is the grammar-like justice of not messing with other people's stuff, which Smith distinguishes as *commutative justice*. But we need more than commutative justice. What, after all, justifies an allegiance to commutative justice? Surely the justification for commutative justice is not again commutative justice. We must go beyond commutative.

To get justice right we need to go to a second justice but not merely that. We must step from one justice to not merely two but to three: The two other justices are distributive and estimative.

Smithian *distributive justice* is not to be confused with the welfare state or 'social justice.' Rather it is one's making a becoming use of what is one's own. Smith says it consists in proper beneficence. Robin adheres to distributive justice when Robin makes a becoming use of what is Robin's own.

Estimative justice is estimating objects properly. The objects for estimation include every object of consciousness. "Nature, by an absolute and uncontroulable necessity has determin'd us to judge as well as to breathe and feel" (Hume T 1.4.1.7).

From Robin's perspective, the objects include those that constitute other people's stuff, which commutative justice tells Robin not to mess with, and those constituting Robin's own stuff, which distributive justice tells Robin to make a becoming use of. But the objects also include objects that are neither Robin's stuff nor anyone else's stuff; they are unowned; they are partaken of by anyone. They are notions, images, ideas. One such object is Smith's liberal program. May we all do it justice. In political theorizing, the chief justice is estimative justice.

The Liberal Program

You wander into an outdoor amphitheater where you find a concert about to begin. You are handed a piece a paper on which is printed a list of the pieces to be performed. After hearing the cellists and violinists tune their instruments, you listen to the performances listed in the program. That sense of "program" is a good way to think of what Smith's moral and political outlook offered, *the liberal program*. (In Smith's time, the word *programme/program* was scarcely used. He used "the liberal plan," "the liberal system," "liberal principles.") As the Melzer quotation above suggests, the liberal program was forming prior to Smith.

Western civilization got more and more with the program. Such was a salient and distinctive tendency of Western civilization, for at least a couple of hundred years.

But since around 1880, not so much.

Back at the outdoor amphitheater, the program finishes up and the auditors depart and head home, carrying the printed program. Now at home, it leaves them without any definite part to play. That is the chief problem with the liberal program: What to fill the page with? A melody is for each to supply in his or her own way. (The point is ably treated by Monty Python, *Life of Brian*, "Yes, we're all individuals".)

Since 1880, the tendency of Western civilization has been to forsake the liberal program.

The word "liberal" did not have a political meaning until the 1770s. It acquired a political meaning for the first time, thanks in part to *The Wealth of Nations*. In one of the important passages establishing the political meaning, Smith speaks of "the liberal plan of equality, liberty and justice." It is the plan of "allowing every man to pursue his own interest his own way," and it is placed in contrast to an organizational view of society, a plan of "restraint and regulation." The stark contrast helps to define "liberal" and thus *the liberal plan*: We share a plan, or follow a program, of engaging one another as liberal individuals acting according to liberal principles, trusting that such an operating system shall give rise to healthy spontaneous order, as opposed to seeing society as an organization directed from the top.

But the liberal plan depends on an allegiance to it, an allegiance with roots in the culture of the society. Such allegiance depends on moral leadership, and hence moral leaders. Today's liberal leaders must animate the liberal conversation of preceding liberal exemplars—the great thinkers, particularly of the original arc of liberalism in the 17ᵗʰ and 18ᵗʰ centuries, such as Francis Hutcheson, Joseph Butler, David Hume, Adam Smith, Edmund Burke, and James Madison. Such thinkers serve as a meeting place for us today; we come together in their discourse—as Christians come together in the Bible. For classical liberals, the discourse of liberal exemplars is focal, their voices are focal. Upon them can we pull together to articulate and stand up for the liberal plan.

Not all of today's leaders need engage in intense scholarship. But some must. Healthy judgment depends on a social network of trustworthy scholarship and reflection—a sociology of judgment. Some members of the network must supply judgments about how exemplars like Smith made sense of modern society and our past. That justifies intensive Smith scholarship. Short essays bring insights to life, but there is need to grasp the fuller outlook that renders them natural. By close reading and meticulous scholarship, we make ourselves more at home in Smith.

The Theory of Moral Sentiments

The Theory of Moral Sentiments (TMS) is about moral duties. It is about virtue. It is highly approachable in its stories and illustrations. On the other hand, it's pretty subtle, even mysterious.

People often say that the central idea of TMS is sympathy. Before Smith, however, others had talked about sympathy. What's distinctive in Smith is how he connects sympathy and moral approval. He says that moral approval always relates to a sympathy.

But, it will be pointed out, someone can be alone in her room and feel moral approval or disapproval. So where is the sympathy if she is alone in her room? Well, Smith will say, the sympathy is with her man within the breast, or conscience. Smith maintains the connection between sympathy and moral approval by speaking of metaphorical beings with whom we share sentiment or sympathize.

Smith posits the idea of a universal benevolent beholder of humankind. Smith says the man within the breast is a representative of such a universal benevolent beholder. Our conscience is a representative of God or a being like God. Our conscience is not necessarily a good representative of God, mind you, but a representative nonetheless.

Smith instructs us toward better alignment with the approval of the benevolent beholder. Smith inspires us to make virtue our supreme concern. Virtue corresponds to better alignment with what the benevolent beholder approves of. He speaks of virtue as cooperation with the Deity.

Smith uses the expression "impartial spectator" in a number of related meanings. One is the universal benevolent beholder, another is the man within the breast or conscience, another is a great sage whom we admire, and another is an ordinary person who seems to be impartial and who happens to be spectating.

But in the quiet of your own room, by yourself in the cool hours, it is the sentiment of the man within the breast that guides your reflection.

By setting out general formulations, Smith provides a framework for ethics. But Smith also gives us many concrete illustrations that communicate what Smith himself approves of and disapproves of. Smith, then, offers a framework that involves guidance from exemplars or sages, and, at the same time, offers himself concretely as exemplar, for us to draw guidance from.

Smith says that we observe instances of conduct and learn to form rules. We learn from seeing how people conduct themselves, especially those we admire. In his published works Smith renders many judgments, providing us with a wealth of particular instances of conduct. From observing the many instances of Smith's conduct we learn some of the contours of good conduct.

www.CartoonStock.com

Think Spiral

When you think about ethics, think spiral. When you think about epistemics, think spiral. When you think about virtue, think spiral.

Why spiral?

"Why?" furnishes an example:

"Why X, Mommy?"

"Because Y, dear."

"Why Y, Mommy?"

"Because Z, dear."

"Why Z, Mommy?"

"I don't know, dear. Eat your ice cream before it melts."

The "Why? Why? Why?" series is not circular. It does not depart from X and return to X, as a circle does. Rather, it goes from X to Y to Z, followed by "I don't know." "I don't know" might be unsatisfying, but if you learn not to expect much of an answer to a question like "Why Z?," then not getting one won't feel so unsatisfying. Mommy may teach the child not to expect much of an answer by saying: "Because Z is how it is, dear. Now play backgammon with your friend."

In the first question posed by the child, X is the thing to be explained, or explanandum. Mommy offers explanation Y. We get a spiral:

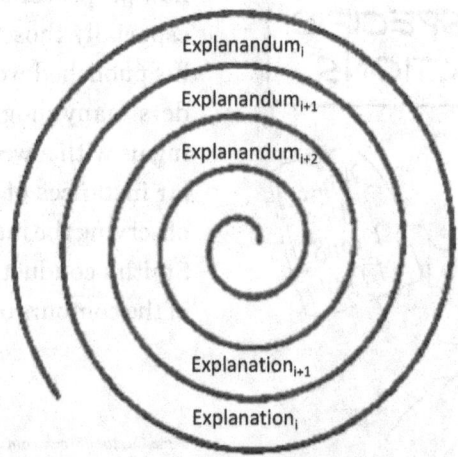

Traveling clockwise, the spiral winds up from the page, we hope. The inner loops are higher, we hope. Our journey raises us in wisdom and virtue, we hope.

In each loop the explanandum is distinct, and that's why we need subscripts. Subscripts are difficult, but such difficulty is to be anticipated. Shirk the difficulty and you doom yourself to stark demarcation and going in circles.

The difficulty comes in minding circumstances particular to the loop. Such difficulties and the conflicts they involve must be met amicably. Edmund Burke said: "This amicable conflict with difficulty obliges us to an intimate acquaintance with our object, and compels us to consider it in all its relations" (*Reflections*, 141). Burke taught us that justness in politics depends on the circumstances, and his lesson goes also for philosophical discourse. Adam Smith preached an attitude of amicability toward philosophical difficulties. Think spiral.

Historians tell stories of cause and effect. They know, however, that a cause can be repositioned as an effect, which might call for a preceding historical cause. We need subscripts on "cause" because each pertains to a particular "effect," also bearing a subscript. There is no definitive starting point in history. Historians pick up with the story somewhere and say: "Z caused Y, which then caused X, which then..."

Smith writes of "that great chain of causes and effects which had no beginning, and which will have no end" (TMS 289.37). Smith offers a cause-and-effect spiral of passions: "all his own passions will immediately become the causes of new passions" (111.3).

If spirals are unavoidable—and I think they are—we should learn to cope with them.

There is one spiral that is most profound and upsetting. It led the Bible, Augustine, and Kierkegaard to speak of "fear and trembling." It is the spiral of moral validation.

Adam Smith taught that, after some basic level of material security, our tranquility and well-being depend mainly on our moral condition. We want moral approval, or validation. But from whom?

For each of us, one of the most important sources of moral approval is that which comes from our conscience. Fear and trembling arise partly from not having that approval, or being unsure as to having it, but also from being unsure that the approval of our conscience is adequate. Should we let our conscience be our guide? How do we know that we should trust *our* conscience?

www.CartoonStock.com

"From now on, maybe we should let somebody *else's* conscience be our guide."

Once one starts asking himself that question, the conscience is already fuzzied up. Smith spoke of the conscience as "the man within the breast." The interesting part of that formulation is the word "man." If we have a man within our breast, does that man have a breast? And does he have another man within his breast? In other words, does our conscience have a conscience?

Yes, I think we should endorse that sort of iterative or recursive way of thinking. And we should embrace the spiral that it would generate: We want moral validation. For such validation we look to our validator. But is our validator valid? Who validates our validator? There's no escaping such self-questioning and the embarrassments and humbleness that come with it.

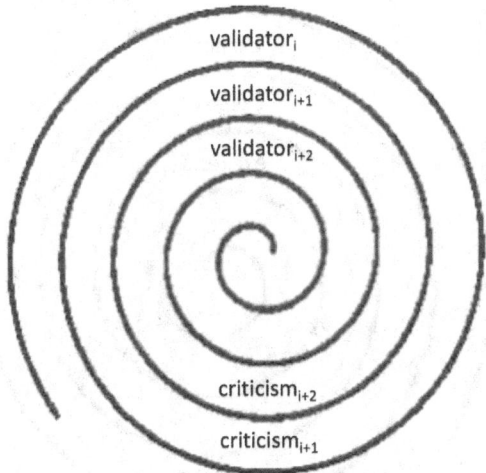

Again, we hope the spiral winds upward. With each round of criticism and reflection, the conscience or validator is slightly reformed, we hope for the better. There is no final loop.

Smith explained that our conscience is formed in part by emulating exemplars. But, in this life, an exemplar is not a guru or cult figure, whose every judgment is sacred and beyond question (as Brian is treated by his followers in the Monty Python "Yes, we're all individuals" scene). One of the notable things about Smith is that his admirers generally do not resemble groupies or cultists. There is no foundational first principle. There is no rigid Smithian moral doctrine.

Reading the works of a great thinker like Smith leads us to another distinction, that between exegesis and eisegesis. Exegesis is when the reader of a text draws the meaning of the text out of the text. Eisegesis is when the reader puts meaning into a text. Let the distinction operate within a loop, and let loops wind recursively, to make a spiral. If a text affords us with an encounter with a great author, then it is natural that the author means for us to find nonobvious meanings in the textual passages—to get a joke, to take a hint, to experience an epiphany, or to feel regret. We then have, at a deeper loop of the spiral, meaning that in one sense is inside the text and in another sense infused into the text by the reader.

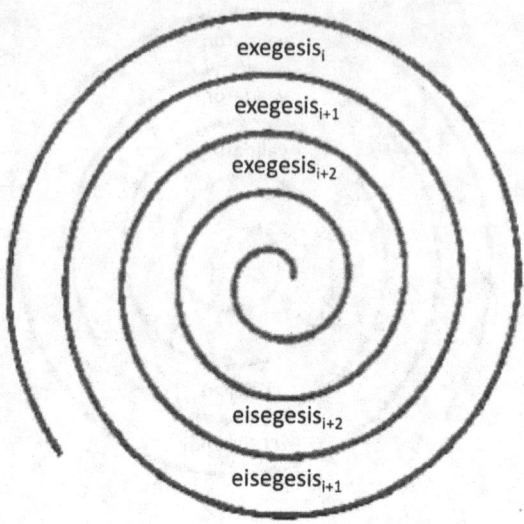

Again, we hope the spiral winds upward, but the term *eisegesis* is often used as a pejorative, insinuating that the eisegete is *not* winding upward. The insinuation is that the eisegete puts meaning into the text irresponsibly or erroneously. Some Smith scholars would say that some of my interpretations of Smith are eisegetical.

A related spiral emerges in theology from the supposition that God wrote two sorts of books, one of scripture, the other of the natural world. Natural religion holds that the two agree, and even that God's intention and guidance can be discerned from the book of nature alone. The distinction operating within a loop is that between one's interpretation of scripture and one's interpretation of nature. To sustain the correspondence between the two "books," one might adjust one's current interpretations, giving rise to the next loop. A Christian who subscribes to natural religion tries to travel the spiral in a way that sustains a correspondence between the Bible and the book of nature. In light of an evolved understanding of nature, one might reinterpret certain verses as figurative or allegorical, or as specially circumstanced, to sustain the correspondence.

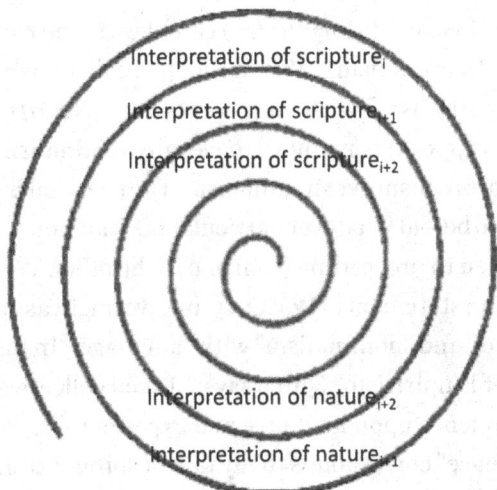

Again, estimative justice is the matter of estimating objects proper-ly, or doing them justice, and objects for estimation include ideas. Episte-mology, then—epistemic justice?—sits within the realm of estimative jus-tice. Here again I encourage one to think spiral: Each loop contains facts, information, interpretation, and judgment. There is wisdom in the adage: *Facts are theory-laden.*

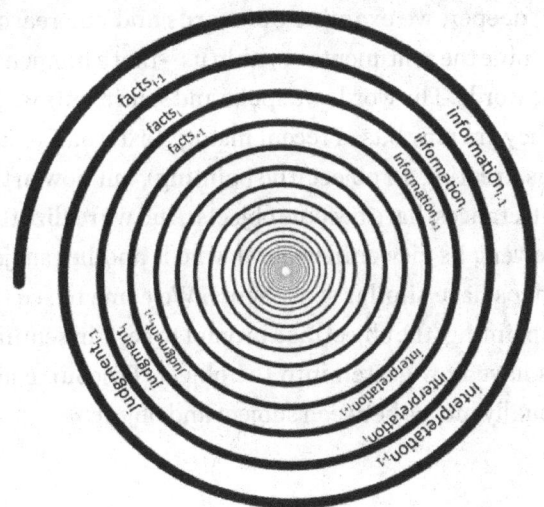

The adage (*Facts are theory-laden*) can likewise be couched in terms of "realism" and "nominalism." Within a loop, "realism" is associated with "facts" and "nominalism" with "interpretation." *Reality is nomenclature-laden.* My proposal is no more to elevate nominalism over realism[1] than it is to elevate realism over nominalism. The proposal is to think spiral. The proposal is to be—at whatever particular position you are within a particular loop—open to proceeding from one to the other. We hope upward.

To relate it to a statement of W.V.O. Quine, we might associate "realism" with "experience," and "nominalism" with "language." In his famous essay "Two Dogmas of Empiricism" Quine says: "Taken collectively, science has its double dependence upon language and experience" (1961, 42). Quine's "double dependence" corresponds to my talk of spiral, I think.

The *Oxford English Dictionary* defines *subject* in the sense of grammar: "The part of the sentence of which the rest of the sentence is predicated." It gives also the following definition: "the conscious mind, esp. as opposed to any objects external to it." Suppose we investigate an object such as a painted portrait and discuss it. In the sentence, *We discussed the painting*, "discussed the painting" predicates "We." We discuss with words. Words depend on nomenclature and tacitly involve theories, if only about the existence of things and relationships between them.

Dwelling deeper, we examine our words and our reasons for using them. We examine the sentiments—within us—that a moment ago brought forward those words. The words we spoke and sentiments we felt now have subscripts. They are now bits of recent history, "external" to us. At first the subject was us, treating an object (the painting), but now artifacts of that subject (our utterances) have become objects. And we realize that the painting's other viewers, its viewer in general, who is another subject, is like us and will perhaps have similar sentiments. We come to see the nature or quality of the painting (the object) as a prompt to certain sentiments. Notice how subjects have now gotten into the object. Discourse about human affairs continually moves between subject and object.

---

1. Hume held that we are destined, as if by Nature herself, to believe in such things as causation and the continued existence of objects, though variability and indeterminacy will mark many of our formulations of causes, effects, and entities (T 1.4.7.4, 1.4.1.7, 1.4.2.1, 1.4.2.51, 1.4.7.9).

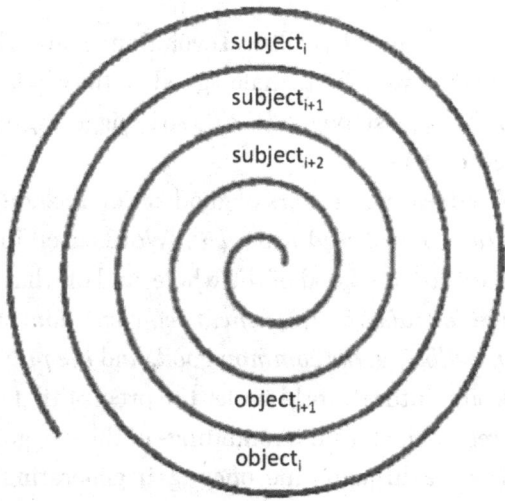

We could likewise look into the portrait and see a painter, of human-ity common with us, who was subject in relation to blank canvas. We find a subject (the painter) in the object (the painting). Spirals wind with every encounter, including those with oneself. Søren Kierkegaard (1989, 43) advised us to think spiral about the self: "The self is a relation which relates to itself."

The Correspondence between the Two Goods

In his theorizing about ethics, Smith maintained an organizing princi-ple of long standing, which I call *the correspondence between the two goods*.

The two goods are:

1. Good conduct of the individual—call her Robin.
2. The good of the whole of humankind (present and future), as that good is affected by Robin's action.

Suppose Robin faces a choice between action A and action B. Suppose you affirm that Robin's doing A is *better for humankind* than her doing B. Is it sensible, then, that you affirm, also, that Robin *ought to do B*, rather than A?

That would not be sensible. Cultural evolution seems to have organized our thinking such that we strive to make "good for the whole" correspond to "good action" or the highest "ought." We do so by jiggering what is on either side of the correspondence.

Words used in treating matters of good action include *ought, should, right, duty, virtue, justice,* and *propriety.* Words used in treating matters of what constitutes the good of the whole, and of what advances such goodness, include *desirable, best, beneficial, efficient, flourishing, thriving, healthy, happy, wellbeing, the common good,* and *the public interest.* We tacitly navigate our cultural world under the precept that *ought* and *beneficial* shall correspond. Our understandings of the two goods work upon each other, and evolve through time, once again generating a spiral shown in Chapter 4. The proposal is no more to elevate consequentialism over deontology than it is to elevate deontology over consequentialism. The proposal is to think spiral. The proposal is to be, at whatever particular position you are at within a particular loop, open to proceeding from one to the other. We hope upward.

As Rivers Are Lost in the Sea

La Rochefoucauld wrote, "it is very hard to distinguish between benignity extended toward all mankind and consummate cleverness" (1959, 153). If wisdom is defined as knowing how to conduct oneself properly, and virtue as acting accordingly, and if one's overriding private, personal passion is to excel in proper conduct, then the correspondence between the two goods would ensure that effective benignity and such consummate cleverness will correspond.

Kierkegaard said that purity of heart is to will one thing. How does one approach purity of heart? "If a man should will one thing, then he must will the Good, for in this way alone was it possible for him to will a single thing" (Kierkegaard 1948, 175). If the one thing were proper conduct, or correspondingly, serving universal benevolence, then, for a man who willed that one thing, his purity would lie in persisting in that act of will for as long as the moment of action lasts.

La Rochefoucauld also said: "Virtues are swallowed up by self-interest as rivers are lost in the sea" (64). Virtue is chiefly the matter of what it is that one makes his self-interest.

An Empty Bag Does Not Stand Upright

"Klein, your spirals make my head spin!"

One gets dizzy just thinking about them. With fear and trembling we ask ourselves:

"What loop am I in?"

"Where am I in the loop?"

"Which way is up? Clockwise? Or is this one of those funky counterclockwise spirals?"

Even if one's attitude toward spirals becomes amicable, by itself the spiral pattern does not provide all that one needs. If all you have is amicability to spirals, you are apt to be lost in clouds and mist.

"Most fortunately it happens, that since reason is incapable of dispelling these clouds, nature herself suffices to that purpose" (Hume T 1.4.7.9).

Here Hume spoke for himself. Here, on this matter, all anyone can do is speak for himself or herself.

But, what is "this matter"? Where is "here"?

As was noted in the Preface to this book, Poor Richard observed: An empty bag does not stand upright.

The matter is: What's in your bag?

The loops of the spiral usually bring only small changes, tweaks, not drastic reformations. As we progress in any of the spirals, from interpretation$_i$ to interpretation$_{i+1}$, or from validator$_i$ to validator$_{i+1}$, or from subject$_i$ to subject$_{i+1}$, the difference from one loop to the next is not necessarily large. Most often, it is small. There is continuity in the evolution of the things within the loops of the spiral. We are not reduced to a series of disjointed moments. We are not reduced to a meaningless series of ontological

infinitesimals. Rather, we cohere. Our experience flows. Our understanding evolves.

It doesn't work to say that the enduring, robust, ever-richer and more
refined thing in your bag is the imperative to serve universal benevolence or
to be virtuous. Being virtuous is an organon constitutive of the spiral. The
virtue organon says: The path to what you want is often a path of vice, but
the road to what *You* want is the road of virtue. You organize your thoughts
on the assumption that everything that rises must converge.

But those broad assumptions are framework. The organon carries the
imperative to serve *better*. The quest is to *better* serve universal benevolence.

Better than what?, you ask.

The answer is sometimes better than how things are going without
your participation, sometimes better than what others are offering, sometimes better than what your performance had been up to a moment ago,
but always better than that other course of action that seems to be the chief
rival to the one you are contemplating. You must contribute something that
mitigates distress, answers a need, solves a problem. You must serve *better*.

Smith showed us how his ethical plexus can stand upright because of
the things that he put inside of his own 'bag.' Think of the bag as an 'item'—a
design—you may buy a unit of at a store. You then show others how they
could use such a bag by exhibiting how you make use of the one you brought
home from the store.

Inside of Smith's bag is the will to promulgate sensibilities favorable
to the liberal program. That was his primary guidance on how, in morals
and politics, to serve better. That spirit in Smith is clear from the start, I
would argue—in the original 1759 edition of TMS and in the 1763 lectures
on jurisprudence. The spirit was, I suspect, in Smith as early as his years
as pupil of Francis Hutcheson. A Glasgow colleague, William Leechman,
wrote of the never-to-be-forgotten Hutcheson:

> As he had occasion every year in the course of his lectures to
> explain the origin of government and compare the different
> forms of it, he took peculiar care, while on that subject, to incul-
> cate the importance of civil and religious liberty to the happi-
> ness of mankind: as a warm love of liberty and manly zeal for

promoting it were ruling principles in his own breast, he always insisted upon it at great length and with the greatest strength of argument and earnestness of persuasion: and he had such success on this important point, that few, if any, of his pupils, whatever contrary prejudices they might bring along with them, ever left him without favourable notions of that side of the question which he espoused and defended. (Leechman 1755, xxxv-xxxvi)

A warm love of liberty animated Smith's work and gave it purpose and direction. The message is a scrupulous yet pragmatic conservative liberalism. That is the program he projects, the tune he plays, the tapestry he sews, the story he tells. Put a subscript on it and advance it through your spiral, always looking upward. Smith advanced that evolving object forward, and I would say upward. That spirit moved his work forward. That kept him going. Smith willed contributions to liberal civilization. We should be grateful.

One can: (1) embrace neither liberalism nor spiral, (2) embrace liberalism but not spiral, (3) embrace spiral but not liberalism, or (4) embrace both.

You are more than your person and more than any spiral drawn on a page. Edmund Burke's relationship with difficulty was exceedingly amicable because he had an exceptional sense of things within the spirals that organized his thinking. You judge how to fill out what is inside any spiral. Since you are beyond the spiral, the objects represented within have determination beyond.

Think spiral, but remember too that an empty bag does not stand upright.

Two Glimpses of Adam Smith

It is Glasgow, December 1763 or January 1764. It must have been chilly outside. The scene is a university classroom, the auditors in their teen years:

When Mr. Smith undertook the charge of accompanying the Duke of Buccleuch to the Continent, it became necessary for him to resign his Professorship in the College of Glasgow, in the middle of his annual course of lectures. He procured a literary friend, in whose talents he had perfect confidence, to finish the course; and furnished him, for that purpose, with the notes [he used] to deliver his prelections; thus providing as well as he could, that his pupils might suffer no disadvantage from the change. But still fearing that there was some injustice done to those young men who had paid the usual fees on the faith of having the benefit of a complete course of his lectures, he resolved to set his conscience at ease upon that score. After concluding his last lecture, and publicly announcing from the Chair, that he was now taking a final leave of his auditors; acquainting them at the same time with the arrangement he had made to the best of his power for their benefit; he drew from his pocket the several fees of the students, wrapped up in separate paper parcels, and beginning to call up each man by his name, he delivered to the first who was called, the money into his hand. The young man peremptorily refused to accept it, declaring, that the instruction and pleasure he had already received, was much more than he either had repaid, or ever could compensate: and a general cry was heard from every one in the room, to the same effect. But Mr. Smith was not to be bent from his purpose. After warmly expressing his feelings of gratitude, and the strong sense he had of the regard shewn to him by his young friends, he told them, this was a matter betwixt him and his own mind, and that he could not rest satisfied unless he performed what he deemed right and proper. 'You must not refuse me this satisfaction. Nay, by heavens, gentlemen, you shall not;' and seizing by the coat the young man who stood next to him, he thrust the money into his pocket, and then pushed him from him. The rest saw it was in vain to contest the matter, and were obliged to let him take his own way. (Tytler 1814, I: 272-3n)

It is Edinburgh, July 1790, at Panmure House:

[A]fter the burning of his papers on that long-ago July Sunday in Panmure House, Smith felt well enough to welcome his friends in the evening with his usual equanimity. A considerable number of them came to be with him then, but he did not have strength to sit with them through supper, so he retired to bed before it. Henry Mackenzie recorded his parting words in the form: 'I love your company, gentlemen, but I believe I must leave you to go to another world.' Hutton gave Stewart some different wording: 'I believe we must adjourn this meeting to some other place.' (Ross 2010, 436)

CHAPTER 2

Who Is Adam Smith's Impartial Spectator?

By Daniel B. Klein, Erik W. Matson, and Colin Doran

Adam Smith encourages us to seek moral coherence. To steel ourselves into better personal moral rules he suggests that we heed the sentiments of impartial spectators. The impartiality of the spectator helps us see how the personal rules can be shared with others, or generalized; such sharing is key to our own moral coherence.

There are different kinds of spectators that Smith refers to as "impartial" in *The Theory of Moral Sentiments* (TMS). Every impartial spectator shares the characteristic of being presumptively emotionally disinterested toward parties to the spectacle. We argue that Smith uses the expression "impartial spectator" in a number of ways, including: a human bystander, a being with superhuman qualities, and "the man within the breast" (or the conscience). For the last, the attribution of impartiality usually remains skeptical: Smith tells us that the man within the breast is only purportedly or *supposedly* impartial.

Suppose that a restaurant patron named Jim has an altercation with his server, and that a bystander, another patron named Rick, observes the incident. Rick is presumed by all to have had no prior personal contact with either Jim or the server. We thusly presume that Rick is impartial, neither friend nor enemy to either party. Any real-life Rick, however, might have some partiality beyond our ken. Suppose Jim and Rick are male, and the server female. Or, Jim and Rick are white, and the server black. Et cetera. Who knows what partiality, invisible to us, Rick might feel toward one or the other. Suppose the server is attractive. In TMS many occurrences of "impartial spectator" describe ordinary practice or offer practical advice, and impartiality is only a presumptive impartiality. There are myriad unknowns that might undo the presumed impartiality; yet we nonetheless speak of someone being "impartial." Smith did likewise.

Another aspect of Rick is his knowledge. We say that Rick "observes" the altercation, but how closely? Does he catch every syllable, every gesture, every glance exchanged? And even if Rick is supposed to have observed closely, there is the matter of interpretive knowledge. Suppose Jim told the server, "But I told you no ketchup." Was that rude of Jim? Besides information on the scene, what Knud Haakonssen (1981) calls "contextual knowledge," there are broader issues of knowledge, of interpreting, and of competence in judging among interpretations, issues that Haakonssen calls "system knowledge" (79). Different Ricks will interpret and judge differently how systems work—systems of propriety, systems of markets, systems of politics, and so on. In the present discourse, the word used to signify a combination of such facets of knowledge is *intelligence*. A key issue is: Must intelligence align with benevolence toward larger wholes? Must intelligence be good?

If we posit that Rick is impartial, does it follow that Rick is aligned with benevolence toward the whole? Can Rick be an "indifferent spectator" and yet capricious toward the whole, or even malevolent? Might Rick judge matters impartially and intelligently, yet malevolently? The Nazis of course had their putative intelligence service, the *Sicherheitsdienst*, and they may have been impartial toward certain local matters, at least in a limited sense of "impartial."

In some key passages, Smith alludes to a higher impartial spectator, a being who not only has superhuman intelligence and benevolence, but whose sentiment, if only it were accessible to us, would never fail us as a guide to what is beneficial for the largest conceivable whole, embracing "all rational and sensible creatures" (237.6).[2] We may posit such a being, and then converse over what her sentiments would be about the matter under discussion. Although the godlike being is by no means directly or reliably accessible, we develop characterizations of her, characterizations ineluctably fragmentary, vague, and contested. It is natural for humans to posit some such being, which takes the definite article *the*.

---

2. The citation 237.6 means page 237, paragraph 6 of the Glasgow edition of TMS.

Some writings on TMS err in treating "the man within the breast" as interchangeable or synonymous with the highest sense of "the impartial spectator." We contend that the man within the breast must be distinguished from the highest sense of "impartial spectator," and here that contention serves as a touchstone. In a passage new to Ed. 6 of TMS, for instance, Smith says that "the prudent man is always both supported and rewarded by the entire approbation of the impartial spectator, and of the representative of the impartial spectator, the man within the breast" (215.11). Such a representative is no more synonymous with what he represents than, say, a representative in Congress is synonymous with his electorate. In several passages, *all of which are also new to Ed. 6*, Smith refers to the man within the breast as the "supposed" impartial spectator. That "supposed" should be understood, not as *sup-pos'd* (meaning posited), but rather as *sup-pos-ed* (meaning purported)—just as a sarcastic report on a Congressional hearing might say: *Next to speak was the supposed honorable gentleman from Kansas.* The representative only *supposedly* serves the good of his electorate.

No consensus in the Smith literature

Some scholars deny the presence of a godlike conception of the impartial spectator in Smith and, moreover, seem not to distinguish the impartial spectator and the conscience or man within the breast. Samuel Fleischacker (2016, 274) emphasizes the "eminently human character" of the impartial spectator. Jack Weinstein (2016) suggests that Smith's impartial spectator does not have "access to any privileged information" (352). Weinstein continues, "[e]ach impartial spectator is...unique to its imaginer" (355). Craig Smith (2016, 328) argues that "the only sense in which the impartial spectator is universal is that all normally functioning humans have it." James Otteson (2002, 73) says, "the conscience is informed by the impartial spectator or 'the man within,'" and that the impartial spectator "serves as one's conscience" (2011, 96). T.D. Campbell (1971) says of "Smith's image of the impartial spectator": "all his characteristics are fully human, and he possesses these only to the degree which is common in the average person" (137). Likewise, David D. Raphael (2007) held that "[t]he impartial spectator is still a man, not a god, and indeed a perfectly normal man" (45). An aspect of our disagreement with these scholars is that our interpretation weakens the definition of "impartial spectator" by expanding the range of its possible significations. The range includes mundane indifferent bystanders, an exemplary person, the man within the breast, and a godlike conception.

Other scholars suggest that Smith does indeed affirm and talk of a godlike spectator, whose beholding spans whatever relates to the discourse situation. Théodore Jouffroy (1840) said that for Smith the impartial spectator "represents God" (191). Knud Haakonssen (1981) says that the high conception of the impartial spectator is distinct from actual, concrete, human spectators. Haakonssen speaks of the higher conception of impartial spectator as "an ideal whom both agents and actual spectators can approach" (56). Our efforts to agree about the judgments of the higher impartial spectator "may never, or very rarely, be completely successful, but the really important point...is that it is the *search* itself which makes social life possible" (Haakonssen 1981, 58; italics original). Jerry Evensky (1987, 452) sees in Smith an impartial spectator who "fully appreciates the Design" and who is "a perfect arbiter among the sentiments." Vivienne Brown (1994) says that the impartial spectator "has been set up as an analogue of the wise Stoic's divine Being" (74). Ross B. Emmett (2011, 128) and Paul Mueller (2016) suggest that the impartial spectator comes to signify a category of ideal impartial spectating and judging. Roderick Firth (1952, 318n2) mentions Smith in expositing "the ideal observer."

Some also seem to distinguish between the impartial spectator and the man within the breast. Jeffrey Young (1992, 74) affirms the place of an ideal or transcendent spectator, and distinguishes that from the man within the breast, who "has feet of clay and so his judgements can be wrong." Charles Griswold (1999, 91) emphasizes that the man within the breast in TMS 130.32 is but an "imagined spectator," consulted through "illusory sympathy." Joseph Cropsey (2001, 21) interprets the man within the breast to be "the vicar and symbol of all spectators." Douglas Den Uyl (2016, 264) says, "the impartial spectator is not one's conscience or probably even, as Smith puts it, 'the man within the breast.'"

Impartial spectators, from Rick to Joy

Smith uses "impartial" to designate multiple kinds of spectators. Smith affixes a variety of articles or modifiers: "the," "this," "that," "the only," "the most," "every," "any," and "no." (An Excel file collects all passages for key terms and codes all cases of "impartial spectator": https://econfaculty.gmu.edu/klein/Assets/ImpartialSpectatorFinal.xlsx.)

Smith's most down-to-earth conception of an impartial spectator is simply of an apparently—hence presumptively—disinterested, at-hand onlooker, a bystander. We call such conception $Rick_1$—based on our example of a bystander, Rick, watching an altercation at the restaurant. In the fourth paragraph of TMS Smith speaks of "every attentive spectator" (10.4). Where Smith first uses the word *impartial* it is coupled with "candid" (22.8); the coupling also occurs later ("every candid and impartial spectator," 148.28). At TMS 69.2 Smith equates "every impartial spectator" with "every indifferent by-stander," like our $Rick_1$. We should not suppose that $Rick_1$ is necessarily particularly intelligent or virtuous. In fact, even as a rather stupid and selfish fellow, $Rick_1$ may be termed an impartial spectator, provided that he is spectating, and that, seemingly, he is partial to no party of the spectacle.

Now consider a "$Rick_2$," of more than average intelligence and competence in judging. Smith evinces such higher conception when he refers to "every *intelligent* and impartial spectator" (249.27, 283.28; italics added). We take the sentiments of $Rick_2$ more seriously than those of $Rick_1$. Smith conceptualizes higher impartial spectators, spectators who are more intelligent or more aligned with benevolence toward the parties observed.

Higher-order human impartial spectators ($Rick_{1+n}$) might inspire us with admiration and serve as exemplars, whom we learn to emulate.[3] Perhaps some $Rick_9$ is one whom we regard to be a "great leader in science and taste, the man who directs and conducts our sentiments, the extent and superior justness of whose talents astonish us with wonder and surprise" (20.3). Our higher conceptions of the impartial spectator, $Rick_9$, are presumed by us to be wiser and better aligned with universal benevo-

---

3. For passages in TMS on admiration and emulation of exemplars see 20.3, 75.3, 114.3, 117.9, 159.7, 192.11, 247.25, 323.10, and 336.24.

lence, and hence more authoritative in judgment. We hold that their wisdom extends to matters of greater complexity and their beneficialness spans larger wholes. Smith clearly seems to have a higher-order impartial spectator in mind when he speaks, for instance, of "the real and revered impartial spectator" (155.43) or "the most impartial spectator" (158.4).

Just as we can imagine a being who runs faster or punches harder than any actual human, we can imagine a being who hears more, sees more, reads more, learns more, and thinks with greater refinement and perspicuity. From the example of wise humans, it is natural for us to step beyond human limitations, to extrapolate beyond what is humanly achievable. We can imagine a being who is more benevolent. We can imagine a being who interprets and judges better. We can imagine a being who has greater intelligence and greater benevolence than any actual human.

FIGURE 2.1: A SPECTRUM OF SPECTATORS WHO MIGHT BE CALLED "IMPARTIAL"

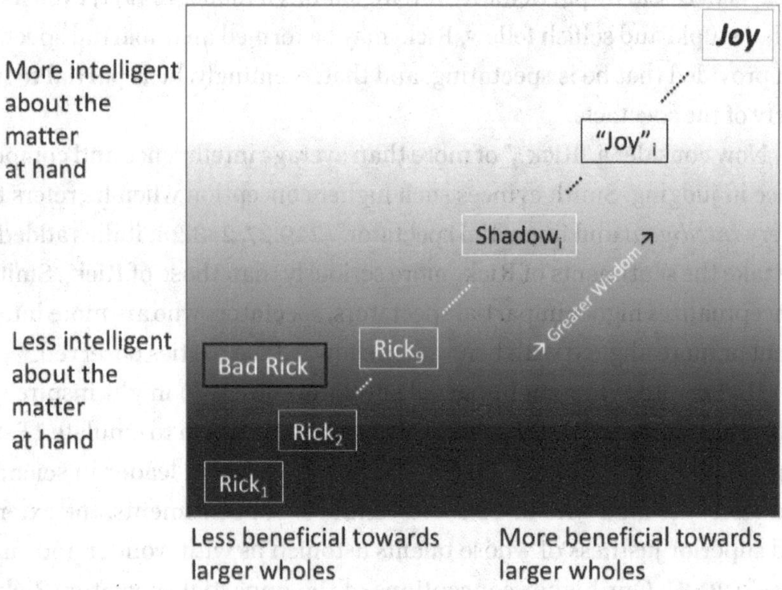

In Figure 2.1, the vertical axis charts intelligence about the matter at hand: Knowledge of what happened, and how such happenings work. Think of the vertical axis as measuring savviness about the spectacle;

upward movement along the vertical axis represents more detailed information about the spectacle, better interpretation of the spectacle as part of larger wholes, or both. But that axis does not broach upon wholes larger than the spectacle: Rick may be termed a spectator of the incident in the restaurant, but he is not presumed to be a spectator of, say, the lived experience of the entire town or country within which the restaurant is located.

Located within the diagram (Figure 2.1) are beings who, firstly, are spectators—they are not part of the matter at hand, they are not party to the spectacle. Secondly, such beings are regarded as presumptively impartial, like the bystander Rick in the restaurant. It could be that such a Rick is pretty savvy about the altercation, and really impartial as regards Jim and the server, but again capricious or even malevolent. Thus, we could have an off-diagonal *bad* Rick, as shown in the diagram. Such a Rick fails in rendering a judgment that is beneficial toward larger wholes—the variable along the horizontal axis.

In speaking of the beneficialness of the spectator (some Rick), we mean that if Jim acts according to the approval of Rick, then Jim's actions will be beneficial to the whole. We mean, then, the Rick is beneficial *qua* spectator and judge of conduct; Rick might not be very beneficial in other respects, for example, he might snore at night.

The diagram shows ascending human spectators (Ricks) and superhuman spectators. The 45-degree diagonal is the stairway of ascending wisdom. In terms of the vertical axis, we have ascending intelligence about the spectacle. In terms of the horizontal axis we have a corresponding accession in beneficialness toward larger wholes.

Greater beneficialness does not necessarily imply greater benevolence. The advance from $Rick_1$ to $Rick_9$ does not imply that $Rick_9$ is remarkably more benevolent. $Rick_9$ may simply be better aligned with benevolence toward larger wholes (i.e., with the judgments of a still higher spectator who really is more benevolent) without himself being remarkably more benevolent—"it is not that feeble spark of benevolence" that induces sacrifice (137.4). Such alignment goes with virtue, but a lively sentiment of benevolence is not necessary for accession in wisdom and virtue—although it is helpful for such accession (152.34-36), and it is agreeable (142–143, 172.4). Contrasting his own system with that of Francis Hutcheson, Smith (301–

306) taught that benevolence is not the only or even necessarily the principal road to beneficialness.

$Rick_9$ wants the approval of his conscience (his man within the breast). We naturally presume that for *our* exemplars—and let's suppose that $Rick_9$ is such an exemplar—that *that* approval (that is, from $Rick9_9$'s man within the breast) depends on $Rick_9$ acting in good alignment with universal benevolence. Thus, we presume that the example of our exemplar $Rick_9$ provides useful—though not infallible—guidance on how we are to pursue such alignment, even if $Rick_9$ in no special way feels a lively benevolence toward larger wholes.

Humans naturally step beyond the human. They naturally imagine personalities, beings, with superhuman qualities. Wonder Woman and Spiderman are superhuman in certain respects. Santa Claus is superhuman in knowing whether you've been bad or good. Think of a superhero with superhuman intelligence about larger wholes. Where Smith speaks of an imagined being knowing Jim's merit "though mankind should never be acquainted with what he has done" (116.5), and then turns it around to an evil "for ever to be concealed from every human eye" (118.9), he posits a knowledge that is superhuman to those other than Jim, and uses in both cases "the impartial spectator" for such a being. At this step, the key ingredient of the imaginary being is knowing "what he [Jim] has done," and no further superhuman wisdom. We denominate this step *Shadow*,[4] after the old radio character—"Who knows what evil lurks in the hearts of men? The Shadow knows!"[5]

Humans naturally step further, to the idea of a judge so intelligent

---

4. The Shadow "possessed many gifts which enabled him to overcome any enemy. Besides his tremendous strength, he could defy gravity, speak any language, unravel any code, and become invisible with his famous ability to 'cloud men's minds'" (Old Radio World).

5. Perhaps economists resort, in effect, to such a Shadow figure when they tell the science-fiction story called "Supply and Demand": The Shadow knows the supply curve and demand curve, and the economist discusses what he might see and know, and feel about outcomes. Even if the story is used chiefly as a foil, economists thereby make points about how markets work (or don't work), without knowing what the Shadow knows.

and so benevolent (or, at any rate, beneficial[6]), and impartial at so high a level,[7] that her judgments, if only they were accessible to us, would never fail to point us toward service to the largest whole. We call such being *Joy*. Built into the idea of Joy is that there is no higher moral authority: There is no being whose approval is more beneficial to the largest whole. Joy, by definition, is morally supreme. Joy may be thought of as allegory, but for monotheists, Joy corresponds to God (although not all attributes commonly attributed to God are necessary for the allegory Joy[8]). Smith speaks of "that supreme wisdom and divine benignity *which we necessarily ascribe to*" the Author of nature (166.7; italics added). Like others before him,[9] Smith speaks of virtue as cooperation with the Deity (166.7). Virtue may be understood as what God approves of. Built into Smith's thought is the correspondence between the two goods: Good conduct corresponds to what is good for the largest whole. In the four Scandinavian languages, *god* means good, and the word for God is *Gud* (in Icelandic, *Guð*).

It is common for people to speak as though intelligence could be brought to completion or perfection— 'omniscience.' But doesn't every interpretation occasion an opportunity for a yet better interpretation? As for benevolence, Smith says: "Benevolence may, perhaps, be the sole principle of action in the Deity... It is not easy to conceive what other motive an independent

---

6. If such being (Joy) were superhumanly beneficial without herself being so benevolent, it would seem natural to explain her *alignment with* benevolence the same way we do for humans: seeking the approval of some higher being, an approval that depends on such alignment. We might content ourselves with such a regress, but it also seems quite natural, and quite satisfactory, to simply make the step to a being who is so benevolent.

7. Superhuman-ness might also be said to mark Joy's impartiality, in that no human could be as disinterested a bystander or spectator to the large wholes that she beholds.

8. Notably, a common attribute of God is his designing/willing/creating of the universe, and that attribute is not necessary to the allegory of Joy. There is, however, a naturalness to attributing providence to a being who is morally supreme. First, the benevolence of such a being (Joy) resembles that of a creator: Creators usually care for their creation, as a parent cares for her child, a homemaker her home, and an author her discourse. Second, we are more likely to take seriously what (we think) a superhuman being thinks if we believe that that being is our creator, analogous somewhat to how a child tends to take seriously what (it thinks) its parent thinks than what some other person might think.

9. The idea of virtue as cooperation with the Deity is very old, of course, but some predecessors recent to Smith included Lord Shaftesbury (2001 II, 201), Joseph Butler (1736, I.I.III), and Francis Hutcheson (2008, 109).

and all-perfect Being, who stands in need of nothing external, and whose happiness is complete in himself, can act from" (305.18). But it also is not easy to conceive how a being acts always from benevolence alone. Smith says that humans naturally ascribe to gods "all their own sentiments and passions...Those unknown intelligences which they imagine but see not, must necessarily be formed with some sort of resemblance to those intelligences of which they have experience" (164.4). Humans have no experience of beings who act always and only from benevolence.

Yet we manage to have Joy while sidestepping 'omniscience' and complete, final notions of 'ideal,' 'perfection,' 'transcendence,' and the like. Each person falls back on a supposition that his highest-to-date characterization of Joy would be aligned with any better-yet characterization well enough to justify his proceeding with his characterization of Joy. It is a supposition of selfhood coherence, of being on a path toward improvement, a path of greater wisdom. Smith describes the usual course of the wise and virtuous man: "It is the slow, gradual, and progressive work of the great demigod within the breast... Every day some feature is improved; every day some blemish is corrected" (247.25). However, as one proceeds diachronically through life on such supposition, he might arrive at a point at which he feels that he has erred drastically, that the supposition is wrong, that his characterization is, not merely blemished, but faulty in a significant way. Then he *backs up* to return to a former crucial fork in the road, and he does significantly revise his moral outlook. But one's usual course in ethical reasoning is to maintain the supposition and carry on.

In Figure 2.1, "Joy"$_i$ denotes a *characterization of* Joy. Since one's characterizations of Joy pertain to vast wholes, to profound issues of their health and well-being, and to vast issues of how well-being is advanced, and since such notions are necessarily vague and complex, and only vaguely distinguished from penultimate-to-date notions, and since people tend to proceed on the aforesaid supposition, it is natural for people to simplify their reference to such characterizations by speaking of that trail-into-the-heavens with a singular, like "God." People often speak of "*the* world" or "*the* universe" without having definitized a world or universe, because it is unnecessary to do so: Tacitly, the world and the universe are already definitized. Likewise, Smith in several instances writes of "the" impartial spectator without having definitized a spectator: He writes of "the" impartial spectator in a way that certainly allows the reader to think that he means an always present and everywhere morally supreme impartial spectator.[10] We use *Joy* in just such fashion. Though each person's sense of Joy, or characterization of Joy, is somewhat different from anybody else's, the concept, or category, is something they have in common. As Haakonssen (1981, 58) says, "it is the *search* itself which makes social life possible; it is the *search* for a common standpoint that is common, not necessarily the standpoint."

Wisdom is the intelligence facet of virtuous conduct. Eleven times in TMS Smith uses the phrase "wisdom and virtue" as a more or less unitary thing, as when he speaks of "the character of the most exalted wisdom and virtue" (241.11), and five times[11] uses the phrase "wise and virtuous."[12] Indeed, Smith says, "virtue is upon all ordinary occasions, even with regard to this life, real wisdom" (298.13).[13]

The man within the breast: A representative of Joy

Jim's exemplars, such as $Rick_9$, are not continuously on-hand for consultation. Jim's developing of his man within the breast entails his extending "in imagination only" (114.3) the judgments of $Rick_9$. Jim must imagine how $Rick_9$ would view Jim's own conduct. And even his revered exemplars

---

10. In the Excel file we have coded all instances of "impartial spectator." Instances especially aptly understood as Joy include ones at 215.11, 225.19, and 294.49.

11. A sheet in the Excel file inventories the 16 instances: https://econfaculty.gmu.edu/klein/Assets/ImpartialSpectatorFinal.xlsx

12. Smith's TMS paragraph that opens section VI.iii "Of Self-command" (237.1) seems to run counter to our suggestion here that the wisdom and virtue are like two sides of the same coin. We propose the following interpretation of it: When Smith posits Jim as having "the most perfect knowledge" of "the rules of perfect prudence, of strict justice, and of proper benevolence," he means rules regarding a set of things that falls short of the passions in Jim that "are very apt to mislead him." A larger set of things, a set that included those troublesome passions, could be made the subject of a yet more extensive body of rules, a body of rules of which Jim, who lacks self-command, does *not* have "the most perfect knowledge." In other words, for any issue of self-command we can extend virtue so as to view the issue as a matter of self-knowledge.

13 And in the same paragraph Smith writes: "Temperance, magnanimity, justice, and beneficence, come thus to be approved of, not only under their proper characters, but under the additional character of the highest wisdom and most real prudence" (299.13).

may be felt defective in some respects. Jim learns to adjust even their sentiments. He joins the personalities, and the adjustments, into a sketchy composite personality, the man within the breast, or conscience.

Ed. 6 of TMS brought Part VI, which includes a bold passage in which
Smith advances a sense of "the impartial spectator" that is not only beyond
any Rick, but is beyond the man within the breast. The passage is remarkable in a number of ways. It reads:

> In the steadiness of his industry and frugality, in his steadily sac-
> rificing the ease and enjoyment of the present moment for the
> probable expectation of the still greater ease and enjoyment of a
> more distant but more lasting period of time, the prudent man
> is always both supported and rewarded by the entire approba-
> tion of the impartial spectator, **and of the representative of the
> impartial spectator, the man within the breast.** The impartial
> spectator does not feel himself worn out by the present labour of
> those whose conduct he surveys; nor does he feel himself solicited
> by the importunate calls of their present appetites. To him their
> present, and what is likely to be their future situation, are very
> nearly the same: he sees them nearly at the same distance, and
> is affected by them very nearly in the same manner. He knows,
> however, that to the persons principally concerned, they are very
> far from being the same, and that they naturally affect *them* in a
> very different manner. He cannot therefore but approve, and even
> applaud, that proper exertion of self-command, which enables
> them to act as if their present and future situation affected them
> nearly in the same manner in which they affect him. (215.11; ital-
> ics original, boldface added)

Call the prudent man Jim. Here, first of all, Smith clearly, unequivocal-
ly distinguishes the impartial spectator from Jim's man within the breast.
Second, Smith describes the relationship between those two: Jim's man
within the breast is a "representative" of the impartial spectator. Third, this
impartial spectator seems to have intimate intelligence of the Jim's present situation, and also of "what is likely to be" Jim's future situation. If this

impartial spectator is a human spectator, some Rick, it seems remarkable that such Rick both has such personal knowledge and is not partial to Jim (or to present-time Jim). What's more, this impartial spectator has such present-and-future intelligence not only about Jim, but about all of "those whose conduct he surveys." This impartial spectator regards each surveyed person's present and future situations "nearly at the same distance, and is affected by them very nearly in the same manner." What human spectator could have such knowledge and such detachment over some unspecified set of surveyed persons? Moreover, what human spectator would "not feel himself worn out by the present labour of those whose conduct he surveys"? But the real clincher is this: *Why would all those who are surveyed by Rick make their man within the breast a representative of Rick?* Who is this Rick that, if accessible, would serve as a guide for everyone's conscience? It seems, rather, that Smith's language here propounds an imaginary, super-intelligent, super-beneficial spectator. This impartial spectator is aptly understood as God/Joy.

Jim's man within the breast, then, is a representative of God/Joy. In Part III, Smith says:

> What is agreeable to our moral faculties, is fit, and right, and proper to be done; the contrary wrong, unfit, and improper... Since these, therefore, were plainly intended to be the governing principles of human nature, the rules which they prescribe are to be regarded as the commands and laws of the Deity, promulgated by those vicegerents which he has set up within us. (165.5–6)

In seeing virtue as cooperation with the Deity (166.7), Smith calls upon us to scruple to avoid any disagreement between what our conscience deems good and what we understand to be good for the largest whole. In Eds. 3, 4, and 5, Smith had referred to "the man within" as "This inmate of the breast, this abstract man, *the representative of mankind, and substitute of the Deity*" (130 note r; italics added).

Some features of our interpretation that might seem peculiar

Our reading of Smith distinguishes between the man within the breast and the highest sense of "the impartial spectator" (viz., God/Joy). As we have seen, that is at odds with some of the scholarship. Before taking up textual challenges, we pause to notice some features of our interpretation, features that the reader might find novel and awkward.

Impartiality might be thought of as a matter of carrying out a given set of standards or rules. "When the first Brutus led forth his own sons to a capital punishment, because they had conspired against the rising liberty of Rome" (192.11), Brutus acted impartially, because the rules did not carve out allowances for the family of the consul. But had the rules been different, had they contained such allowances, *sparing the sons* would have been in keeping with an impartial execution of *that set of rules*. Impartiality deserves little more veneration than does the set of rules that it carries out. Impartiality rises to a venerable wisdom only when, first, the ascription ("impartial") is reasonably sound, but, secondly and more importantly, only when it runs up to large wholes and high planes of interpretation and judgment (corresponding to higher position along the vertical axis in Figure 2.1). Whereas Brutus's decision quickly met a definitive set of rules that predicates impartiality, other decisions lack such definitiveness. Rick's decision about Jim's propriety in the restaurant altercation leave us pondering and debating the different *levels* of rules that govern propriety or politeness in such a situation; we ponder the higher rules governing *the conditions under which* a lower rule becomes operative.

Because the adjective *impartial* can modify the spectating of a wide range of spectacles, from narrow to immense, from trivial to momentous, our interpretation proliferates significations of "impartial spectator." We have spoken of Ricks (which run from "every indifferent by-stander" all the way up to our most admired exemplar), the Shadow, characterizations of Joy/God, and Joy/God—and, next, we consider text in which the man within the breast is an "impartial spectator." By recognizing the weakness of the definition of "impartial" and the wideness of the range of spectacles, our interpretation recognizes many sorts of spectators signified as "impartial spectator." The expression "the impartial spectator" is not only polysemous, but its range of meanings is quite elastic.

That elasticity parallels an interesting contrariety in Smith, a contrariety that should be borne in mind as we explore the man within the breast—MwB, for short.

The contrariety is that Smith's attitude toward humankind's potential or essence often seems reverential, yet his attitude toward the bulk of humankind often seems scornful. Does Smith regard Jim's MwB to be loftier than Jim the complete human being? Smith speaks of the MwB as a "demigod," "partly of immortal...extraction," "divine extraction," "the great judge and arbiter...capable of astonishing the most presumptuous of our passions," etc. (TMS 131.32, 137.4). If everyone's MwB is a demigod etc., and if everyone is pretty much as lofty as his MwB, how is it that Smith so often expresses a rather blanketing scorn? Suppose that Jim is one of the basest among "the great mob of mankind" (62.2, 253.30).[14] Does that mean that Jim's MwB is not a demigod worthy of reverence? Is Smith's reverential talk of the MwB confined to those Jims high on the wisdom-and-virtue staircase? Another possibility is to say that the basest Jim the complete human being is *far below* that Jim's own MwB: Divine extraction is in Jim, but coming through only very poorly; great potentialities are in Jim, but being realized only very poorly. In *The Lion King*, the spirit of Mufasa calls to Simba: "You are more than what you have become." Perhaps the reverential view is a perspective that every Jim assumes, or is encouraged to assume, in communing with his own MwB: The reverence expresses an intrapersonal, not interpersonal, comparison.[15]

Even the man of highest wisdom and virtue, usually painted with grandeur and dignity, an object to be regarded with reverence and admiration, is at times regarded otherwise. In the opening chapter, "Of Sympathy,"

---

14. Other scornful remarks in TMS include: "the present depraved state of mankind" (77.8), "so weak and imperfect a creature as man" (77.9), "The coarse clay of which the bulk of mankind are formed" (162–3.1), "the noisy applauses of ten thousand ignorant and enthusiastic admirers" (253.31).

15. A shift between intrapersonal and interpersonal comparison might be a way to resolve a contrariety appearing in the Chinese earthquake paragraph (137.4): While pondering whether to sacrifice his little finger, the man hears his "inhabitant of the breast" call to him that he is "in no respect better than any other in [the multitude]" and yet he sacrifices his little finger from the love of the "superiority" of his own character—though no better than others, the man, by making the sacrifice, is superior to what he would otherwise be.

Smith, wandering momentarily into the most fateful issue of the coherence of consciousness, drops the remark that an infant's thoughtlessness and want of foresight provide it with "an antidote against fear and anxiety, the great tormentors of the human breast, from which reason and philosophy will, *in vain*, attempt to defend it, when it grows up to a man" (12.12; italics added). Are even our exemplars but other vain and irredeemable creatures?

The man within the breast as "supposed impartial spectator"

We take to heart Smith's unequivocal statement (215.11) that Jim's MwB is a representative of "the impartial spectator," which we there interpret as God/Joy. Now we turn to text in which MwB is rendered a sort of "impartial spectator."

In expositing the idea of an identified human being, Rick, deemed "impartial," we have maintained that the attribution is always only presumptive. As a practical matter, we are never sure that Rick is not partial to any of the parties to the spectacle. Moreover, the matter of judging conduct within the spectacle, such as the altercation between Jim and his server, presupposes some sense of the moral principles or rules that apply: Was Jim *rude* to the server? Here we apply the principles of common civility. But we have suggested that the interpretive scope can be widened so as to make an issue of judging principles of common civility. We must then imagine a much vaster spectacle—one to which Rick is *not* an actual spectator—at a higher level of intelligence. We ask then, not simply whether Rick is partial to either Jim or the server, but whether Rick is partial to certain groups in judging principles of civility. Even if Rick has connection to neither Jim nor the server, maybe Rick has chosen his principles partially, and thus, in a larger sense judges the altercation partially. At both levels (not to speak of still higher levels), any impartiality attributed to Rick is at best presumptive. Save only when impartiality is *built into* the being as with God/Joy, any attribution of impartiality can be questioned. Indeed, in "so imperfect a creature as man" (25.8, 305.18), everyone fails impartiality at some level.

In *English: Meaning and Culture*, Anna Wierzbicka (2006) discusses what she calls epistemic adverbs, including *supposedly*. She writes that "*supposedly* has a somewhat sarcastic ring" (281). For example, a 1731 book on skin diseases, authored by Daniel Turner and published in London, speaks of medical procedures "by whose Means many desperate and **supposedly** invincible Diseases have been conquer'd" (Turner 1731, 332, boldface added). The same author also wrote a book on surgery, and sarcasm is on full display when Turner writes of "the vain Arrogance of such as fancy nothing to be insolvable by their (**supposedly**) unbounded Comprehension" (Turner 1729, 251; boldface added).16 As for the adjective *supposed*, Wierzbicka (pp. 280-1) explains one of its usages: "the speaker who qualifies something as *supposed* dissociates himself or herself from the original statement ('I don't say I know') and in fact expresses some skepticism ('I think that it is not true')." *The Oxford English Dictionary* provides numerous quotations up through Smith's time containing the skeptical adjective *supposed*, including Shakespeare's "Let the supposed Fairies pinch him" (1623) and Richard Montagu's "The onely true God…no supposed, false, subintroduced God or Gods" (1641).

Collins Dictionary (2018) shows that the pronunciation of the skeptical adjective *supposed* is səpoʊzɪd–a three-syllable pronunciation, *sup-po-sed*. *Collins* says that this pronunciation goes specifically with the skeptical definition: "You can use *supposed* to suggest that something that people talk about or believe in may not in fact exist, happen, or be as it is described."

The adjective *supposed* has, of course, a meaning directly from the past-tense and participle forms of the verb *to suppose—supposed*, namely, posited, assumed, and *Collins* indicates that that is pronounced səpoʊzɪd—just two syllables, *sup-pos'd*.

The two different meanings—*sup-po-sed* and *sup-pos'd*—pertain to our issue. In a generous and searching podcast interview with one of the present authors, Samuel Fleischacker (2016b; 13:00f) takes up the matter of the numerous instances in which Smith renders the MwB as "supposed impartial spectator," and, maintaining interchangeability between MwB and "impartial spectator" in any sense beyond a Rick, he suggests that

---

16. When we chart "supposedly" in Google's Ngram viewer, 1600-2000, we see that the word was used a bit up to the early 1700s, fell into disuse, and then revived after 1890. Nonetheless, it appears that there was awareness of *supposedly* and its sarcasm prior to Smith. Incidentally, none of Turner's works appear in Bonar's catalogue of Smith's library.

Smith meant *sup-pos'd*, or posited.[17] We argue the contrary, that is, that Smith meant *sup-po-sed*.[18]

In Ed. 6 of TMS there are fourteen occurrences of the adjective *supposed*, here listed in the order in which they appear in the work:

1. "this supposed impartial judge" (85.4) (also in Ed. 5, p. 145)
2. "this supposed equitable judge" (110.2) (also in Ed. 5, p. 198)
3. "his supposed disgraceful conduct" (120.11)
4. "the supposed murder of his own son" (120.11)
5. "the supposed impartial and well-informed spectator" (130.32) – MwB
6. "The supposed impartial spectator" (131.32) – MwB
7. "the supposed impartial spectator" (134.1) – MwB
8. "the real or supposed spectator of our conduct" (145.21)
9. "the supposed physical connection between the parent and child" (223.14)
10. "the supposed impartial spectator" (226.22) – MwB
11. "the supposed beauty of his own ideal plan of government" (233-4.17)
12. "the supposed impartial spectator" (262.1) – MwB
13. "the supposed impartial spectator" (262.2) – MwB
14. "the supposed impartial spectator" (287.34) – MwB

17. Here we would like to express thanks to Professor Fleischacker for engagement on these matters. In fact, it was not until the podcast that we noticed that the two different meanings corresponded to two different pronunciations.

18. Here we should note that, although it is clear that the skeptical meaning of *supposed* clearly existed well prior to Smith (and Fleischacker acknowledges that in the podcast), we have had difficulty confirming that in Smith's time that meaning would have been phonetically expressed as *sup-po-sed*. We have searched old dictionaries and thus far found neither confirming nor disconfirming evidence of the hypothesis that our differentiation in pronunciation corresponding to the different meanings extends back to Smith's time.

Of these fourteen occurrences, the last twelve in the list are new to Ed. 6.[19] Of those twelve, seven are signifying MwB (as marked in the list). We contend that those seven cases should be understood as *sup-po-sed*.

To assess whether Smith might have used *supposed* that way, we look at the other occurrences of the adjective *supposed* newly introduced into Ed. 6. Four of the five are clearly *sup-po-sed*.[20] Let's look at those four.

Smith's first two new occurrences come together in a poignant discussion of the innocent man accused of a great crime:

> The innocent man...is struck with horror at the thoughts of the infamy which the punishment may shed upon his memory, and foresees, with the most exquisite anguish, that he is hereafter to be remembered by his dearest friends and relations, not with regret and affection, but with shame, and even with horror for his **supposed** disgraceful conduct: and the shades of death appear to close round him with a darker and more melancholy gloom than naturally belongs to them. Such fatal accidents, for the tranquillity of mankind, it is to be hoped, happen very rarely in any country; but they happen sometimes in all countries, even in those where justice is in general very well administered. The unfortunate Calas, a man of much more than ordinary constancy (broke upon the wheel and burnt at Tholouse for the **supposed** murder of his own son, of which he was perfectly innocent), seemed, with his last breath, to deprecate, not so much the cruelty of the punishment, as the disgrace which the imputation might bring upon his memory. (120.11; boldface added)

The first occurrence here, "his supposed disgraceful conduct" shows Smith using "supposed" where we might today think "supposedly" more apt—that is, we would probably say "supposedly disgraceful conduct." As noted previously, *supposedly*, though finding usage prior to Smith's day, was

---

19. Or, presumably new to Ed. 6: They are not in Ed. 5 (1781). We have not checked Eds. 1–4, but presumably the twelve occurrences would not be found in any of them.

20. The exception is item 8 on the list ("real or supposed spectator," 145.21) which we think is better understood as *sup-pos'd*.

scarcely used at all in Smith's day, and apparently *supposed* functions here either as an adverb (modifying "disgraceful") or as a second-order adjective (that is, modifying the noun phrase "disgraceful conduct"). Either way, the usage in "supposed disgraceful conduct" perfectly parallels how one should, on our interpretation, read "supposed impartial spectator."

Next, in expounding the social-distance theory in Part VI, Smith tends to account for familial sympathy as arising from habitual sympathy, affection born of familiarity, more than from mere blood relatedness. Smith writes: "I consider what is called natural affection as more the effect of the moral than of the **supposed** physical connection between the parent and the child" (223.14; boldface added); here again Smith uses "supposed," not only as *sup-po-sed*, but in place of where today we might say "supposedly" (as a modifier to "physical").

Finally, also in Part VI, Smith speaks of the man of system, who "is apt to be very wise in his own conceit; and is often so enamoured with the **supposed** beauty of his own ideal plan of government" (233.17; boldface added). This *supposed* is not merely skeptical but downright sarcastic.

And as for Smith's other writings, they too show the skeptical *supposed* (see the Excel file), for example: "In both regulations the sacred rights of private property are sacrificed to the **supposed** interests of publick revenue" (WN 188.27; boldface added).[21]

It is clear, then, that the skeptical meaning of *supposed—sup-po-sed—* not only functioned in Smith's day, but that he himself employed it, and notably in the additions introduced in Ed. 6 of TMS—even in signal ways, as he doubles up on *sup-po-sed* in the Calas paragraph, and he uses it with significant sarcasm in the important man-of-system paragraph. Indeed, Smith's changes to Ed. 6 seem to have been especially concerned with differentiating MwB and the highest meaning of "impartial spectator," as signaled especially by the remarkable paragraph 215.11, and we think it conceivable that Smith inserted these other occurrences of *supposed* quite consciously, to clue us in to how he meant "the supposed impartial spectator"—*a 4-gram that first appeared only in Ed. 6, and that appears there six times.*

---

21. There are 37 instances of the adjective *supposed* in WN, and in the Excel file we have coded five as clearly and four arguably better understood as *sup-po-sed*.

Consider a further point. It seems to us that the adjective *supposed* in the sense of *sup-pos'd* is used when one posits something quite definite and well defined, as in figuring out how many bottles of wine are need for a supposed (*sup-pos'd*) number of guests. The supposition put in place (the number of guests) is definite. But for the MwB the impartial spectator is not definite and well defined. Reading "supposed impartial spectator" in the sense of *sup-pos'd* would almost seem like a way of stating that the supposition puts Rick or some other definite being in place as the impartial spectator—as though Rick, rather than some definite alternative, say, Mary, is the impartial spectator supposed. But that is not what Smith means when he speaks of MwB as the "supposed impartial spectator."

The MwB and his shortcomings

Jim may tout that his conscience achieves impartiality, and Jim's conscience may purport (to Jim) that it achieves impartiality. But the rest of us are inclined to grant only *supposed* impartiality. Further discussion of MwB's shortcomings may help to elucidate the differentiating of MwB and Joy.

Smith tells us: "The man within the breast, the abstract and ideal spectator of our sentiments and conduct, requires often to be awakened and put in mind of his duty, by the presence of the real spectator" (153.38). One shortcoming of MwB, then, might be that he nods off, or perhaps other passions or elements within Jim suppress the MwB. When MwB reports to Jim, he is true and sound, but sometimes the report is absent, or only faintly heard, or faintly heeded.

Smith tell us, moreover, in describing self-deceit, "In order to pervert the rectitude of our own judgments concerning the propriety of our own conduct, it is not always necessary that the real and impartial spectator should be at a great distance" (156.1). Even when he (a Rick) "is at hand, when he is present, the violence and injustice of our own selfish passions are sometimes sufficient to induce the man within the breast to make a report very different from what the real circumstances of the case are capable of authorising" (156–7.1). We diagram the passage in Figure 2.2.

FIGURE 2.2: SELF-DECEIT AT 3 AND 4, RESULTING IN A FAULTY REPORT FROM MWB.

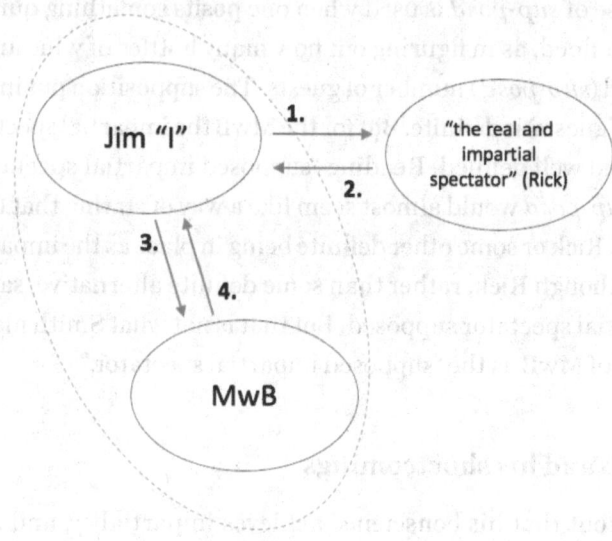

After consulting Rick, Jim communes with his MwB. But that communion (3 in the diagram) is greatly affected by "the violence and injustice" of Jim's "selfish passions," inducing the MwB to return to Jim a report (4 in the diagram) "very different from what the real circumstances of the case are capable of authorising." Here, MwB does something that God/Joy would never do.

Smith leaves us wondering as to why the MwB is so affected by the selfish passions so as to return to Jim a faulty report. But, however we might construe that perversion, does it not make sense to say that that perversion shows, or constitutes, a lack of impartiality on the part of MwB? Does it not make sense to say that the MwB *allows himself* to be swayed by the selfish passions? If such susceptibility to selfish passions does not show partiality, what would? Even though Rick is at hand, *the MwB returns a faulty report.* In our view, Smith is here telling us that the MwB may be partial. Any impartiality attributed to MwB is only a *sup-po-sed* impartiality.

Although Smith does not, we might carry his allegory yet further. If Jim has a man within his breast, then *that* man presumably also has a conscience—yet another man within *his* breast. In such iteration, we get the conscience's conscience. We suggest that Smith's contrariety about human beings can be thought of this way: We may not have much regard for or confidence in Jim's conscience, but we should revere Jim's conscience's conscience's...conscience—or Jim's nth-order conscience. In fact, if the ellipsis represents a long enough iteration, that is, if n is large enough, Jim's nth-order conscience is nearly the same as our own nth-order conscience. They both converge to God/Joy, whom surely we revere. Smith's invitation to wisdom and virtue is to the call to refine and revise our deeper spirits so as to make our conduct more aligned with God/Joy's approval. Smith helps us to do that—for example, by identifying many sources or syndromes of corruption.

Indeed, there are passages where the MwB is termed an "impartial spectator" without the presence of the skeptical *supposed*. Such occurs most notably when Smith describes "The man of real constancy and firmness, the wise and just man" (146–7.25)—which also is new to Ed. 6. The wise and just man excels in cultivating his MwB, and in making his conduct conform to the approval of his MwB. The superior impartiality of *his* MwB, *his* representative of God/Joy, is something for us to admire, not something to throw a skeptical *supposed* upon. This wise and just man is like our Rick$_9$ and is what Smith has in mind when he says a few pages later that "The real, revered, and impartial spectator, therefore, is, upon no occasion, at a greater distance than amidst the violence and rage of contending parties" (155.43).

"Ideal"

In five passages, the MwB is called "ideal" (147.26, 148.28, 148.29, 153.38, 158.4), and these passages might be used to challenge our differentiating MwB and God/Joy. But in Smith's time "ideal" generally meant ideational, notional, as opposed to real or actual. The OED says of this meaning: "Now rare." Today, the prominent meaning is perfect. But that meaning does not appear in Johnson's *Dictionary* (1755, 1039), as the following image shows:

FIGURE 2.3: IDEAL AND IDEALLY ENTRIES FROM JOHNSON'S DICTIONARY

IDE'AL. *adj.* [from *idea.*] Mental; intellectual; not perceived
by the senses.
   There is a two-fold knowledge of material things ; one
real, when the thing, and the real impreſſion thereof on our
senſes, is perceived; the other *ideal*, when the image or idea
of a thing, abſent in itſelf, is repreſented to and conſidered
on the imagination.   *Ch yne's Phil. Prin.*
IDE'ALLY. *adv.* [from *ideal*] Intellectually; mentally.
   A tranſmiſſion is made materially from ſome parts, and
ideally from every one.   *Brown's Vulgar Errours.*

In two of the passages (147.26, 153.38), Smith pairs the "ideal" with a
"real" for another spectator (a Rick, in our scheme), and at 158.4 with "the
most impartial spectator," which we are inclined also to interpret as a Rick.
We acknowledge that two of the passages are more ambiguous (namely
148.28 and 148.29 about the man whose leg is shot off by cannon fire), and
that some of the twelve instances of "ideal" in TMS may be understood to
mean perfect, but we think that Smith's usages of "ideal" does not pose a
significant challenge to our interpretations. (The Excel file shows the twelve
"ideal" passages.)

Yet other new Joys of Ed. 6

Not only are all of the occurrences of "supposed impartial spectator" new to
Ed. 6, but what we regard to be the most signal significations of Joy are, too.
They occur at 215.11, 225.19, and 294.49. We have already quoted 215.11.
Let us look at the other two.
   In Part VI, Smith writes:

> Nature, which formed men for that mutual kindness, so neces-
> sary for their happiness, renders every man the peculiar object of
> kindness, to the persons to whom he [Jim, say] himself has been
> kind. Though their gratitude should not always correspond to
> his beneficence, yet the sense of his merit, the sympathetic grat-

itude of **the impartial spectator**, will always correspond to it. (225.19; boldface added)

Although this impartial spectator could perhaps be understood otherwise, we suggest that it is quite apt to understand it as God/Joy. The sympathetic regard of this being "will always correspond" to Jim's kindness—yet Smith himself had expounded on how the basic rule of gratitude (returning equal value for any kindness) will "Upon the most superficial examination...appear to be in the highest degree loose and inaccurate, and admit of ten thousand exceptions" (174.9). Yet the impartial spectator here "always" gets it right. Moreover, this impartial spectator is getting right not merely one occasion of Jim's kindness, but many occasions spanning multiple "persons to whom he himself has been kind." This impartial spectator seems to have superhuman contextual knowledge and always estimates Jim's kindness rightly.

Next, the following is a new and complete paragraph that Smith inserted near the end of the long chapter on "Systems which make Virtue consist in Propriety":

> None of those systems either give, or even pretend to give, any precise or distinct measure by which this fitness or propriety of affection can be ascertained or judged of. That precise and distinct measure can be found nowhere but in the sympathetic feelings of **the impartial and well-informed spectator**. (294.49; boldface added)

Smith had expounded on how the rules of all the virtues, except commutative justice, are loose, vague, and indeterminate (174-5.9–11; cf. 327.1), that is, that there is no accessible "precise and distinct measure." Only God/Joy achieves such precision, and that obtains by definition, as it were. Smith's purpose in this paragraph is not to suggest that a source for precise guidance is readily "found," but, rather, to tell us how to conduct our search for guidance. The search should not focus on what "those systems" (are said by Smith to) point to—Dr. Clark: "the relation of things;" Mr. Woollaston: "the truth of things, according to their proper nature and essence;"

Lord Shaftesbury: "a proper balance of the affections" (293.48). Rather, it should strive to commune with beholders, and to formulate, refine, and select beholders. The newly inserted paragraph is telling the reader to study beholders to ascend the staircase of wisdom, with a God/Joy concept lending coherence to the ascent.

In examining the passages just treated, as well as 215.11, the reader may wish to try an experiment: Insert "supposed" before "impartial." Such an insertion may strike the reader as quite inappropriate. If so, the reason, we suggest, is that "supposed impartial spectator" signifies MwB, while these passages are, rather, about God/Joy.

Concluding remark

The correspondence between the two goods is the proposition that Jim embrace the program of sustaining correspondence between *good* conduct and what is *good* for the largest whole. Each of these goods involves God/Joy: For Jim to achieve good conduct is for him to "act so as that the impartial spectator may enter into the principles of his conduct, which is what of all things he has the greatest desire to do" (83.1). The good of the largest whole is what God/Joy finds beautiful, for God/Joy beholds that whole and is universally benevolent.

By embracing the correspondence, Jim does not avail himself of a formula dispensing ready answers to his continuous duty of good conduct. Rather, the correspondence is a program of exploration: (1) of coming to better understandings of what the beholder finds beautiful, or what constitutes the good of the whole and how that good is served, (2) of sensing what conduct on his part is approved of, and (3) of understanding how these two wings meet in the coordinated sentiments of God/Joy, or at least in the best representatives of that being. The staircase of wisdom and virtue calls to Jim to develop his man within the breast so as to refine, revise, and reformulate his understanding of the entire correspondence, and in that way cooperate with the being.

In pursuing good conduct, we heed exemplars, the "particular instances" of their judgment, their approval and disapproval, their estimation of objects (159.8, 187.2). Smith's writings provide a wealth of particular instances. Smith paints the program in its fullness, and provides an exemplar (like our Rick9) to work with within it.

Appendix: An Excel file collects all passages for key terms and codes all cases of "impartial spectator": https//econfaculty.gmu.edu/klein/Assets/ ImpartialSpectatorFinal.xlsx.

CHAPTER 3

Beholderism: In Praise of Adam Smith's Organon and Allegory

A young woman is watching a set of weighing scales gradually settle their equilibrium in a noiseless, curtain-drawn room. The objects on the table suggest that she is about to value the worth of various coins and pearls, but the presence of a painting hanging directly behind her suggests a more profound unfolding of events.

Her head obscures most of the painting, but its exposed upper section reveals Christ in Judgement. In this painting-within-a-painting, Jesus is doing what the woman is doing—he is weighing something. Except his work is deliberating souls on Judgement Day.

—Matthew Wilson (2023), on symbols in Vermeer paintings.[22]

---

22. Woman Holding a Balance (1662-64) by Johannes Vermeer, owned by the National Gallery of Art, Washington, Widener Collection.

In this chapter, I explain Adam Smith's organon and Smithian allegory. I then turn to the issue: Are they good? I maintain that they are. A significant portion of their goodness comes from their working together.

Such goodness is not binary, like an on/off switch. Goodness is a matter of degree, of how readily—how pervasively, deeply, habitually—we should think in this Smithian manner. By "good," I mean pretty darned good— better than skeptics think.

Does this chapter contribute to Smith scholarship or intellectual history? What debates does it contribute to?

This chapter contributes to two issues: (1) whether Smith's ethics are nonfoundationalist; (2) supposing they are, whether that is good.

What I mean by *organon*

An organon is a principle for organizing thought. That comports with a definition in the *Oxford English Dictionary*: "An instrument of thought or knowledge; a means of reasoning, discovery, etc.; *esp.* a system of rules or principles of demonstration or investigation." I use "organon" to mean, more specifically, a 100-percent-of-the-time principle maintained and used to organize discourse and inquiry. The statement "The triangle has three sides" or "The child was born of a mother" might be thought of as true by definition, and in that respect like organons, as I use the term.

In 20th century economics, Gary Becker may be thought of as having maintained the organon of utility maximization in interpreting human behavior. It is presupposed; it is the manner of Becker-speak. In terms of the analytic/synthetic distinction, one would say that, in Becker-speak, the statement "the action was undertaken in maximizing utility" is an analytic statement; it is necessarily true by the ground rules of Becker's discourse.

In Becker-speak, that some fellow Jim endeavored to maximize his utility is not to be demonstrated or evidenced. What does call for demonstration and evidence, however, is that Becker-speak is good. The claim that Becker's organon is good—a claim, by the way, that, in my view, Becker oversold—would be a synthetic statement. But the important point here is that a rejection of the organon's goodness must ponder what Ronald Coase (1960) called "the total effect," the pluses and the minuses.

A case for rejecting an organon will necessarily be discursive, as will a case for embracing it. It would be improper for one to criticize the present chapter on the grounds that the arguments are discursive. This chapter is an endeavor in contemplation, expression, and exhortation: I do not cite much relevant literature. Also, in treating Smith's organon and allegory, I do not address their distinctiveness and originality in relation to other thinkers.

Organons are used to organize thought, like accounting identities. They serve as frameworks within which elements are made to fit. Let's return to Gary Becker's organon: In the case of the man who commits suicide, Becker might admit that it is odd to say that he endeavored to maximize his utility, but Becker would note that sometimes people or their situations are odd. The world is a buzzing, blooming confusion, and if our ways of sense-making are to get anywhere we have to share some ground rules. If one looks closely into an accounting system, I suspect that one might see some odd designations.

Before moving on, it might be useful to list two other organons:

- Here is an organon associated with Darwinism: *It survived because it was fit*. That organon can be sustained 100 percent of the time by contouring, as necessary, "fit," "survived," and "it."

- Here is an organon associated with a foil used in Ronald Coase's 1960 article "The Problem of Social Cost": *If transaction costs were negligible and parties were aware of the relevant opportunities, those parties achieved an efficient outcome*. That organon can be sustained 100 percent of the time, notably by contouring "transaction costs" and "efficient," two terms which may be thought of as mutually constitutive, each containing the other in its definition.

Smith's Organon

Smith's organon is that inside of every moral sentiment there lurks a sympathy. For any moral sentiment that a person has, there is another being who shares that sentiment as a "fellow-feeling" (10.5); there is a communion of sorts behind any moral sentiment. The sympathy might be vestigial, but its impression or echo makes it a living sympathy of a sort.

Smith advanced the organon abundantly. In the first edition of *The Theory of Moral Sentiments* he wrote:

> But in whatever manner it [i.e., our past conduct] may affect us, our sentiments of this kind have always *some secret reference*, either to what are, or to what, upon a certain condition, would be, or to what, we imagine, ought to be the sentiments of others. We examine it as we imagine an impartial spectator would examine it. (110.2; italics added)

Other prime statements from the first edition are found, for example, in the third chapter of the book (quoted in this footnote[23]) and at the end of Part IV (quote in this footnote[24]). The first edition included at least seven passages that seem to at least imply the organon, namely at 17.3, 110.2, 163–65.4–5, 193.12, 306.21, 311.10, and 325.14. Others were added subsequently (e.g., at 46n*, 133ff). Shortly after the appearance of the first edition, Smith showed Gilbert Elliot draft emendations confirming "my Doctrine that our judgements concerning our own conduct have always a reference to the sentiments of some other being" (Corr. 49).

Suppose our fellow Jim has a sentiment about the beauty of someone's conduct—a moral sentiment. Smith's organon holds that with Jim's moral sentiment there lurks a sympathy between Jim and some other being, a sympathy in which the sentiment is a fellow-feeling between the two of them. That such can be said to hold 100 percent of the time requires the conjuring of some such being who shares the sentiment. For when no actual walking, talking human being is present, or at least none sharing the sentiment, the sympathizing being must instead be some other sort of being, such as:

- a figure from the past, such as Jim's mother or father or teacher, perhaps now deceased, or,

---

23. "A little attention, however, will convince us, that even in these cases our approbation is ultimately founded upon a sympathy or correspondence of this kind" (17.3).

24. "All such sentiments suppose the idea of some other being, who is the natural judge of the person that feels them; and it is only by sympathy with the decisions of this arbiter of his conduct, that he can conceive either the triumph of self-applause or the shame of self-condemnation" (193.12).

- a figure who happens to be absent, perhaps someone Jim admires, an exemplar, or,

- Jim's conscience, which Smith terms "the man within the breast," or,

- a being that Jim imagines, perhaps a characterization of God or of an allegorical being God-like in certain respects, or,

- God.

These uncarnate beings intertwine: The exemplars of Jim's life figure into the development of his conscience, which is a "representative of the impartial spectator" (215.11)—"impartial spectator" here meant in a highest or supreme sense. You will not see the being clearly and distinctly, but figure that *some* being of fellow-feeling lurks there for Jim.

Just as we can see the world through the lens of Gary Becker's organon of utility maximization, we can see the world through the lens of Smith's organon. But saying that we can see through Smith's lens is different from saying that we should.

I need to acknowledge that my expounding on the beneficialness of Smith's organon would seem to collide with Smith's own words in paragraph 315.3 of TMS. That paragraph seems to imply that the issue of whether one embraces his organon, though possibly "of the greatest importance in speculation, is of none in practice." The present paper rejects the exoteric message of that paragraph. Elsewhere, I suggest that we should consider that paragraph an instance of esoteric writing (Klein 2023a, 194–195).

Smithian allegory

The second feature of Smith's ethical thought to be praised is Smithian allegory. Allegorical beings, such as Pinocchio or the characters in *Animal Farm*, are clearly not human, but they illuminate human conditions and teach human lessons.

Those who read Smith as theological—who read Smith as meaning by "the impartial spectator" in the highest sense *nothing short of* God—might object to my "allegory" talk, because allegory is short of God. I concur: For all that I have to say, God works, too. My "allegory" talk should be read as "at least allegory" or "allegory if not religion," except when I explicitly distinguish allegory from religion or theism.

Smithian allegory is not singular, but there is a master allegory, namely, that:

good ~ pleasing to the supreme benevolent beholder of the whole

The symbol ~ should be read as "corresponds to."

I call the allegorical being of the master allegory Joy. Joy is superhuman, perhaps even God-like in certain respects, always including at least the following two respects: (1) She is super-knowledgeable, in "contextual" and in "system" knowledge, to use terminology of Knud Haakonssen (1981, 79). (2) She is benevolent toward the whole of humankind. Like God in some respects but not necessarily others, Joy is God-light.

Smith strove to make his works work for both theists and non-theists. His ethical thought does not depend on the full kit of God. A less-than-theistic option is available, a merely allegorical option. Joy accommodates non-theists. Also, Joy affords theists a way of promoting certain patterns of thought to mixed audiences.

Smith affirms divine providence[25] and certainly allows the reader to associate the impartial spectator, in the highest sense, with God. But Smith also allowed his readers to take the ideas allegorically. I do not elevate a non-theistic allegorical interpretation above a theistic interpretation. The things that matter here are shared by both. To coalesce both interpretations, I refer to the being corresponding to "impartial spectator," in the highest sense, as "God/Joy." Again, my "allegory" talk—as in the title of this chapter—may be understood as "allegory if not religion."

Let me add that many of my theistic friends agree that casting God as the beholder does not necessarily bring great precision or certainty to our moral theorizing. Smith wrote:

25. Do we slough off divine providence in the Joy approach? If I am to imagine a universally-benevolent Joy, how shall Joy learn to feel universal and impartial love for humankind but by imagining the love that would be felt by a providential creator of the whole?

That to obey the will of the Deity is the first rule of duty, all men
are agreed. But concerning the particular commandments which
that will may impose upon us, they differ widely from one another. (176.12)

God too is remote, inaccessible, and superhuman. God does not necessarily make matters more foundationalist.

Now, some Smith scholars might reject the claim that Smith maintained God/Joy. Consider paragraph 215.11, which was new to Ed. 6 of 1790.

In paragraph 215.11, Smith does three things: (1) He explicitly distinguishes "the man within the breast" from "the impartial spectator"; (2) he
specifies the relationship between the two, saying that the first is a "representative" of the second; and (3) he imbues "impartial spectator" here with
superhuman and universalistic elements. Here is the first sentence:

In the steadiness of his industry and frugality, in his steadily
sacrificing the ease and enjoyment of the present moment for
the probable expectation of the still greater ease and enjoyment
of a more distant but more lasting period of time, the prudent
man [Jim] is always both supported and rewarded by the entire
approbation of the impartial spectator, **and of** the **representative** of the impartial spectator, the man within the breast. (215.11;
boldface added)

Thus Smith distinguishes the impartial spectator from Jim's man within the breast. Further, Jim's man within the breast is a "representative" of
the impartial spectator. In the remainder of the paragraph, Smith uses the
pronouns *they* and *them* without ambiguity but with a testing difficulty.
The result is a paragraph of intensity and challenge. To make things easier, I insert clarifications:

The impartial spectator does not feel himself worn out by
the present labour of those [let's say: Jim, Jill, Sue, and Tom]
whose conduct he surveys; nor does he feel himself solicited by
the importunate calls of their present appetites. To him their

> present, and what is likely to be their future situation, are very
> nearly the same: he sees them [that is, *situations*, future and
> present] nearly at the same distance, and is affected by them
> very nearly in the same manner. He knows, however, that to the
> persons principally concerned [Jim, Jill, Sue, Tom], they [situa-
> tions, future and present] are very far from being the same, and
> that they [situations, future and present] naturally affect *them*
> [Jim, Jill, Sue, and Tom] in a very different manner. He cannot
> therefore but approve, and even applaud, that proper exertion
> of self-command, which enables them to act as if their present
> and future situation affected them nearly in the same manner in
> which they affect him. (215.11)

Smith here speaks of a being who has intimate intelligence of Jim's
present situation and also of "what is likely to be" Jim's future situation.
This being is not the man within Jim's breast. Smith says, rather, that it is
"the impartial spectator." If this being is a human spectator, some Rick, it
seems remarkable that such Rick has such personal knowledge and is not
partial to Jim (or to present-time Jim).

What's more, this being—"the impartial spectator"—has such present-and-future intelligence not only about Jim, but about all of "those
whose conduct he surveys"—say, Jill, Sue, and Tom, in addition to Jim. This
impartial spectator regards each's present and future situations "nearly at
the same distance, and is affected by them very nearly in the same manner."
What human spectator could have such knowledge and such detachment
over some unspecified set of surveyed persons? Moreover, what human
spectator would "not feel himself worn out by the present labour of those
whose conduct he surveys"?

Smith makes that being singular, while Jim, Jill, Sue, and Tom are
plural. "The impartial spectator" of whom Jim's man within the breast is
a representative is *not* Jim-specific. Here, there are four representatives—
one in Jim, one in Jill, one in Sue, and one in Tom—but the being variously
represented is singular.

If "the impartial spectator" here is some guy Rick, why would all those
who are surveyed by him make their man within the breast a representative

of him? Who is this Rick that, if accessible, would serve as the principal of each's conscience? Does Smith imply that Jim, Jill, Sue, and Tom are siblings, and that "the impartial spectator" is Mom or Dad?

We might also ask: In extolling Jim for his prudence, why introduce Jill, Sue, and Tom at all?

Smith is suggesting something along the lines of Jim, Jill, Sue, and Tom as the children of God. Smith's language here propounds an imaginary, super-intelligent, super-beneficial spectator. This impartial spectator is aptly understood as God/Joy. God/Joy is like a common parent in that God/Joy has contextual knowledge, is benevolent, and is impartial toward all whom He or She surveys. God/Joy hopes and fears for His/Her children and perhaps communicates with them.

In the construct, there is time and story. There are hopes and fears. Joys and tragedies. Sympathy. And God/Joy, is not a human being; Erik Matson (2022, 277–278) elaborates and shows the enlargement of such God/Joy features in Ed. 6. These features make *allegory* apt.

It should not be a matter of controversy in Smith scholarship that Smith maintained God/Joy. In Eds. 3, 4, and 5, Smith had referred to "the man within" as "This inmate of the breast, this abstract man, *the representative of mankind, and substitute of the Deity*" (130 note r; italics added).

The master allegory of God/Joy as super-knowledgeable benevolent beholder is joined by other allegories, such as the allegory of "the man within the breast," who is a representative of God/Joy, the allegory teaching that to be virtuous is "to co-operate with the Deity" (166.7), and the allegory teaching that our companions are "vicegerents" of God/Joy (130.31, 165.6, 166.6). These are extensions of the master allegory.

Smithian allegory, Smith's organon, and Smith's plexus

We may see God/Joy, the man within the breast, and the sympathy of the man within the breast as parts of a plexus. The plexus combines the organon and Smithian allegory, in particular renditions.

It would be possible to embrace an allegory of God/Joy without embracing Smith's organon: One would maintain the idea of a benevolent super-knowledgeable beholder, but not the idea that a sympathy lurks in every moral sentiment. And it would be possible to embrace Smith's organon without embracing Smithian allegory: One would maintain the idea that a sympathy lurks in every moral sentiment, but not the idea of a benevolent super-knowledgeable beholder. Strictly speaking, then, one does not imply the other. Smith, however, does combine them in developing a plexus of thought—involving particular allegorical constructs and particular renditions of the organon. That plexus is rich and rewarding. Smithian allegory deserves praise even apart from the fact that it makes possible that plexus. But the goodness of Smith's plexus warrants yet more praise for Smithian allegory. The case for Smith's plexus enlarges the case for Smithian allegory.

Related literature

The issues taken up in this paper have an intellectual history that is protracted and diffuse, but the issues have not ripened into a scholarly debate.

The 1759 reviewers David Hume, Edmund Burke, and William Rose gave TMS a warm welcome. According to Smith's friend Samuel Romilly, Smith much preferred TMS to WN. For a long time, however, almost everyone thought that TMS was much inferior to WN. TMS was discounted, disparaged, disrespected, and dismissed. In 1927, Glenn Morrow (1927, 336) lamented that TMS had long been consigned to "oblivion." What prompted the consignment was, among other things, Smith's organon and Smithian allegory. In Chapter 10, I quote 35 authors, the earliest of which are Thomas Reid, Lord Kames, and Adam Ferguson, and the latest is Arthur N. Prior (1949). All of the 35 authors express at least one of the following sorts of criticism: TMS was said to err by relying on allegory, metaphor, and figurative language at crucial points in the theory; at those points it was said to invoke principles themselves vague or, even worse, circular; it was said to lack foundations; it was said to violate foundational demarcations. The most elaborate critiques of Smith are perhaps those by Thomas Brown (1820), Théodore Simon Jouffroy (1840), and James Anson Farrer (1881).

With only a few exceptions,[26] commentators recognized TMS's nonfoundationalism and damned it for that.

After 1976, readers began to approach TMS without holding its nonfoundationalism against it. Some explicitly note its nonfoundationalism, including Charles Griswold (1999, 165), Emma Rothschild (2001, 231, 238; 2004,152), and Samuel Fleischacker (2004, 23–26).

Ryan Hanley explains in *Our Great Purpose: Adam Smith on Living a Better Life*: "the end of our goodness…isn't simply our own happiness but the promotion of the happiness of all, and thereby God's will, here on earth" (2019, 132). Roderick Firth (1952), Paul Oslington (2012), and Jeffrey Young (1992) likewise interpret the supreme impartial spectator as God or ideal. Deirdre McCloskey (2008) highlights the role of exemplars in what she calls virtue ethics (pp. 48–49, 60, 65). Her description of a circa-1790 shift in ethical thinking toward some preeminent principle (reason, categorical imperative, greatest happiness, etc.), as opposed to talking of the virtues of human beings, dovetails with my "oblivion" narrative.

Broadly speaking, however, the two attitudes toward Smith's nonfoundationalism have not engaged one another, and in that sense there has not been a scholarly debate. For the longest time Smith's nonfoundationalism was, to almost all, objectionable, and then, after 1976, it was, to many, unobjectionable. This chapter argues that it is not only unobjectionable but positively good. I do not directly engage critics like Brown, Jouffroy, and Farrer, but I mount a case against their objections.

Understanding the allegorical in TMS helps us understand why TMS fell into oblivion. It helps us understand developments after 1790. Also, it also helps us ponder whether Hume and Smith differ from much of the rest of the Scottish enlightenment, as suggested by Knud Haakonssen (1996, 7, and related chapters) and Nicholas Phillipson (1973).

---

26. There are a number of works/authors between 1790 and 1976 that I regard as being exceptional in seeming not to hold TMS's nonfoundationalism against it or in expressing an on-the-whole highly favorable estimation of TMS, including James Clerk Maxwell (see Campbell and Garnett 1882, 143, 212), Harald Höffding 1900, I, 443–446; Wilhelm Windelband 1901; Francis Hirst (1904); Albion Small (1907), Edward Westermarck (1914/2023), Glenn Morrow (1923, 1927), Henry J. Bitterman (1940a, 1940b), J.N. Findlay (1950, 25n1), Roderick Firth (1950), Overton H. Taylor (1960), Alec L. Macfie (1967), J. Ralph Lindgren (1969, 1973), Ronald Coase (1976), and E.G. West (1976).

In praise of Smithian allegory

Compared to what?

Saying that Smithian allegory is good prompts the question: Compared to what?

Those who roll their eyes and scoff at God/Joy presumably feel that they have a good way of thinking about the good, a way without God/Joy. Well, what is it?

Maybe they think they have a "principle." Some will invoke science-sounding principles like "net benefits," "utility," "efficiency," others, more aesthetic-sounding principles like "beauty," "happiness," "flourishing." Such formulations, it is said, need not or even should not involve any notion of a super-knowledgeable benevolent beholder.

Let's briefly consider the word "efficiency." Efficiency can be thought of as a ratio of outputs to inputs, as in fuel efficiency—that is, vehicle miles traveled to gallons of gasoline. When the scoffer invokes "efficiency" as the criterion for goodness, the input is something like the alternative courses of action. But what is output?

The scoffer—perhaps an economist—might invoke willingness-to-pay notions, which on blackboards have a semblance of precision. But the semblance is false for things of importance. Blackboard notions involve a slew of suppositions. One concerns the individual's wealth level. We point out that a dollar means more to a poor person than it does to a rich person, a truth not accounted for in the efficiency standard. The scoffer says, "Yes, of course. So efficiency is a first approximation, and we tweak from there as necessary." But that is an admission that the good is more than "efficiency." He is admitting that he makes "efficiency" focal only because it helps with the good, which is still larger and undisclosed. And wealth levels are but one of myriad relevant presuppositions. How one identifies the "efficient" course—if elaborated—turns out to be a discursive, blooming harangue.

About this matter I once wrote a footnote, which I reproduce in part here.[27]

As for the term *utility*, it was originally more strictly synonymous with *usefulness*, which Hume distinguished from *agreeableness*. Chocolate ice cream is agreeable; the immediate pleasure is its main benefit. A wheelbarrow is not agreeable, but it is useful. Jeremy Bentham himself had misgivings about "utility." A better term is *beneficialness*.[28] *Bene-* is Latin for well; from the same source came *bonus*, good.

There is no benevolence in a wheelbarrow. But a benevolence lurks in our saying that it is beneficial. My plea—like that of Ryan Hanley (2019), Erik Matson (2022), Francis Hutcheson, and many others—is to understand that beneficialness corresponds to what a super-knowledgeable benevolent beholder finds beautiful.

In saying that Smithian allegory is good, I do not propose that we speak expressly of God/Joy whenever we speak of beneficialness. But it would be misguided to banish God/Joy. Philosophies that purport to do so throw the baby out with the bathwater.

---

27. Here is part of a footnote from Klein (2012, 216n6):

> Some points one might make about why efficiency/willingness-to-pay concepts are often ambiguous would include: 1) The diminishing marginal utility of wealth; 2) The hypothetical nature of propositions, giving rise to ambiguities in, for example, the time-to-adjustment in deciding one's willingness to pay; 3) The collective action problems that might matter to the individual's contemplation of how much he would be willing to pay; 4) The issue of deeper, truer preferences, as opposed to unenlightened preferences, which is especially relevant in considering policy reforms; 5) Identity factors involved in changing policy; 6) In as much as a policy reform would alter future preferences, perhaps of the new and future generations, we have to consider what preferences are worth fostering; 7) The Smithian distinction (TMS: 68, 83, 137, 188–192) between passive experience of the effects of a change and moral agency for the change; and 8) Economists often, perhaps usually, do not have good data on the willingnesses to pay that are most pertinent to their theoretical arguments.

> And, where "economic efficiency" is confined in such a way as to make it relatively precise and accurate, it really is a lower-level criterion for overall judgment. That is, narrower, more precise notions of economic efficiency are not a final arbiter of the social good.

28. It is especially in the second enquiry that Hume distinguishes agreeable and useful. On Bentham's misgivings about "utility," see below pp. 113–15..

A venerable doctrine

Smith allowed that "our good-will" may be "circumscribed by no boundary, but may embrace the immensity of the universe" (235.1). Such good will, however, is a far cry from the universal benevolence of God/Joy, a "benevolent and all-wise Being" (235.3). Smith writes:

> Benevolence may, perhaps, be *the sole principle of action in the Deity*, and there are several not improbable arguments which tend to persuade us that it is so... But whatever may be the case with the Deity, so imperfect a creature as man...must often act from many other motives. (305.18;, italics added)

Smith tells of a man of humanity in Europe who can prevent the amputation of his pinky but only by causing a dreadful earthquake in China. The man acts beneficially. Why? "It is not the soft power of humanity, it is not that feeble spark of benevolence" (137.4).

If universal benevolence, as opposed to mere good-will, is to play a central part in our ethics, our ethics will need to give a part to God/Joy. Smithian allegory, or, more broadly, the tradition upon which it builds—what Alexis de Tocqueville called "the spirit of religion"—is the only way to give universal benevolence an honest place in our pursuit of wisdom and virtue. Tocqueville (39, 43, 282) held that the spirit of religion and the spirit of liberty stand together and fall together. If he was right—and I think he was—that means that the dignity of man stands or falls with the spirit of religion.

A wheelbarrow is a lever. A lever has four components: The **lever arm** (in blue in the diagram at right below), the **force or effort**, the **fulcrum**, and the **load**, which the person applying the force aims to lift. (Levers vary by which of the last three components is situated between the other two, along the lever arm.)

FIGURE 3.1: TWO IMAGES OF A LEVER WITH THE LOAD BETWEEN THE FULCRUM AND THE EFFORT/FORCE.

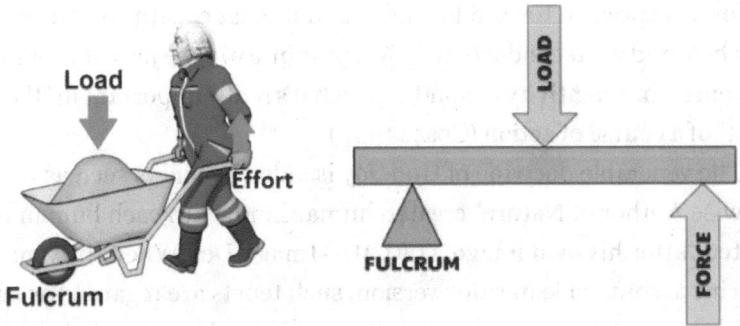

Smith presumed that he lifts humankind in lifting the **load** of his conscience; he applied the **force** of his will in doing so, and part of that will was "that feeble spark of benevolence." The **lever arm** includes bodies of learning, for example as contained in *The Wealth of Nations*. The **fulcrum** includes Smith's plexus (allegory + organon). Within the fulcrum is God/ Joy's universal benevolence; within the force is a feeble spark of benevolence. A spark can, with tending, produce abiding warmth and light.

After telling of the man who forgoes his pinky, Smith ridicules "whining and melancholy moralists" who instruct us to share the feelings of humankind, especially pain and suffering. "[F]irst of all, this extreme sympathy with misfortunes which we know nothing about seems altogether absurd and unreasonable," since, among 20 persons taken at random, 19 are in tolerable circumstances. Second, "[t]his artificial commiseration, besides, is not only absurd, but seems *altogether unattainable*," not least from knowledge problems. And third, "this disposition of mind, though it could be attained, would be perfectly useless, and could serve no other purpose than to render miserable the person who possessed it" (140.9; italics added). A lively sense of benevolence with every person of the world would not only be in vain, but a vanity: "That we should be but little interested...in the fortune of those whom we can neither serve nor hurt, and who are in every respect so very remote from us, seems wisely ordered by Nature" (140.9).

By getting God/Joy into a human lever we make honest use of universal benevolence. We contemplate how a being with a capacity for universal benevolence would feel about things in the world. We try to better align with what serves his or her benevolence, prompted by the man within the breast;

magnanimity in the job calls not only for persistence and self-command, but for a skepticism toward formulas about what constitutes the good of the whole and what conduces to it. Magnanimity in the job calls for imaginativeness and creativity in pondering what's really important in "the total effect" of a course of action (Coase 1960).

The venerable doctrine of God/Joy is aided by tenets such as that the "all-wise Author of Nature" created humankind, with each human being created "after his own image" (130.31)—Imago Dei. When the venerable doctrine assumes a leaner Joy version, such tenets are regarded as agreeable extensions. In particular, Joy communicates her allegorizing of such extensions and explains that you may understand her sensibilities in those ways—that is, ways that are second-order allegories: Within our allegory she explains hers: "As if I created the world. As if there will be eternal justice in the afterlife." Sing to the tune of John Lennon:

> Imagine Joy as well as
>
> Her imagination

Thus, our allegory of Joy may be a compounded allegory: We tell an allegory of Joy within which Joy tells an allegory of the Creator, who, within Joy's allegory, communicates to each of us by His book of nature, a book that each of us must interpret. Creation, then, is an element of the compounded allegory. Thus, we have an allegorical figure (Joy) allegorizing the Creator. The Creator can also be called Joy: That is, Joy is saying: "Suppose I created the cosmos, to communicate to each of you, by the book of nature."

Smithian allegory mitigates self-deceit

One advantage of Smithian allegory is that it mitigates certain forms of self-deceit. By properly locating universal benevolence in the fulcrum, rather than in our effort or force, Smithian allegory may spare one a faux benevolence.

Back in the day, inferiority and superiority were better reckoned. There are three being-to-being postures: upward, on-a-level, and downward.

In a work in Latin of 1738, translated by George Turnbull in 1741,

Johann Gottlieb Heineccius explained love in each of the three postures:

> [L]ove always tends towards good. But whatever we embrace
> with affection as good, must either be a more perfect being than
> our selves, equal, or inferior to us, and less excellent. Love of the
> first kind, we call *love of devotion or obedience*; love of the second
> kind, we call *love of friendship*; and love of the third sort, we call
> *benevolence*. (Heineccius 2008, 66)

In the *Lectures on Jurisprudence*, Smith says: "In a civilized nation
the man who gives the presant [sic] is superior to the person who receives
it" (LJ(B), 405). Jim, qua benefactor, looks downward to his beneficiary.
Acknowledging Jim's benevolence, the grateful beneficiary looks upward
to Jim, perhaps gratifying Jim's sense of superiority. Such gratification also
may come by what Smith calls "illusive" gratitude (78.11), and such illusive
gratitude may be delusive (158.5).

In learning to shed faux benevolence, we may avoid the condescension
that comes with it, and others may be spared the mischiefs which such
wickedness gives occasion to. An honest approach may spare the world of
"innumerable delusions" (WN 687.51).

Smithian allegory affords us the prospect, however, of being of good
will and public spirit. Smith writes: "There have been men of the greatest
public spirit, who have shown themselves in other respects not very sensible to the feelings of humanity.... Who had ever less humanity, or more
public spirit, than the celebrated legislator of Muscovy [Peter the Great]?"
(185–86.11). Virtue calls for competently aligning with God/Joy's benevolence. Moreover, pondering that benevolence kindles and instructs the feeble spark inside of us.

Smithian allegory impels us to mind the most important things

Coase (1960) told us that in judging a course of action, we must consider
its total effect, as opposed to treating certain particular effects as dispos-
itive. Smithian allegory makes us mindful of the things really of greatest
importance in both courses of action, such as the long-term cultural, insti-

tutional, and moral effects. It urges us to reach up and out, in the manner of Iain McGilchrist's right-hemisphere, to get a more synoptic sense of the larger whole, to improve our sense of what is most important in and for that whole. It prompts us to ask: How does the matter, including the effects of our activities in relation to the matter, look in the eyes of God/Joy?

Smithian allegory chides us for shirking the responsibility to face up to the total effect. It tells us to say "No" to double standards—such as that pernicious deceit that treats one course of action (such as liberalization) as failing if it doesn't work perfectly and an alternative course of action (such as governmentalization) as succeeding if it works at all. Smithian allegory rebukes us for squandering attention on "vain subtilties" that "authorise innumerable evasive refinements" and "teach us to chicane with our own consciences" (340.33).

Smithian allegory impels us to confess the looseness of our aesthetic-like sensibilities

Smithian allegory impels us to confess embarrassments about our thinking about the most important things, such as about the long-term cultural, institutional, and moral effects of a course of action. Allegorization calls to us: How does it all look to God/Joy? What does she think of the course of action? These questions concern God/Joy's knowledge and aesthetics.

The higher and deeper that our thinking goes, the less articulate and conscious things are. People don't know how they ride a bicycle, nor how they assess large wholes. Ask someone to tell you the standard for rating a movie, and he will not know what to say. Smithian allegory calls on us to sift and weigh the warrants for positions on vying courses of action. It is bound to prompt us toward a certain candor and humility. "Frankness and openness conciliate confidence" (337.28). Smithian allegory fosters openness about the looseness of the sensibilities that occasion our judgments.

Some people seem to want to flatten science or truth or knowledge down to what is precise and accurate—hence to what is not a matter of much contention. They tout the positive/normative distinction. Such cant emerged during the time of TMS's consignment to oblivion. Smith's thought flowed from many traditions, some ancient, but notably from moral and jural thinkers, who assumed a Christian outlook. Such figures as Grotius, Pufendorf, Butler, Gershom Carmichael, and Hutcheson approached the good of the whole not as proud scientists but as humble, contemplative servants of God.

Smithian allegory shows us that we explore both ends of inquiry

Suppose we discuss whether *Roman Holiday* is a good movie. There are two objects there. We discuss the relation between them. Should we put *Roman Holiday* into the good-movie category? In discussing the matter, we focus on *Roman Holiday*. But really we explore both objects. Besides exploring particulars of *Roman Holiday*, we explore the good-movie category. Our sensibilities about movie goodness grow and improve by watching movies and talking about their goodness.

Smithian allegory helps us see that in doing economics, political science, or any other flavor of moral philosophy, it's the same. Suppose we are discussing the total effect of the minimum wage, as compared to no minimum wage. In discussing the matter, we explore both particularistic aspects and consequences of the minimum wage and broader sensibilities about the good of humankind and what conduces to it. Our sensibilities about the social good grow and improve by studying issues and talking about the goodness of vying positions.

Smithian allegory makes it perfectly natural for us to see the parallel just drawn between discussing *Roman Holiday* and discussing the minimum wage. Both discussions are about sentiments inspired by a spectacle, that is, about an aesthetic experience. The scoffer who would banish God/Joy would also banish His/her aesthetic experience in beholding the minimum wage. That scoffer often uses language that obstructs the natural parallel, often by invoking unhelpful demarcations between kinds of sentiment, thought, and experience.

Smithian allegory impels us to confess the by-and-large status of certain generalizations and maxims

Smithian allegory impels us to see that our interpretations of the world—

the "lever arm" in my earlier analogy—are themselves courses of action, which again we must judge and choose for their service to God/Joy. We may then see that those interpretations involve central principles of two different kinds, first, those that by construction hold 100 percent of the time, and, second, those that are generalizations, referring to many more particular statements located about the web of statements. The generalizations hold by and large. Such central generalizations will relate to certain maxims or precepts, and those too are by and large. They are not axiomatic. They admit of exceptions. In the 18th century, British thinkers pervasively acknowledged the place for exceptions, recognizing that exceptions did not undo a principle's principlehood. Smithian allegory, then, may abate the follies of axiomatic systems such as the image of economic science propounded by Ludwig von Mises and the political ethics of Murray Rothbard. The Misesian tradition of "apodictic certainty" is misguided: Instead, people should recognize each of their so-called apodictic statements either as organonic, in which case its worthiness is not a matter of conclusive logic but remains a matter for broad reflection and ethical judgment, or as enthymemic, in that it is qualified, admits of exceptions, admits looseness, and so on. In Klein 2012 (ch. 15), Jason Briggeman and I argue that some of the statements propounded by Israel Kirzner as apodictic ought to be reconstrued as enthymemic. Likewise, liberals ought to take a "by and large" or presumptive stance on the liberty principle, not an axiomatic stance.

Smithian allegory prompts us to understand the correspondence between the two goods

Smithian allegory facilitates our awareness and understanding of the correspondence between good conduct and the good of the whole. When ethicists discuss the goodness or propriety of conduct, we might call the approach deontological. When they discuss that conduct's consequences for the good of the whole, consequentialist. Smithian allegory helps us see that they are yin and yang, two sides of a single spiral. Deontology and consequentialism differ in framing and procedure, but both tacitly involve God/Joy, who approves of good conduct and who is pleased by good consequences.

By getting people to recognize the correspondence between the two goods as an organon, Smithian allegory can help people escape the cul-de-sacs that suggest some kind of tension or disjunction between deontology and consequentialism. Such cul-de-sacs were constructed after 1790. The two goods are the two wings needed to fly. The two are complements, not rivals. We may enlarge and naturalize ethical thought by unlearning spurious post-1790 teachings.

Smithian allegory enables our talk about coordination, communication, error, and correction throughout the system

By allegory, and only by allegory, we may elaborate and sustain talk of communication, cooperation, error, correction, etc., throughout the system, for example in the manner of Friedrich Hayek's talk of coordination and communication. Such talk gets us to focus on the mechanisms: What are the signals, etc.? What makes them function better rather than worse?

Simple metaphor such as "the high price told me to buy less than I usually do" is like "the cloudiness told me to take an umbrella." *It does not suffice* to elaborate Hayek's "communication" and the other important terms. One could say, "the pristine snow around the house told the burglar to break in." The do-X message that Hayek says is communicated is something other than simply "do X for your own miserable good." It is a more elaborate system of communication, emanating from a benevolent being (allegory), of quarterbacking, of cooperation, not just simple metaphor about the price telling you "buy this thing" or "don't buy this thing." That would be on par with the pristine snow telling the burglar to break in.

Models (blackboard, equilibrium, agent-based) are metaphor, but not allegory. Allegory is somewhat distinct from other figurative devices that create a comparison between the target and the figure (metaphor, simile, analogy, parable). Allegory seems to entail an entering into, or sympathy, between the target's unfolding experience and the allegorical being's unfolding experience; the two unfolding experiences cannot simply be two human beings (as with a parable). One has to be other than a human being. As for models, the figurative unfolding experience is too mechanistic, too cold. The Walrasian auctioneer is a metaphor, not an allegory; we don't enter into the experience of the auctioneer.

By allegory, and only by allegory, can we sustain the idea that to be virtuous is "to co-operate with the Deity" (166.7). Only by allegory can Jeremy Bentham sustain his statements: "The work of Adam Smith [*WN*] is a treatise upon *universal benevolence*.... [N]ations are associates and not rivals in *the grand social enterprise*" (1843, 563; italics added). All such statements, even the pervasive expression "price signal," can be sustained only by allegory. If you would banish God/Joy without expunging "price signals" from your active vocabulary, you display a dissonance. Hold on to "price signals" and welcome God/Joy's invisible hand into your science of economics.

In Akira Kurosawa's *The Hidden Fortress* (1958), two scruffy companions stick together throughout the film, but during the first 98 percent of the film they ceaselessly carp at one another and distrust one another. Only when they find, together, something higher, and personified, in the final moments of the film, is the road to virtue opened up to them; their interaction changes strikingly.

Next, we praise Smith's organon. Again, the organon is part of Smith's rich and rewarding plexus, which also involves Smithian allegory. What follows therefore enlarges the case for Smithian allegory.

In praise of Smith's organon

Smith's organon says that Jim's moral sentiment relates to and reflects a sympathy between Jim and another being. We can sustain that principle by conjuring moments of sympathy, perhaps tacit, subconscious, or vestigial, and including especially sympathies with an imaginary being. Sympathy lurks inside of moral sentiment.

To praise Smith's organon, I need to say more about the role of exemplars in Smith's plexus. Much of my praise of Smith's organon rests on the large and vital role it gives to exemplars.

Exemplars, emulation, and the man within the breast

The prophet in the comic below receives the wholesome central platitude:

The coarse clay of humankind, however, needs more than bare platitude:

Instruction is offered in scripture and in (the rest of?) the book of nature, notably social experience, "the great school of self-command" (145.22). In that school we learn proprieties, and our sense of propriety is raised, we trust, by the conduct of those we particularly like and admire. We look up to exemplars. The "upness" of their conduct means higher in virtue, better aligned with serving the good of the whole, more approved of by God/Joy. We make God/Joy proud of us by emulating virtuous exemplars. Smith expounds on the vital role of exemplars and emulation throughout TMS (20.3, 48.14, 75.3, 114.3, 117.9, 159.7, 192.11, 247.25, 323.10, 335–336.23–24). He emphasizes that we take pointers from "particular instances" of rightness and goodness (187-88.2 and 159.8), and that we entertain a vague notion of perfection, unattainable but not altogether unapproachable (25–6.7–9, 247–249.23–26).

Exemplars ought not be idolized. Idolatry is veneration or reverence taken too far or acted upon too simplistically. But don't throw the baby out with the bathwater. Too often, the place of reverence is done less than justice. If we do not regard certain figures as great, we simply will not be moved to emulate their conduct. We must sense greatness; otherwise there is no "looking up" and nothing taken to heart.

But we also must learn accuracy in perceiving greatness. Michael Polanyi (1959, 96) wrote (as I noted in the first chapter): "We need reverence to perceive greatness, even as we need a telescope to observe spiral nebulae." Spurners of reverence are like astronomers without telescopes, poor perceivers of greatness.

Learning from exemplars, mentors, and authorities, we grow our man within the breast, incorporating the examples they set, but none of them whole cloth without alteration. On the road of wisdom and virtue, "[e]very day some feature is improved" (247.25). Virtue implies upward vitality.

Where one is coming from

Jim's man within the breast is a unique development. Even if its uniqueness is known to Jim, that uniqueness is scarcely known to others. Suppose that Jim takes some action, which is observed by Hank and Samantha, who then discuss Jim's action. The organon helps Hank and Samantha communicate with one another. It enhances their peaceful and productive conversation.

Hank approves of Jim's action. Samantha asks: Hank, wherein do you find sympathy for your approval of Jim's action? Hank must be ready to lead Samantha to his moral authority, such as a teacher or mentor they both know or a thinker they both know of. It might be a thinker of the past, such as Adam Smith. The procedure prompts Hank and Samantha to talk about how Hank's moral authority sees matters like that of Jim's action.

When Hank and Samantha come together in that moral authority, Samantha may then say, "Sorry, I think that thinker is all wet on the matter." "Well, Samantha," Hank replies, "wherein do you find sympathy for that disapproval of my moral authority?" Samantha answers by citing a different thinker, whom she regards as a moral authority. Now the conversation grows to the matter of how the two cited thinkers view matters like that of Jim's action. By layers, the procedure opens us up to different views of things.

Hank may say, "Oh, Samantha, you cannot slavishly follow that thinker!" And Hank is right, of course.

In referring to that thinker, Samantha does not so much identify the one with whom she finds sympathy, but characterizes that one in a way that Hank will find meaningful. The one with whom Samantha finds sympathy is, most notably, the man within the breast. By referring to her moral authority, she gives Hank a flavor of her man within the breast. She communicates by reference to cultural landmarks.

A goodness in the adversary's soul

"Well, Samantha," Hank might say, "even though your man within the breast resembles your authority in matters like Jim's action, my man within the breast does not. Mine resembles my moral authority, so where does that leave us?"

Smith urges them on. He says to Hank:

> Hank, your man within the breast is the representative of a super-knowledgeable, benevolent spectator. And Samantha's man within the breast, too, is a representative of the same spectator. (In fact, that goes for everyone, so the spectator is universal.) Now, as you and Samantha have not found sympathy in the matter of Jim's action, it would seem that there is a problem in the representations developed in your breasts. We all know that none of us has full or direct access to God/Joy. Talk with Saman-

tha about how you think God/Joy would look at your man within the breast vis-à-vis her man within the breast.

Smith's organon proposes that we knowingly buy into two procedures. First, we see all moral approval as related to a sympathy. Second, we mutually seek a common standpoint to address our moral differences. The procedures prompt us to come together to enter into each other's ways of seeing, to tolerate our differences, to consider that maybe our man within the breast should change somewhat. In embracing Smith's proposition we better accommodate our differences, maybe resolve them to some extent. By being good Smithians and receiving others as good Smithians, we overcome stereotypes and come together to improve judgment in matters of common concern. Smith's organon humanizes our intellectual adversaries. It makes us ashamed of demonizing them. We ought to try to sustain an organon that every soul is good, even if the current mind that belongs to it is not.

Smith's organon makes us more accountable to others and to ourselves

Smith's rendition of the organon, and the allegories it involves, gets us to take moral authorities seriously, to enter into their outlooks. One speaker embraces "the Locke alternative" or "the Aquinas alternative"—tweaked, no doubt. But one develops an understanding of Locke, of Aquinas, as the case may be. Such figures have emerged as focal; their texts are focal points upon which traditions can be built. Their outlooks can serve as focal sets of sensibilities, and with them identifiers and faiths. Moral philosophizing naturally involves intellectual history.

Smith's organon impels us to read great thinkers seriously, scrupulously, and to argue over them. Wayne Booth (1974, 221) wrote: "The notion that values are found and established *in valuers* entails the notion that some valuers are better at the task than other—not a popular notion these days but one we cannot avoid."

The scoffer professes to serve a principle (rationality, reason, truth, efficiency, greatest happiness, etc.) unaided by sympathizing spirits who supposedly represent "God" or "Joy" or other such fairy tales. This scoffer understands that the good is not simple or formulaic. He admits that the good is not simply what he happens to favor at the moment, for he recognizes that sometimes he reconsiders his judgment, deciding that he had previously been wrong. He admits that there are deeper sensibilities at play. He might say: "The good is what would win the favor of my deeper sensibilities about the principles I adhere to."

Okay, scoffer, can you give us a flavor of those principle-based sensibilities? Are there certain traditions they draw from? Are there principal thinkers that guide those sensibilities? Was it principals that led you to principles?

The leading citizen was once called the *princeps*, a word that relates to the English word *prince*, as well as *principal* and *principle*. The scoffer's sensibilities follow certain interpretations of the good of the whole and of the best means of promoting it. There are principals behind the scoffer's principles. The scoffer is not really so far from Smith's organon.

If the scoffer would stop scoffing, he could then pursue the questions naturally prompted by the organon, as in the dialogue between Hank and Samantha, and make his own thought and sentiment more accountable. By embracing the organon, he can make himself more upwardly vital.

Smith's organon calls on us to make our prejudices and affiliations more just

It is not the case that humans are born good and learn corruption. They are born savage and must learn goodness. We must learn to resist savagery. We are instinctively affiliated with our personal history and prejudiced toward our past conduct: "The opinion which we entertain of our own character depends entirely on our judgment concerning our past conduct. It is so disagreeable to think ill of ourselves, that we often purposely turn away our view from those circumstances which might render that judgment unfavourable" (158.4). We are instinctively vain, self-important, and prideful.

Those who deny prejudices and affiliations are delusional. They do not proceed free of prejudice and affiliation. They proceed with prejudices and affiliations less examined, less candid, and less just.

Edmund Burke's criticism of the thinking of revolutionaries seems pertinent:

We are afraid to put men to live and trade each on his own private stock of reason; because we suspect that this stock in each man is small, and that the individuals would do better to avail themselves of the general bank and capital of nations, and of ages. Many of our men of speculation [perhaps, Hume, Smith, Blackstone?], instead of exploding general prejudices, employ their sagacity to discover the latent wisdom which prevails in them. If they find what they seek, (and they seldom fail) they think it more wise to continue the prejudice, with the reason involved, than to cast away the coat of prejudice, and to leave nothing but the naked reason; because **prejudice**, with its reason, **has a motive to give action to that reason, and an affection which will give it permanence**. Prejudice is of ready application in the emergency; it previously engages the mind in a steady course of wisdom and virtue, and does not leave the man hesitating in the moment of decision, sceptical, puzzled, and unresolved. **Prejudice renders a man's virtue his habit**; and not a series of unconnected acts. **Through just prejudice, his duty becomes a part of his nature**. (Burke 1999, 182, boldface added)

Smith said that "the real and steady admirers of wisdom and virtue" are "a select, though, I am afraid, but a small party" (62.2). But a party they are. They affiliate in their shared appreciation of the wise and virtuous; they cultivate their prejudices with care. We may begin by confessing our prejudices and affiliations. Smith's organon leads us to do just that.

Here is Burke again, on the revolutionaries:

Nothing is left which engages the affections on the part of the commonwealth. On the principles of this mechanic philosophy, our institutions can never be embodied, if I may use the expression, **in persons**; so as to create in us love, veneration, admiration, or attachment. But that sort of reason which banishes the affections is incapable of filling their place. (Burke 1999, 171, boldface added)

As the revolutionaries destroy traditions, emblematicized in persons, and the communities, identities, and faiths organized around them, they reduce us to instinctive selfishness and a lesser lot of moral authorities, often highly transient.

One does not have a formula or articulated system for sensing the virtues of the exemplar. You need to see and imagine the persona, the personality, the conduct. Would the exemplar frown or smile? Are you making the exemplar proud of you?

The costs and benefits of estimating objects properly

How is the badness of bad policy to be felt as costs—in a forgone-opportunity sense—for the policymakers and intellectuals who might otherwise espouse the bad policy? When deciding whether to support a bad policy, how might they have skin in the game?

One hope is the pain of disapprobation. Complaints of pundits and commentators quickly get lost in the din. Complaints of friends and colleagues linger longer. What hurts most is disapproval from the conscience. The man within the breast. Notice how Smith made the conscience a being, the *man* within the breast.

The policymaker or intellectual with a conscience faces a genuine cost when he endorses a policy that he knows too well to be bad: He forgoes a reality without painful disapproval from the man within the breast. That is the central point of David Rose's *Why Culture Matters Most* (2019; see also Rose 2011). A good culture calls on us to justly regard beings, incarnate and otherwise.

The badness of a policy is often pretty obvious to anyone with some scruples. The pain of disapprobation has an effect with many policymakers and intellectuals. Those who perpetually espouse obviously bad policy obviously have a man within the breast who is weak and corrupt.

God/Joy has been pushed off the stage, and virtue has retreated. The organon has been abandoned by much of the clerisy, and virtue has retreated. The retreat is not surprising. The approval or disapproval of the man within the breast is the chief way in which social consequences can be transfigured into costs and benefits for the policymaker and the intellectual. The

ideas and imagery of a universal and benevolent beholder are essential—
that is, beholderism is essential. The conscience is essential.

Knowledge of time and place is dispersed throughout the human stations; in each station, someone is watching. Researchers have suggested
that images of eyes watching can influence behavior (Bateson, Nettle, and
Roberts 2006). A meta-analysis (Dear, Dutton, and Fox 2019) seems to
validate an effect against antisocial behavior.

**FIGURE 3.2: EACH WEEK BATESON, NETTLE, AND ROBERTS (2006) HUNG DIFFER-
ENT PICTURES IN A UNIVERSITY COFFEE ROOM AND MEASURED HOW MUCH PEOPLE
CHIPPED IN FOR DRINKS CONSUMED.**

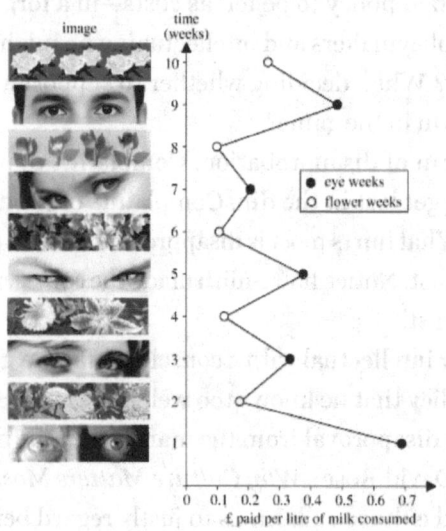

With God/Joy, we have a sense of a superior whom we are obliged to
obey. Michael Zuckert (1994, 189) writes: "Only if one can find in nature
the will of a superior can there be said to be a law of nature, as opposed,
say, to a natural good. Obligation, and thus law, can ensue only when
there is an antecedent superior/subordinate relationship." Allegorization
inspires an allegiance and affiliation.

Matthew 25: 40 is quoted in Leo XIII's *Rerum Novarum*: "As long as
you did it to one of My least brethren you did it to Me." According to Smith's

plexus, we are responsive to the man within the breast, who is a representative of God/Joy, who loves each human being. Act like we were created by God/Joy, each with a divine spark within. Thus, the plexus leverages our interests so as to induce respect for the rights and interests of every other human being. The praxis of respect for the dignity of the individual depends on Smith's plexus. It depends on a certain sense of awe for God/Joy and his or her representative within us. Recall the words that Heinnecius used for love in the upward posture: *"love of devotion or obedience."*

Where Smith speaks of "the devout and contemplative virtues" (134.35), he suggests that God has often been bundled up with bad tenets and practices, which have soured people on religion—"have exposed it to contempt and derision" (134.35). Smith suggests that, in rejecting the beholderist bundles they find on offer, many have thrown the spirit of religion out with the bathwater.

CHAPTER 4

Hume and Smith on Utility, Agreeableness, Propriety, and Moral Approval

By Erik W. Matson, Colin Doran, and Daniel B. Klein

> [William] Robertson's Book has great Merit; but it was visible
> that he profited here by the Animosity against me. I suppose the
> Case was the same with you.
>
> ... it mortifies me that I sometimes hurt my Friends.
>
> – David Hume, letter to Adam Smith, 28 July 1759 (Corr. 44)[29]

Ⅰ n 1759, shortly after the publication of Adam Smith's *The Theory of Moral Sentiments*, David Hume wrote an anonymous abstract of it, appearing in Smollett's *Critical Review* in May of 1759.[30] David Raynor (1984) aptly describes it as "highly complimentary," though it consists mostly of quotations from TMS.

Commenting briefly on TMS's Part IV, Hume writes:

> Our author subjoins many irrefragable arguments, by which he

---

29. Also, in a March 3, 1748, letter to Charles Erskine, Hume said that his essay on the Protestant Succession, which he and Erskine decide to hold back from the public, was "extremely dangerous, & sufficient, not only to ruin me for ever, but also throw some Reflection on all my Friends, particularly those with whom I am connected at present" (Greig, Letters of David Hume, 1:112–13).

30. Hume's abstract is reproduced in Reeder (1997: 33–50) and here is referred to as *"Abstract,"* followed by page number. Note that on page 50 of the Reeder reproduction there is a typo: "digest himself" should read "divest himself."

refutes the sentiments of Mr. Hume, who founded a great part of his moral system on the consideration of public utility. The compass to which we are confined, will not allow us to explain them at full length; but the reader, who will consult the author himself, will find, that philosophy scarcely affords any thing more undeniable and conclusive. (*Abstract, 45*)

The quotation begins with "Our author," which clearly signifies Adam Smith. Afterward we read that the present occasion "will not allow us to explain *them* at full length" (italics added) and, then, a suggestion that the reader consult "the author himself." The exoteric signification of "them" is Smith's irrefragable arguments and of "the author himself," again Smith, thus: *Philosophy scarcely affords anything more undeniable and conclusive than the moral writings of Smith.*[31]

But "Hume was capable of using ambiguity or irony for ulterior purposes" (Raynor 1984, 161). We believe that Hume has a sly signification of "them," namely "the sentiments of Mr. Hume," and of "the author himself," namely David Hume, thus: *Philosophy scarcely affords anything more undeniable and conclusive than the moral writings of Hume.*

Hume's *Abstract* highlights the mystery of the relation between Smith's moral theory and Hume's, and how Smith and Hume themselves conceived of that relation. Several authors have treated the matter.[32] In this paper we offer a fresh examination of Smith's moral theory in relation to Hume's. In Part IV of TMS, Smith presents a foil against which he develops his own theory, a foil supposedly representing Hume. According to the foil, moral approval derives from "utility." But, as a characterization of Hume's theory, that foil is misleading.

The foil is misleading in several ways. One conspicuous way, which is not really germane to the larger issues that we deal with in this piece, comes with Smith's "chest of drawers," where Smith gives the impression that Hume's moral theory draws no distinction between human beings

---

31. Such seems to be the reading of James Fieser (2005, I: 117).

32. Authors who have treated Smith's moral theory in relation to Hume's include Campbell (1971), Haakonssen (1981, esp. 39–44, Raynor (1984), Martin (1990), Pack and Schliesser (2006), Rasmussen (2017, 86–112).

and inanimate objects.[33] But Hume says just the opposite in his *Enquiry Concerning the Principles of Morals* (EPM), published eight years prior to TMS.[34] Such a misrepresentation is curious, and it might be a tip-off that something is up.[35]

One of the more important misrepresentations stems from the fact that Smith used the words *utility* and *useful* differently than Hume did—Smith quietly stretched them to include species of agreeableness, thereby obscuring the importance of agreeableness in Hume's theory.

But the most significant problem with Smith's representation of Hume concerns Smith's advance on Hume. The conspicuous aspect of Smith's advance is to insert something in between moral approval and beneficialness ("utility" in Smith) and to emphasize that something. Smith inserts another phase: the approver's *sense of propriety*. With that phase now finding formulation, Smith then generates *a spiral* of beneficialness and propriety, a spiral shown in Figure 4.7 (located toward the end of this chapter). We consider Figure 4.7, illustrating the spiral, to be the most important arrival point in the present chapter.

But Smith gives a somewhat misleading impression about the extent to which his propriety phase is at variance with Hume's account of moral approval. Whereas Smith allows the impression that in Hume moral approval derives quite determinately from "utility," in fact Hume conveys the interpretive spaciousness of the operations that generate moral approval; here, Hume even speaks repeatedly of "proper sentiments."

But the propriety phase in Smith opens up to a key facet of Smith's development on Hume: He poeticizes a locus of sympathy not emphasized in Hume—namely, the relation between the moral judge and her own man within the breast—, but that locus enters the theory in addition to the

---

33. Smith writes: "[It] seems impossible that the approbation of virtue should be a sentiment of the same kind by which we approve of a convenient and well-contrived building; or that we should have no other reason for praising a man than that for which we commend a chest of drawers" (TMS 188.4; see also 327.17).

34. Hume says (EPM 5.1): "We ought not to imagine, because an inanimate object may be useful as well as a man, that therefore it ought also, according to this system, to merit the appellation of *virtuous*. The sentiments, excited by utility are, in the two cases, very different; and the one is mixed with affection, approbation, &c. and not the other."

35. On conspicuous errors as a device of esoteric writing, see Melzer (2014, 55, 314–315).

sympathies emphasized in Hume, not in lieu of them. We distinguish lateral sympathy, which is important in Hume's thought, and vertical sympathy, which is especially characteristic of Smith's more inner-directed and allegorical thought. Smith embraces Hume's lateral sympathy and enhances moral theory by adding formulations ("the man within the breast," "the impartial spectator") that elaborate vertical sympathy. Smith's propriety phase is a vertical enhancement to Hume's account. Smith vertical dimension gives rise to a spiral of beneficialness and propriety.

Next, we come to something of a twist in the whole matter: We show that—as Smith well knew all along!—propriety is a species of agreeableness! Smith's propriety phase represents another dimension within which such agreeableness lives. In treating the matter, we introduce a distinction between propriety-agreeableness and otherwise-agreeableness.

Agreeableness forms a part of beneficialness. Smith's vertical dimension thus gives rise to a spiral representing development of the judge herself, of her man within the breast. It is a spiral of beneficialness and propriety: Each propriety phase in the next loop of the spiral engenders a species of agreeableness—"all his own passions will immediately become the causes of new passions" (111.3)—*now as a part of beneficialness*. Figure 4.7 shows the spiral, and it highlights the nonfoundationalism of Smith's moral theory.

Smith's developments on Hume, then, involve the following three facets: (1) formulation of the propriety phase; (2) the poetic elaboration of vertical sympathy; (3) the diachronic spiral of propriety and beneficialness.

The three facets come together, especially in Ed. 6 of TMS. The whole development goes beyond Hume, but, really, is agreeable to Hume—though Smith himself portrays his developments as *disagreeing* with features of Hume's moral theory.

We speculate that Smith was more or less aware of all that that we say, including the absence of any significant disagreement. Why, in that case, would Smith have proceeded as he did? We address that question at the end of the piece. Our speculations about why Smith proceeded as he did suggest a method in the madness.

Before treating Smith's representation of Hume, we present Hume's thinking on utility, agreeableness, and moral approval, particularly in EPM. We offer an interpretation that nests moral approval within Hume's conception of "understanding" and "taste." We portray Hume's thinking on moral approval as more capacious than as represented by some others, including Smith.

We treat EPM, not the *Treatise*, as the Hume work that Smith has chiefly in view in constructing the foil to represent Hume. Smith, for example, employs the phrase "why utility pleases"—a section title of EPM (and absent from the *Treatise*)—in both of Part IV's complimentary allusions to Hume (TMS 179.2, 188.3). The editors of the Glasgow edition of TMS, D.D. Raphael and A.L. Macfie, note the connection to EPM, but remark "Smith seems to be thinking more of the *Treatise*, II.ii.5" (TMS 179.2 n1). But the present piece, we suggest, amply shows that, despite the terminological twist, Smith made the schematic portion of EPM—we call it the "four-factor account"—a cornerstone of the foil.36 As Smith was surely aware, Hume thought EPM his finest piece of writing and repeatedly repented of the *Treatise*, even explicitly disavowing "that juvenile Work."37

Hume's moral theory

Hume's four-factor account in EPM

Hume develops his thought concerning the relation between utility, agreeableness, and moral approval schematically in EPM. He relates judgment of an action or character trait to its usefulness and agreeableness. Hume's four-factor account can be expressed as follows: Mary deems Jim's conduct or action praiseworthy based on Mary's understanding of whether it is (1) useful to Janet or other non-Jim persons (i.e., serves public utility), (2) useful to Jim, (3) agreeable to Jim, or (4) agreeable to Janet. (In this paper we often say "Janet" as synecdoche for all non-Jim persons.) Each of the four factors of moral approval in Hume's account is treated in a separate section

---

36. Hume's four-factor account finds articulation at T 3.3.1.30 but is made strongly schematic only in EPM.

37. Hume refers to the *Treatise* as "that juvenile Work" in the "Advertisement" disavowing it, penned in 1775, published in 1777, and reproduced in T 586-587. Hume's repeated regrets are presented by Norton (2007), vol. 2 of T 582-588. We agree with Beauchamp (2000, xvi) that "it is probable that his 'repenting' of his early work was unfeigned."

of EPM. These criteria of praiseworthiness are, of course, not unrelated to one another. Some of Jim's actions could be useful to Jim and agreeable to Janet, and so forth. Hume says that honesty, fidelity, and truth are praised initially as social virtues contributing to public utility, but are also approved of for their private benefit to individuals who possess them (EPM 6.1.3).

Figure 4.1 shows the four factors, numbered counterclockwise (1), (2), (3), and (4) to match the order presented in EPM. In our presentation of Figure 4.1, notice that we provide an explanatory sentence, and notice an important feature of that sentence: Mary's approval depends on *Mary's understanding* of Jim's action as viewed through the four lenses. Smith's development on Hume chiefly lives in the realm of Mary's understanding, a realm we dub the "vertical" dimension.

FIGURE 4.1: HUME'S FOUR-FACTOR ACCOUNT

Mary's assessment of the praiseworthiness of Jim's action is based on Mary's understanding of four factors:

	Jim's action is **Useful** to	Jim's action is **Agreeable** to
Janet	(1) EPM 5 E.g.: justice, fairness, kindness	(4) EPM 8 E.g.: wit, politeness, chivalry
Jim	(2) EPM 6 E.g.: industry, discretion, prudence	(3) EPM 7 E.g.: cheerfulness, courage

Public utility and social virtue

Virtues that are approved of largely for their public utility (factor 1) are called the social virtues, and include justice, kindness, gratitude, and public spirit (EPM 2.5, 3.1). Utility to Hume is synonymous with usefulness to the purposes that people have, ordinary peaceable purposes, treated as presumptively morally legitimate. When Hume says that Jim's virtue or action is approved of for its public utility he means that it is understood to be useful to purposes of non-Jim persons. We might say that the approval-points of useful action are imputed from the value—or agreeableness—of achieving the purposes that the action conduces to. The useful action *assists* purposes, even if such "assistance" is not mutually known and recognized by the actual agents. Thus the approval-points of usefulness do not flow directly from the action; they are dependent on the value of the assisted purposes. Similar to how the value of a capital good, such as a wheelbarrow, is imputed from the final goods it helps produce, the merit of utility is imputed from the agreeableness it conduces to.

Hume writes of the social virtues: "the end, which they have a tendency to promote, must be some way agreeable to us, and take hold of some natural affection" (EPM 5.1.4). He holds that the natural affection that bonds the moral approval of the social virtues to public utility is fellow-feeling and a desire for the prosperity of humankind. Hume, like Grotius, Hutcheson, and Smith, has a roundly social conception of the self and holds that we are genuinely good-willed toward others, saying (EPM 5.2.17): "Here is a principle, which accounts, in great part, for the origin of morality: And what need we seek for abstruse and remote systems, when there occurs one so obvious and natural?"

Sympathy underlies a general fellow-feeling with human happiness or misery (EPM 7.29). Public utility in Hume is understood by imagining the sentiments and passions of a person who is affected by a particular virtue or action of another. Thus when Mary is judging a particular action of Jim's and considering its contribution to public utility, she imagines, for instance, how Janet is affected by Jim's action. If she imagines Jim's action as being useful in a process that brings about pleasure, benefit, or comfort for Janet, Mary understands it to contribute to public utility. The same process occurs in the assessment of inanimate objects, which fall outside the realm of morals, but are subject to similar aesthetic judgment:

> Thus, suppose a man, who takes a survey of the fortifications
> of any city; considers their strength and advantages, natural or
> acquir'd; observes the disposition and contrivance of the bastions, ramparts, mines, and other military works; 'tis plain, that
> in proportion as all these are fitted to attain their ends, he will
> receive a suitable pleasure and satisfaction. This pleasure, as it

arises from the utility, not the form of the objects, can be no other than a sympathy with the inhabitants, for whose security all
this art is employ'd ... (T 2.3.10.5)

Understanding in Hume, at least as pertains to moral approval,
involves the sympathetic imagination. In Hume we have an emphasis on
lateral sympathy, sympathy with actual rather than figurative or allegorical beings. Think of Mary on a field of social affairs. In judging Jim's action,
she enters multilaterally into Jim's situation, into Janet's situation, and into
any other non-Jim's situations. She relies upon her understanding. Friedrich Hayek (1967, 58) noted that the moral-sense school's idea of sympathy
corresponds to the later notion of *verstehen*—which is German for understanding.

Private utility and selfish virtue

Hume calls the category of Jim's virtues that are approved of for their usefulness for Jim's purposes "selfish" virtues. Since Hume's time the word
selfish has developed more definite connotations that make it self-contra-
dictory to speak of "selfish virtues." Hume simply means character traits
useful for achieving one's own purposes, which are, again, presumptively
perfectly legitimate. As with social virtue, Hume relates moral approval to
sympathy and sociability. When we observe Jim to act in a manner that we
understand to be useful for bringing about his own joy and happiness, e.g.,
acting industriously, diligently, prudently, reflectively, we sympathize with
him and approve his action and character (see EPM 6.1.3). Hume maintains
that such approval of selfish virtue cannot stem from self-love in that "[no]
force of imagination can convert us into another person, and make us fancy, that we, being that person, reap benefit from those valuable qualities,
which belong to him" (6.1.2).

Agreeableness

Agreeableness is that which is immediately agreeable. When Hume
employs the adverb "immediately" in front of "agreeable," he does not mod-

ify "agreeable" but simply accents a key feature of agreeableness. "Immediately agreeable" and "agreeable" are one and the same to Hume (as well as to Smith). Hume writes: "Whatever is valuable in any kind, so naturally classes itself under the division of *useful* or *agreeable*, the *utile* or the *dulce*" (9.1.1). Latin for *sweet*, *dulce* highlights the immediateness of agreeableness, as with chocolate ice cream. In addition to agreeableness of the taste buds, we should point out that agreeableness is fruitfully associated in Hume with pleasing sensation more generally, with something *feeling* good or right—as opposed to "rubbing us the wrong way," as idiom has it.

Hume treats the agreeableness of Jim's action under two heads: agreeableness to Janet (i.e., non-Jim's) and the agreeableness to Jim himself. Qualities that are immediately agreeable to Janet include manners, wit, and politeness. Qualities that are immediately agreeable to Jim include cheerfulness, courage, and tranquility. Things that we judge to be immediately agreeable to their possessors are approved of from basically the same source as with the so-called selfish virtues. It pleases us to see other people happy. "These [characteristics and actions] are immediately *agreeable* to others, abstracted from any consideration of utility or beneficial tendencies: They conciliate affection, promote esteem, and extremely enhance the merit of the person, who regulates his behaviour by them" (8.1). Moreover, virtues and actions that please their possessors spread and become naturally agreeable to onlookers: "WHOEVER has passed an evening with serious melancholy people, and has observed how suddenly the conversation was animated, and what sprightliness diffused itself over the countenance, discourse, and behavior of every one ..." (7.1). Agreeableness in morals immediately engages our approbation and spreads "by a contagion or natural sympathy" (7.2).

The Role of the Understanding

Hume's four-factor account is not a simple formula for moral judgment, but an explanatory process embedded in contexts of understanding, imagination, and judgment that vary *with Mary*. Mary's understanding—as we use the term—can be broadly interpreted as the complex interaction of her portfolio of available interpretations and her faculties of reflection and judgment. Reflection involves reason and imagination. As pertains to reason, Mary's understanding instructs her "in the tendency of qualities and actions, and point out their beneficial consequences for society and to their possessor" (Appendix 1.2). Mary's reason can progress over time, giving her a more or less sound sense of the consequences of a characteristic or action. Hume says: "But though reason, when *fully assisted and improved*," implying that it is coherent to talk about *better* or *worse* reason, as accords with our own sensibilities and higher-level judgments.[38]

Hume says that sentiment plays a role when Mary judges an act praiseworthy or blameworthy (EPM Appendix 1.3). A sentiment is generated by the sympathy that arises from an imaginative component of Mary's understanding. Her ability to imagine herself in the situation of others is a function of her experience and of the degree to which she has cultivated her imagination and moral sensibilities. Hume illustrates the sympathetic imagination:

> Nay, when we run over a book with our eye, we are sensible of such unharmonious composition; because we still imagine, that a person recites it to us, and suffers from the pronunciation of these jarring sounds. So delicate is our sympathy!... In every judgment of beauty, the feelings of the person affected enter into consideration, and communicate to the spectator similar touches of pain or pleasure. (EPM 5.37, 38)

The sympathetic imagination and the operations of reason are codependent in Hume's account. The combined operations of reason and imagination give rise to moral judgment. Together reason, imagination, and judgment comprise Mary's understanding, or assessment, of Jim's action. The understanding is a spacious faculty that encompasses Mary's various interpre-

---

38. EPM Appendix 1.3; italics added. Hume uses the word "reason" in a number of senses. His primary use of "reason" refers to an inferential faculty that operates upon relations of ideas, leading to demonstrations, and matters of fact, leading to probabilities. But at other points, he uses "reason" to refer to a stricter faculty of intuition and demonstration. From the perspective of the second, stricter sense of reason, our primary faculty of reason—particularly its mode of probable reasoning—is not *reasonable*. On similar interpretations of "reason" in Hume see Winters (1979), Owen (1999), and Matson (2017a, 2017b).

tive frameworks. Once we grasp the social interpenetration residing within Hume's conception of the understanding, we see its adaptability not only to diverse contexts that Mary might take into view, but to diverse *Marys*.

The Sense of Taste

In treating agreeableness in EPM, Hume speaks of taste and sentiment. In the moment, Mary senses whether she likes a particular object, whether it accords with her sense of taste. But Hume says that Mary can foster what she thinks constitutes a *better* sense of taste, and that bettering her sense of taste is itself an agreeable quality: "The very sensibility to these beauties, or a DELICACY of taste, is itself a beauty in any character; as conveying the purest, the most durable, and most innocent of all enjoyments" (EPM 7.29). Mary's taste in one particular moment might reflectively become an object of her future estimation. So Mary might think to herself, "how agreeable is my sense of what is agreeable?" On our interpretation, there is a naturally occurring recursivity in Hume's conception of agreeableness. His account of agreeableness can allow for conscious development of moral approval. As Mary can strive to develop good taste in music and art, she can strive to develop good taste in character and morals by working off her exemplars and experience. She can cultivate agreeable sensibilities regarding objects that she thinks *should* be agreeable, independent of whether she finds them to be particularly agreeable herself at a given time. Mary ponders what sort of conduct on Jim's part she *should* find agreeable, or how Jim's conduct accords with her developing sense of taste.

Our interpretation of Hume's conception of taste does not draw particularly on EPM. His essays "Of the Delicacy of Taste and Passion" and "Of the Standard of Taste" show the importance he ascribed to taste in literature and morals, and his general interest in the ongoing 18th-century discussion regarding whether a standard of taste could be established. When Smith alludes to Hume, he does not specify particular works by Hume, so it is perhaps fair on our part to draw from Hume's essays, with which Smith was surely familiar. It might be objected that Hume's essays on taste speak solely to the issue of connoisseurship and cannot be generalized to morals and understanding. But Hume seems comfortable with such generalization, saying that the function of taste is to "give the sentiment of beauty and deformity, vice and virtue" (EPM Appendix 1.21). Moreover, early in his career (T 1.3.8.12), Hume generalized taste to the enterprise of philosophy itself: "'Tis not solely in poetry and music, we must follow our taste and sentiment, but likewise in philosophy." For both Hume and Smith, moral sensibility is the matter of beauty of human conduct.

In "Of the Delicacy of Taste," Hume speaks directly of cultivating taste as a way of forming sound judgment:

> In order to judge aright of a composition of genius, there are so
> many views to be taken in, so many circumstances to be com-
> pared, and such a knowledge of human nature requisite, that no
> man, who is not possessed of the soundest judgment, will ever
> make a tolerable critic of such performances. And this is a new
> reason for cultivating relish in the liberal arts. Our judgment
> will strengthen by exercise: We shall form juster notions of life
> ... (EMPL, 6)

Hume's idea that we can form more or less just notions of life parallels the idea of the recursive nature of propriety in Smith. The sense of taste in Hume allows us, as does the sense of propriety in Smith, to think about how proper or just Mary's moral sensibilities regarding Jim's action are. We can hold Mary's judgment up against the judgment of others. So Hume holds that taste allows us to swap our sense of beneficialness (a composite of usefulness and agreeableness), which is inevitably linked to our exemplars' sense of beneficialness, for Mary's. Hume tacitly endorses and encourages this move: "One accustomed to see, and examine, and weigh the several performances, admired in different ages and nations, can alone rate the merits of a work exhibited to his view, and assign its *proper rank* among the production of genius" (EMPL 238; italics added).

Thus, Hume relates agreeableness to a sense of taste, to a conception of what is justly, or *properly*, considered agreeable. Hume says, "But when these obstructions are removed, the beauties, which are *naturally fitted* to excite agreeable sentiments, immediately display their energy; and while the world endures, they maintain their authority over the minds of men"

(EMPL 233). Hume writes of a sense of agreeableness that is blameworthy: "Particular incidents and situations occur, which either throw a false light on the objects, or hinder the true from conveying to the imagination the *proper sentiment* and perception." He continues: "One obvious cause, why many feel not the *proper* sentiment of beauty, is the want of that *delicacy* of imagination, which is requisite to convey a sensibility of those finer emotions" (234; italics added).

Hume's use of the word *proper* prefigures Smith's propriety phase. Indeed, Smith himself uses "taste" in a way that parallels his propriety phase: in developing our sense of taste we look to the exemplary taste of others (TMS 20.4). Smith particularly links taste to the formation of intellectual virtues. In terms of our distinction between the lateral dimensions (a two-dimension plane) and the vertical dimension, Hume's thought was by no means devoid of the vertical dimension. Smith, we shall see, downplays, among other things, the vertical dimension—i.e., the role of interpretation and sentiment in moral deliberation—in Hume, allowing for the impression that Hume mechanically flattened matters down to the lateral dimensions of the plane. However, what Hume did *not* (much) do in the vertical dimension that Smith does do is treat it in *terms of sympathy*— Hume's conception of *sympathy* does not entail higher-level considerations of "the situation in which the original passion [of the actor] and its expression occurred" (Haakonssen 1981, 46). (Though, later, we show hints of vertical sympathy in Hume.)

The foil that supposedly represents Hume

Smith sets up a foil and attributes it to Hume. The foil serves Smith's purposes, perhaps, but as a representation of Hume it is misleading in a number of ways.

"Utility" and "Useful": Smith's curious semantic deviation from Hume

In several signal passages in TMS, Smith represents Hume's account as holding that Mary's moral approval of Jim's conduct flows from Mary's view of the "utility" of Jim's conduct. That is, Smith specifies "utility" but not "agreeableness." The utility-without-agreeableness representation is very pronounced: The very title of Part IV begins it and then immediately the very title of the first chapter continues it (in relation to the beauty of non-moral objects), and then immediately the first sentence of the first chapter affirms it again, as does the very title of the second chapter (on moral objects). Indeed, in Part IV it is but once that agreeableness is mentioned as a factor in beauty judgments, coming more than halfway through the Part, and quite in passing (188.3).

If one were to assume that Smith uses the word *utility* (and *useful*) as Hume does, then one would have to conclude that Smith simply misrepresents Hume. In all of Smith's representations except at 188.3, it would seem that Smith has simply overlooked, or lopped off, the agreeableness parts of Hume's four-factor account, like cutting off the agreeableness arms and leaving only the usefulness legs (see Figure 4.2). Such a view of the matter seems to be held by Raynor (1984, 59), who says "Smith evidently misrepresents Hume's moral philosophy, which...identifies four independent sources of value, only two of which involve utility."

FIGURE 4.2: THE AGREEABLENESS ARMS AND USEFULNESS LEGS, IN HUME'S SEMANTICS

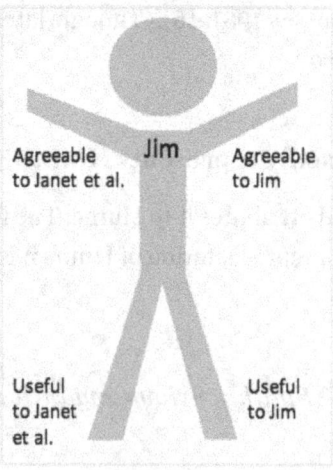

But we read Smith as using the terms differently than Hume does: If only implicitly, Smith *does* preserve the agreeableness arms, but he denominates all four limbs' "utility," whereas Hume denominates only the useful legs "utility." The agreeableness arms are intact, but Smith denominates them, too, "utility."[39] Thus, the arms, for Smith are agreeable, useful, and have utility, whereas for Hume the arms are agreeable but not useful nor have utility. For Smith, this extending of the semantic deviation down to "useful" is really the only way to see Smith as preserving Hume's four-factor thesis while handling the passages saying that according to Hume's system "qualities which are approved of as virtuous...are originally valued as useful to ourselves as well as those which are esteemed on account of their usefulness to others" (TMS 188.5).

Suppose Smith knows that Hume likes chocolate ice cream. Smith might say: "Hume finds usefulness, or utility, in chocolate ice cream." To this, Hume might object: "Well, I find utility in chocolate ice cream only in that, as against other sustenance, it is useful to me, should I have a purpose to satisfy an impulse to it; in that sense agreeableness can always be said to entail such a usefulness, and hence a utility; but I prefer to strip away such a trivial usefulness and preserve 'useful' and 'utility' for purposes aside from such immediate agreeableness."

The one instance within Part IV in which Smith speaks of "agreeableness" as a factor involves an ambiguous "or" but seems to support our interpretation:

> The same ingenious and agreeable author [i.e., Hume] who first explained why utility pleases, has been so struck with this view of things, as to resolve our whole approbation of virtue into a perception of this species of beauty which results from the appearance of utility. No qualities of the mind, he observes, are approved of as virtuous, but such as are u*seful or agreeable* either to the person or to others.... (TMS 188.3; italics added)

Elsewhere, in Part VII, Smith more clearly subsumes agreeable under

---

39. Cf. Campbell (1971, 118), who notes that Smith "does include the *immediate* effects of action."

"utility": "According to [that system which places virtue in utility], all those qualities of the mind which are agreeable or advantageous, either to the person himself or to others, are approved of as virtuous, and the contrary disapproved of as vicious" (305–306.21). Likewise, in reviewing "that principle which gives beauty to utility," Smith speaks of society as "an immense machine, whose regular and harmonious movements produce a thousand agreeable effects" (316.2).[40]

Smith's semantic deviation from Hume is curious. One might suspect that Smith had simply misunderstood Hume, that he had somehow overlooked the agreeableness factors in Hume's account. But select passages show that Smith recognized agreeableness in Hume's account. Indeed, in the one such passage in TMS Part IV, Smith (188.3) even calls Hume "agreeable"! In fact, in Part IV's second paragraph (179.2) Smith introduced Hume as "an ingenious and agreeable philosopher," so it is twice that Smith calls Hume "agreeable." We believe the semantic deviation was knowing and deliberate. Indeed, we fancy that there is an inside-joke quality to Smith's calling Hume "agreeable" (as well as to the passage of Hume's abstract quoted at the outset of the present paper). Hume's wonderfully affectionate letter to Smith on the reception of TMS (12 April 1759) begins: "I give you thanks for the agreeable Present of your Theory" (Corr. 33).

One can see why Smith would like to have a single term that covers all four factors in Hume's account, so that he can then augment that with the propriety phase. But he could have avoided using *utility*, instead using, for example, *beneficialness*, including both agreeableness and usefulness (in Hume's narrower sense). Swapping "beneficialness" in for "utility" in Smith's Part IV would work nicely, and throughout. Smith is then saying that our understanding of the relation between moral approval and beneficialness needs to be enlarged with the idea of propriety.

Another curious aspect of Smith's semantic deviation is that *he does*

---

40. As for material in TMS outside of Part IV, there are yet more passages in which "utility" can be interpreted to encompass both usefulness and agreeableness, for example 52.3, 199.9, 238.4, 327.17. Related passages also occur at LJ 338, 401ff. In TMS 305–306.21, Smith separates useful and agreeable but immediately brings them together under "utility." Although Smith often seems to signify what we call "beneficialness" when he says "utility," we note that there are passages in TMS in which "utility" seems to signify only (or, at least, especially) Hume's usefulness, e.g., TMS 20.4, 35.4, 86.2, 199.9.

not alert the reader that he shoehorns agreeableness into "usefulness" and "utility." If Hume's stronger definition (hence, narrower signification) of "utility" were at all the norm, then Smith does a very poor job of conveying to the reader that he uses "utility" in a sense that is weaker than they are accustomed to. At any rate, Smith never calls attention to the fact that Hume himself does not talk "useful"/"utility" as Smith does.

Because "useful" and "utility" play such a central role in Hume's discourse, not calling attention to the semantic deviation from Hume, not flagging it, makes for a representation of Hume that is downright misleading. The reader of *TMS* would have to be very familiar with Hume's thought not to be led into thinking that Hume uses "utility" as Smith does. Even worse, the innocent reader of *TMS* might conclude that Hume's account does not include the agreeableness factors at all.

By stretching "utility" to mean beneficialness, Smith now has a concise term to represent his foil, and to add propriety to. But the stretching of "utility" is the shoehorning of agreeableness. Agreeableness is de-emphasized. People might get the false impression that Smith has a drab moral vision, giving no weight to chocolate ice cream, wit, charm, manners, and other merely immediately agreeable human experiences. This problem, indeed, was pointed out to Jeremy Bentham, years after he had adopted the stretched "utility," and beginning about 1823 he publicly expressed regret about the choice he had made.[41] The confidante and editor of Bentham, John Bowring, said the following in "History of the Greatest-Happiness Principle":

> An observation made to Mr Bentham by Lady Holland produced a great impression upon him. She said that his doctrine of utility put a *veto* upon pleasure; while he had been fancying that pleasure never found so valuable and influential an ally as the principle of utility. It was clear, therefore, that the word 'utility' not only failed in communicating to other minds the ideas which Bentham attached to it, but that to some minds it communicated ideas wholly different and opposed to them. And true it is, that unless the

---

41. On Bentham's regret appearing as of 1823, see Burns (2005, 49). Also, in an 1822 writing Bentham (1954, 439, 458) speaks of "reasons derived from the principle known by the name of the *principle of utility*; more expressly say *the greatest-happiness principle*" (italics added).

Greatest-Happiness Principle be recognized as the end, the doctrine of utility might be represented as *useful* to some other end....
Dissatisfaction, therefore, with utilitarian phraseology, gradually
increased in Bentham's mind. (Bowring 1843, I: 318–319)

In his later years, Bentham said that he had adopted the term "principle of utility"[42] "in compliance with custom...from *David Hume* and *Helvetius*" (Bentham [1830], IV: 447).[43] It is entirely possible that Smith had
set Bentham[44] (and others)[45] onto the "utility" semantic path. Suppose that
Smith had not deviated from Hume's semantic practice on "utility" (using,
say, "beneficialness" instead);[46] suppose that Smith had not led the reader

---

42. Bentham used "principle of utility" and the like in his 1776 Fragment on Government and 1789
An Introduction to the Principles of Morals and Legislation.

43. Bentham (1843, I: 242), explaining why he used "utility," writes: "for that was the name adopted from David Hume."

44. Searching online resources, we have found no direct evidence that Bentham had read TMS;
still, it seems plausible to us that, even if he hadn't, Smith's moves there would have filtered down
to Bentham. As for Hume: Nowhere in his earlier works does Bentham show awareness that
Hume had separated usefulness (utility) and agreeableness; he does show such an awareness in
Deontology, included in vol. 1 *Works of Jeremy Bentham*, 223, 250–251, published two years after
his death in 1832.

45. It is perhaps not unreasonable to think that Smith may have influenced Cesare Beccaria, *Dei
Delitti e delle Pene*, trans. H. Paolucci (New York: Bobbs-Merrill, 1963) and William Paley, *The
Principles of Moral and Political Philosophy* (Indianapolis: Liberty Fund, 2002), both of whom
talk "utility" in the vein of greatest happiness. Also, Dugald Stewart, by his account of Smith,
helped to ensconce Smith's talk of "utility" (Stewart in EPS 279, 289). As for Helvetius, his work
De L'Esprit was published in 1758, one year prior to TMS; our French is not adequate to judge the
utilité talk found there; but that word is what Google gives as the French translation of *usefulness*,
whereas Google gives *utilitaire* as the French translation of *utility*, and *utilitaire* does not appear
in *De L'Esprit*.

46. Trained as we are in economics, where "benefit" has taken on willingness-to-pay meaning, it
struck us as odd that Hume, Smith, and Bentham did not make "benefit," "beneficial," and "beneficialness" central to their formulations. But we have come to realize that "benefit" derived etymologically from "well done," and was thus originally a good deed, a benefaction, the product of beneficence. Thus Pufendorf (2003, 106) says (as originally rendered in English): "[I]t is a higher Degree
of Humanity, out of a singular Favour *to do a good Turn freely*... [a]nd these...are called *Benefits*,
and are the fittest Matter for rendring Men Illustrious." On such original understanding, consum-
er/producer surplus from mere market exchange would not constitute benefit. Though the OED
indicates that the wider modern meaning does go back at least to 1606, perhaps the original meaning was still too dominant for Hume et al. to follow the word choice that seems so natural to us.

into think that Hume too used "utility" in the stretched sense: In that case, maybe the term "utilitarian" never would have come into existence. We do not mean to suggest that Bentham would not have developed his greatest-happiness thinking as he did, only that it might have gone by some other name.[47]

Our Own Word Choices

Going forward, we shall use *agreeable* and *useful* as Hume does, and beneficialness for the composite of agreeableness and usefulness, and avoid *utility* altogether. Notice, by the way, that the word *beneficialness* bears resemblance to "universal benevolence."

Smith allows an impression of Hume both speculative and determinate

A number of scholars say that Smith criticizes Hume for having an overly philosophical or speculative theory of morals.[48] Charles Griswold (1999, 54) says that "Smith thinks that Hume looks [of moral judgment] *too philosophically* or 'abstractly'" (italics added). Knud Haakonssen (1981, 69) likewise notes that Smith views Hume's idea of beneficialness as a "speculative philosophical construction and not a true reflection of how men in fact judge." Marie Martin (1990, 107) says that Smith and Hume's views on such matters are in "practically diametrical opposition," and D.D. Raphael and A.L. Macfie (1982, 13) similarly speak of a "sharper difference" between Smith and Hume. Spencer Pack and Eric Schliesser (2006, 53) tell us that "Smith devotes the whole of Part IV of TMS to a respectful criticism of Hume's views, which he thinks more suitable to "men of reflec-

---

47. Indeed, Bowring, "History of the Greatest-Happiness Principle" (321) treats at length Bentham's agonizing over terminology, saying, "there is no topic on which his mind was more habitually occupied than in the search of fit terms to convey his ideas." Bowring indicates that Bentham pondered alternatives including *Eudaimonologian, Feliotarian,* and *ipse-dixitism.*

48. For an elaboration on the meaning of speculative and philosophical in this context, and Hume's view on speculation, see T 1.4.7, Livingston (1984, 1–33), and Baier (1991, 1–27). Criticizing Hume for being overly speculative is odd in that it is a charge Hume levels at metaphysicians throughout his work. For an exposition of the Humean nature of Smith's criticism of Hume, particularly regarding Hume's account of justice, see Pack and Schliesser (2006).

tion and speculation," and James Otteson (2002, 8) likewise argues that Smith prides himself on his "superior" understanding of the role of utility in moral approval. In terms of modern psychology and behavioral economics, we might say that Smith represents and criticizes Hume for framing moral approval as a conscious, calculative, System 2 process, rather than an immediate, effortless, System 1-type process (Kahneman 2013, 21).

We agree that Smith represents Hume as having an overly philosophical, speculative, System 2-type account of moral judgment. Smith prefigures such representation in TMS Part I: "The idea of utility...is plainly an afterthought, and not what first recommends [intellectual virtues] to our approbation" (20.4). And he does so again in a section called "Of the utility of this constitution of Nature": "When led by natural principles we are led to advance those ends, *which a refined and enlightened reason* would recommend to us, we are very apt to impute that reason, as to their efficient cause, the sentiments and actions by which we advance those ends, and to imagine that to be the wisdom of man, which in reality is the wisdom of God" (87.5; italics added). By *TMS* Part IV, it seems that Smith's theory is indeed, as Griswold (1999, 140 n23) tells us, "a running critique of Hume's view of the role of utility in moral evaluation." Smith, as against his representation of Hume, says that although there is an important link between beneficialness and moral approbation, moral judgments by no means spring directly from understanding beneficialness: "This utility, when we come to view it, bestows upon them, undoubtedly, a new beauty, and upon that account still further recommends them to our approbation. This beauty, however, is chiefly perceived by *men of reflection and speculation*" (191.11; italics added). Smith says that our moral judgment springs, rather, first from immediate feelings, which then loom over the completion of our judging.

There is yet another critical aspect of Smith's impression of Hume that we think has gone largely unnoticed: Smith allows for a *determinate* impression of Hume's moral theory. That is, Smith allows the reader to see Hume as thinking that moral judgment is a matter of a determinate mapping from inputs to outputs, as opposed to mapping rules that are "loose, vague and *indeterminate*" (TMS 175.11; italics added). On the determinate impression, given that they have the same inputs, all Marys will come to the same judgment of Jim. Smith's determinate impression appertains to how the foil regards knowledge. For the foil, knowledge seems to be interpretively fixed, common-to-all. Hence, knowledge is flattened down to information. A critic of the foil might then say that the foil neglects the interpretation and judgment facets of knowledge; it neglects that interpretations are not symmetric but asymmetric, not common but disjointed (Klein 2012, xi-xiii, 144–56). It is important to consider that different Marys have differently formulated sets of information *and* different interpretive frameworks through which they are processed.

As evidence of this determinate impression, Smith represents Hume as suggesting that: "The spectator enters by sympathy into the sentiments of the master, and *necessarily views* the object under the *same* agreeable aspect" (179.2; italics added). Mary enters into Jim's situation and *necessarily* views things in the same determinate way as he does; she automatically and mechanically shares his interpretation—which implies that all Marys would agree. Smith provides an implicit example in treating the virtue of public spirit: "It is not commonly from a fellow-feeling with carriers and waggoners that a public-spirited man encourages the mending of the high roads." The implication here is that the foil might see the public-spirited man entering into and necessarily agreeing with the interpretation of the waggoners. The impression that Smith gives of his foil has, then, a flat, determinate conception of the sympathetic imagination, taste, and understanding.

In one of the passages where Smith most directly engages his foil, he says: "No qualities of mind [the foil observes] are approved of as virtuous, but such as *are useful or agreeable*" (188.3; italics added). He could have said "but such as are *considered* to be useful or agreeable," which would be closer to Hume's actual position. But he did not. By saying "are useful or agreeable" instead of "are considered useful or agreeable," Smith suggests that Hume sees the things that are useful or agreeable in the universe as fixed. He portrays Hume as a sort of moral and imaginative objectivist. Subsequently in the same passage, Smith tells us that his foil resolves "our whole approbation of virtue into a *perception*" of the beauty deriving from beneficialness (188.3; italics added). The word "perception" here suggests, again, a kind of fixedness of knowledge and a flatness of interpretation. The sentence seems to read as if the beneficialness of Jim's action is fixed and would be correctly understood by Mary if she but had sufficient access to information. Whereas the moments reviewed here allow a determinate impression of Hume, Smith never portrays the foil contrariwise, that is, as acknowledging disjointedness of interpretation in understanding benefi-cialness. Indeed, in a subsequent section we shall suggest that one of the reasons Smith sets up the foil as he does is to accentuate an advantage of his own enhancement to the foil's theory: that enhancement highlights the problem of indeterminateness, and it proposes means to deal with it.

The Knowledge/processing matrix

With Smith's twofold representation of the foil in mind, we can conceive of a set of terms to describe Mary's act of judgment. The terms might be said to sit under the rubrics knowledge and processing. Figure 4.3 shows both rubrics and their corresponding terms combined in what we call "The knowledge/processing matrix." Under the knowledge rubric, we place two broad conceptions of knowledge: determinate and indeterminate. The hallmark of "determinate," again, is commonness (and fixedness) of interpretation—thought is then a matter of logical processing within the interpretation, automatic or computational—so the first row of Figure 4.3 corresponds to "determinate." The hallmark of "indeterminate" is asym-metry in interpretation and loose, vague rules, corresponding to the sec-ond row of Figure 4.3.

The processing rubric corresponds to dual process theory in modern psychology and behavioral economics, which has been elaborated by Dan-iel Kahneman (2013) and applied to Adam Smith by Nava Ashraf, Colin F. Camerer and George Loewenstein (2003). The dual process theory differ-entiates between conscious, reflective, and speculative acts of judgment (System 2) and instinctive, reactionary, and immediate judgment (System 1). Thus, under the processing rubric, we have speculative and immediate, the columns in Figure 4.3.

Smith gives the impression that Hume sits largely in cell (1), where interpretation is common and the process is speculative. We think that Smith himself teaches that moral reflection and judgment range over all four cells, and he develops that extensive sense of moral judgment partly against a foil ascribed to Hume and put in cell (1). Ashraf et al. suggest that Smith has a well-developed sense of dual process-like thinking that runs through his work, placing himself, at times, in different columns. We believe that each of the four cells makes sense as a distinct depiction of morally judging—that is, that there is a meaningful distinction between the two rubrics.

FIGURE 4.3: THE KNOWLEDGE/PROCESSING MATRIX

Processing / Knowledge	Mary's approval is **Speculative**	Mary's approval is **Immediate**
Determinate: Mary's interpretation is common to other's	(1) The foil 'Hume'	(3)
Indeterminate: Mary's interpretation is disjointed with other's	(2)	(4)

Is Hume speculative and determinate?

We agree with T. D. Campbell (1971, 118) that "Smith is somewhat misleading in the way in which he draws a sharp contrast between his own views and those of Hume." We think that Hume is, by and large, neither speculative nor determinate in the way that Smith makes him out to be. We would recast Griswold's statement to say that *TMS* appears as "a running critique" of the *foil's* "view of the role of utility in moral evaluation" (54). Hume is not confined to cell (1). Although, *compared to Smith*, Hume is *relatively* speculative and perhaps *relatively* determinate in his approach to morals, his conception of moral judgment, like Smith's, clearly extends to the other three cells.

A careful reading of Hume—which Smith undoubtedly had—makes it clear that Hume does not hang moral approval on speculative processing. Hume has, rather, an evolutionary conception of moral approval, such that beneficialness is enveloped into general moral rules over time.

Thirdly, experience sufficiently proves, that men, in the ordinary conduct of life, look not so far as the public interest, when they pay their creditors, perform their promises, and abstain from theft, and robbery, and injustice of every kind. That is a motive

[i.e., of understanding beneficialness] too remote and too sublime to affect the generality of mankind, and operate with any
force in actions so contrary to private interest as are frequently
those of justice and common honesty. (T 3.2.1.11)

The basis of moral judgment in Hume more often stems from a sense
of the conformity of an action to evolved general rules than from conscious
speculation. Moreover, at times, moral judgment in Hume even explicitly
occurs apart from considerations of beneficialness. Hume writes: "These
[qualities agreeable to ourselves] are some instances of the several species
of merit, that are valued for the immediate pleasure, which they communicate to the person possessed of them. *No views of utility or of future beneficial consequences enter into this sentiment of approbation*" (EPM 7.20;
italics added). And Hume goes to lengths to makes it quite clear throughout his corpus that moral distinctions necessarily involve *feeling* (T 3.1.1;
EPM Appendix 1). Succinctly put, "morals and criticism are not so properly
objects of the understanding as of taste and sentiment" (EHU 9.1).

The matter is messier when it comes to the determinate impression.
There are moments, especially in EPM, where Hume seems like his moral
theory entails a determinate conception of knowledge. For example, he calls
his moral theory "so simple and obvious" (EHU 9.1); he elevates the power
of "natural unprejudiced reason" in moral deliberation (9.2); he suggests, in
something of a rationalistic fashion, that civil laws "extend, restrain, modify, and alter the rules of natural justice, according to the particular con-
venience of each community" (EHU 3.34).

We think that the determinate impression is generally an inaccurate
characterization of Hume. The determinate impression cuts against the
grain of Hume's understanding of knowledge. Hume speaks of the indeterminateness of knowledge when he says: "We must, therefore, in every
reasoning form a new judgment, as a check or controul on our first judgment or belief; and must enlarge our view to comprehend a kind of history
of all the instances, wherein our understanding has deceiv'd us, wherein
its testimony was just and true" (T 1.4.1.1). He is leery of finality in interpretation: "The most perfect philosophy of the natural kind only staves off
our ignorance a little longer.... Thus the observation of human blindness

and weakness is the result of all philosophy, and meets us, at every turn, in spite of our endeavours to elude or avoid it" (EHU 4.1.12). His indeterminate conception of knowledge famously culminates in the moving conclusion to Book 1 of the *Treatise*, where he confesses his despair: "all my opinions loosen and fall of themselves.... Every step I take is with hesitation, and every new reflection makes me dread an error and absurdity in my reasoning" (T 1.4.7.2). Such skepticism implies an indeterminateness of knowledge, where reasoning proceeds experientially, instinctively, and passionately. In philosophy, then, Hume calls for modesty and limited pretense (EHU 4.2.14).

In his *Essays*, Hume hints at indeterminateness when it comes to moral judgment. He says good judgment is rare and requires cultivations: "[the delicacy of taste] enlarges the sphere both of our happiness and misery, and makes us sensible to pains as well as pleasures, which escape the rest of mankind" (EMPL 5). In "The Platonist," he speaks—though not explicitly in his own voice—to the indeterminateness of judgment and self-assessment:

> To some philosophers it appears matter of surprize, that all mankind, possessing the same nature, and being endowed with the same faculties, should yet differ so widely in their pursuits and inclinations...To some it appears matter of still more surprize, that a man should differ so widely from himself at different times; and, after possession, reject with disdain what, before, was the object of all his vows and wishes. (EMPL 155)

There are, as we have mentioned, parts of EPM that seem to be quite determinate. But when EPM is viewed in the larger context of his thought, the determinate impression fades. In his melancholy conclusion to Book 1 of the *Treatise*, Hume determines to press on in his philosophical pursuit of, among other things, moral theory (T 1.4.7.12). The nature of his practice of philosophy within an unverifiable yet unavoidable frame of belief has been called by Donald Livingston (1984) his "philosophy of common life." His moral theory in EPM should be understood against such a backdrop. Hume's tone in EPM can, perhaps, be interpreted as abstracting from the indeterminateness problem, strewn throughout Hume's work and immortalized by T 1.4.7. Indeed, he hints at the indeterminateness problem in morals at the end of EPM:

> [R]eason...can instruct us in the tendency of qualities and actions, and point out their beneficial consequences to society and to their possessor. In many cases, this is an affair liable to great controversy: Doubts may arise; opposite interests may occur; and a preference must be given to one side, from very nice views, and a small overbalance of utility. (EPM Appendix 1.2)

It bears repeating that in offering his foil "Hume" Smith does not single out EPM. Although he does seem to use EPM as a cornerstone for the foil, what his representation of Hume is offered as a representation *of* is in no way said to be confined to any particular, but rather would run to the whole of Hume's moral theorizing, and in that whole the indeterminateness problem appears.[49]

Propriety of propriety of propriety: Smith's enhancements

If only implicitly, Smith offers a dialectic that gives rise to a spiral—a virtuous spiral, we hope.

The propriety phase: between moral approval and beneficialness

Smith sets a stage of two concepts, moral approval and beneficialness, as a pair of phases. His conspicuous move is then to insert, between those two phases, propriety.[50] "[I]t will be found, upon examination, that the usefulness of any disposition of mind is seldom the first ground of our approbation" (188.5). By the words "the first ground," Smith means the immediacy of a moral orientation that wells up in us upon our spectating or considering Jim's quality or action. In the moment, our sense of propriety is to our evolved understanding somewhat like a receptionist or clerk is to the

---

49. Indeed, editors Raphael and Macfie note in TMS, 179 n1, that in Smith seems to be referring more to T, 2.2.5 than to EPM.

50. Smith reiterates a sort of propriety phasing at 238.4 and 316.2.

institution he serves. Our sense of propriety is "first" in the sense that it first meets the event, and it then prompts our response; it influences which interpretations we entertain and how we judge. Smith gives the example of the propriety we sense in cases of admirable heroism, and says that, also, "when we come to view" the usefulness of the heroism, we yet find "a new beauty" and such new beauty "still further recommends them to our approbation." But this additional beauty, he says, "is by no means the quality which first recommends such actions to the natural sentiments of the bulk of mankind" (191.11). Two other passages convey the same in-the-moment priority of propriety:

> [I]t is not the view of this utility or hurtfulness which is either the first or principal source of our approbation and disapprobation. These sentiments are no doubt enhanced and enlivened by the perception of the beauty or deformity which results from this utility or hurtfulness. But still, I say, they are originally and essentially different from this perception. (188.3)

> The idea of the utility of all qualities of this kind [delicate taste, accurate reasoning, etc.], is plainly an after-thought, and not what first recommends them to our approbation. (20.4)

Between Hume's two phases of moral approval and beneficialness, then, Smith inserts a third phase: propriety (see Figure 4.4). He says: "the sentiment of approbation always involves in it a sense of propriety quite distinct from the perception of utility" (188.5). The clerk of an institution has developed modes of reception, and employs those modes without rethinking their lineage, derivation, or justification; the cleric of a church practices modes of communion and worship without rethinking their lineage, derivation, and justification. The propriety phase is the clerical office of the individual's evolved moral constitution.

FIGURE 4.4: THE THREE PHASES IN SMITH'S MORAL THEORY (TMS IV)

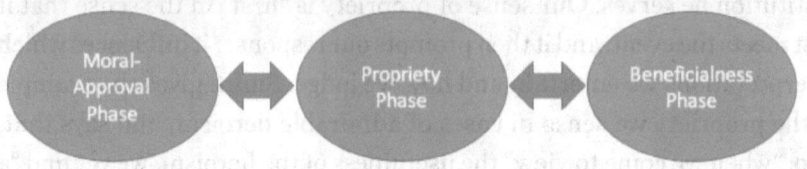

Hume's account holds that Mary's moral approval of Jim's action is linked to Mary's understanding of its beneficialness. But Smith's foil, supposedly representing Hume, omits the sensibilities that clerk for the evolved understanding. The omission creates a wide-open space into which Smith may then insert the propriety phase—the clerk that, in the moment, serves the evolved understanding.

The propriety phase as vertical sympathy

In Figure 4.4, the first link, between moral approval and propriety, is, for Smith, preordained by his formulations. He posits that moral approval relates to a sympathy—an organon that is sustained by resorting as necessary to the man within the breast as the being with whom one finds sympathy[51]—and the sympathy in question regards the judging of Jim's action.[52]

The second link is that between propriety and beneficialness. Smith is, as it were, saying that Mary's sense of propriety has evolved from her understanding of the beneficialness of actions such as Jim's. Here we may enumerate three key elements of Smith's system: (1) Mary's moral approval reflects (not necessarily faithfully) the sentiment of her man within her breast; (2) the man within Mary's breast is a representative (not necessarily a good one) of the impartial spectator in the highest sense of the term (TMS 215.11); (3) the impartial spectator in the highest sense is universally benevolent. There is thus a link between Mary's "clerk"—i.e., her man within the breast or conscience—and Mary's evolved understanding of beneficialness.

The chief development of Smith's propriety phase is the location of

---

51. Smith affirms the organon at TMS 17.2, 46.9 n*, 109.2 ("some secret reference"), 163.4-165.5, 193.12 (final sentence), 306.21 (final sentence), 325.14 (last three sentences). He also does so in a letter to Gilbert Elliot (Corr. 48–50).

52. Indeed, Smith explicitly says that, within his own system, sympathy is "the natural and original measure" of propriety (306.21).

sympathy between Mary and her man within the breast, or her conscience (see Figure 4.5). So whereas Hume's account locates sympathy (chiefly) laterally, Smith's propriety phase implies lateral *and vertical* sympathy. Smith writes:

> It is not commonly from a fellow-feeling with the waggoners that a public-spirited man encourages the mending of high roads. When the legislature establishes premiums and other encouragements to advance the linen or woollen manufactures, its conduct seldom proceeds from pure [i.e., lateral] sympathy with the wearer of cheap or fine cloth, and much less from that with the manufacturer or merchant. The perfection of police, the extension of trade and manufactures, are noble and magnificent objects. The contemplation of them pleases us, and we are interested in whatever can tend to advance them. (TMS 185.11)

FIGURE 4.5: LATERAL AND VERTICAL SYMPATHY

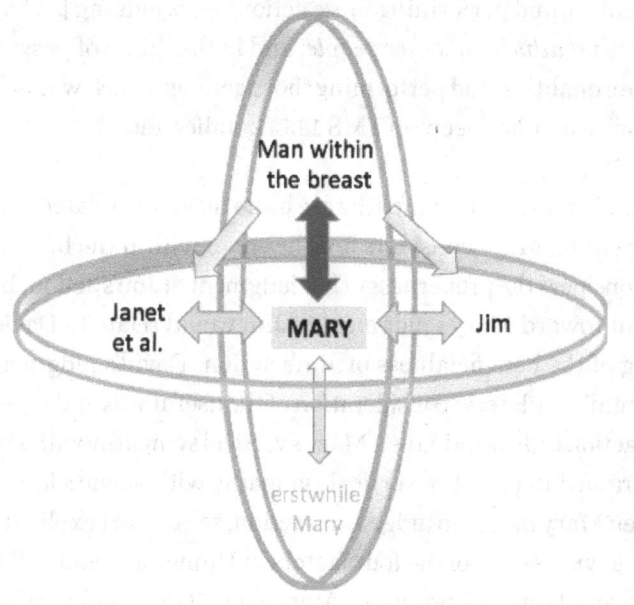

The beneficialness of the high roads does not directly trigger Mary's approval of Jim for mending them. It is the sympathy *with her man within the breast* that calls her, leads her, to consider the meritoriousness, the justness, the beauty of the project. Again, such a sympathy is preordained by Smith's formulations; Mary will not approve Jim's action unless her man within the breast sympathizes with, or can enter into, her judgment—a judgment that we may think of as presumptive or provisional, as potentially up for reconsideration—just as a dissatisfied customer may squabble with the clerk or say, "I'd like to speak with the manager." When judging Jim, Mary tacitly considers whether her man within the breast smiles upon her judgment of Jim's action. The man within the breast embodies the practice and judgments of Mary's homemade, evolved composite of exemplars, the deepest-to-date best practice, by her lights, so to speak.

> The jurisdiction of the man within [the man within the breast], is founded altogether in the desire of praise-worthiness, and in the aversion to blame-worthiness; in the desire of possessing those qualities, and performing those actions [e.g., judging], *which we love and admire in other people*; and in the dread of possessing those qualities, and performing those actions, which we hate and despise in other people. (TMS 185.11; italics added)

Lateral and vertical sympathy are by no means unrelated. In fact, they interpenetrate. Mary considers how her man within the breast, call him David, considers the properness of her judgment of Jim's action. But David's sentiment toward Mary's judgment of Jim would relate to David's understanding of the beneficialness of Jim's action. David's judgment of Jim's action entails his lateral consideration of the usefulness and agreeableness of Jim's action to Jim and Janet. Mary's vertical sympathy with David, then, can be framed in part as a vertical sympathy with David's lateral sympathy. When Mary moves to judge Jim's action, she doesn't explicitly consider how David views each of the four factors in Hume's account. All is blended into an overall sense of propriety. Mary asks: "How would David view my judgment of Jim's action?" But David's view of Mary's action is, in part, a function of his lateral sympathy with Jim and Janet. It should be noted that

Mary's four-factor lateral sympathies still yield points for moral approval. But her sense of the propriety of her judgment, the vertical sympathy with David, looms large.

What is to stop us, one might ask, from extending the recursion? We might ask after the propriety phase between beneficialness and *David's* moral approval of Jim's action. David consults *his* man within the breast, call him Paul, and tacitly asks: "How would Paul view my judgment of Jim's action?" And so on. In principle, we can ask after the exemplars of exemplars, and try to excavate traditions of moral philosophy, as well as the diachronic evolution of the sage, such as Adam Smith. But obviously the higher-order figurative beings grow faint. Actual human beings, like Adam Smith, leave records and give signs that are much more focal than figurative beings. But even an Adam Smith has to judge himself, and that feature points to figurative beings.

Smith's propriety phase provides a serviceable interpretation of the substance of Hume's conception of taste and understanding. Smith develops on Hume by fashioning a moment or phase—the propriety phase—within which we may consider taste and understanding. Though the propriety phase is marked out in relation to the other two phases, what goes on *within* the propriety phase remains loose, vague, and indeterminate: How does the evolved understanding generate its "clerks"? How do clerks serve the institution? Within the propriety phase there will be hardy maxims, but they float in the constellation of practices and habits; propriety is not a determinate all-covering formula or algorithm.

Smith's propriety phase opens the way for consideration of the beneficialness of Mary's judgments. Who, or what, is the deep constitution behind the clerk who serves at Mary's counter? We swap in our own sense of propriety for hers and formulate an opinion on the soundness and goodness of her judgment and the quality of her exemplars.[53] Thus the propriety phase in Smith lends itself to deeper cultural judgments and viewpoints. It opens up the situation to broader social considerations, to apprise ourselves of differing senses of propriety and to estimate the properness of each. It

---

53. For a discussion on Smith on a sense of propriety and selection in interpretation and reasoning, see Matson (2017a).

spirals us up towards considerations of how the impartial spectator would view Jim's action and Mary's judgment of Jim's action as we consider the justice of action and judgment (269.10). It enables us to integrate our judgments about Mary's approval and Jim's behavior with higher and deeper considerations of "that general taste for beauty and order which is excited by inanimated as well as by animated objects" (327.17).

TMS IV puts the propriety phase at the center of the work. Throughout TMS, Smith elaborates on the importance of propriety and the power of the formulation of propriety for thinking about judgment and moral philosophy. The first part of TMS is called "Of Propriety." But by Part IV *it is not Jim but Mary who has become the first-person actor*, the person principally concerned: Her action is the judging of Jim's action. Inserting propriety between the beneficialness and approval phases of Mary's judgment improves our ability to talk about Mary's judgment and sensibilities as a whole. It puts the vital dialectic—the vertical-sympathy dialectic—at the center of the discourse.

Propriety as a species of agreeableness

We are now in a position to move into a further consideration, one that opens a road to a sort of final resolution to interpreting Hume-cum-Smith moral theory: The agreeableness arms in Hume had, all along, included considerations of propriety within his formulation of lateral sympathy. Propriety is a species of agreeableness.

Smith often talks about the *agreeableness* that necessarily accompanies propriety. In fact, once one goes hunting for it, one is struck by how abundant such talk is in TMS, and from the outset. Figure 4.6 presents some textual evidence from TMS of our interpretation. Also, it dawns on the reader of TMS how elemental in Smith is the agreeableness of propriety. Propriety is agreeable by construction, for propriety entails a sympathy, which is always pleasant and agreeable in the awareness of the sharedness of the sentiment, even if the sentiment itself, e.g., grief, is disagreeable (13.1–16.6, 46.9 n*). When Mary senses Jim's motive or intention to have been proper, she sympathizes with Jim. But that is just one of several touchstones in judging the propriety of Jim's action, and at each touchstone Mary finds a sympathy—or agreement—if only with her man within the breast. In a passage that appears to engage Hume and prefigures Part IV, Smith says: "Originally, however, we approve of another man's judgment, not as something useful, but as right, as accurate, as *agreeable* to truth and reality: and it is evident we attribute those qualities to it for no other reason but because we find that it *agrees with our own*" (20.4). Thus we say that propriety can be considered as a species of agreeableness.

FIGURE 4.6: PROPRIETY AS A SPECIES OF AGREEABLENESS IN TMS

Snippet Quote	Citation in TMS
"has exactly observed those measures...which are generally agreeable, reflects with satisfaction on the propriety"	116.5
"bestows a certain propriety...and renders...it agreeable"	179.1
"why the appearance of inconveniency should render any object disagreeable"	179.2
"What is agreeable to our moral faculties, is fit, and right, and proper"	165.5
"the fitness for the useful purposes for which it was intended...renders it agreeable to us."	199.9
"the power or faculty of the mind which renders certain characters agreeable or disagreeable to us"	314.1
"Conscience...properly signifies our consciousness of having acted agreeably"	326.15

Understanding Smith as formulating propriety as a species of agreeable prompts us to distinguish two categories of agreeableness: (1) the agreeableness of something from its striking us, in the moment, as proper—hereafter, "propriety-agreeable"—and (2) the agreeableness of something from it otherwise being agreeable—hereafter, "otherwise-agreeable." The combination of propriety-agreeable and otherwise-agreeable make for an overall sense of the agreeableness of an action or character.

Suppose that Jim steals chocolate ice from Bob and gives it to Janet. Janet knows that the ice cream was stolen. Under Hume's scheme, Mary judges Jim's act of stealing the ice cream by considering whether the theft and subsequent gifting is useful and agreeable to Jim, and whether useful and agreeable to non-Jims. For simplicity, let's not even consider Bob (or any other non-Janet/non-Jims). And, with respect to the individual Janet, let's focus on the agreeableness-to-Janet arm of moral approval.[54] In one sense, Janet might find Jim's theft and gifting to be otherwise-agreeable in that she accepts and enjoys eating the stolen comestible. So, by Hume's original scheme, Mary might award Jim's conduct some otherwise-agreeable points. But when Mary thinks about Janet's sense of the agreeableness of Jim's action, she thinks both about the otherwise-agreeableness and the propriety-agreeableness of Jim's theft *as she imagines they are for Janet.* Janet's sense of the otherwise-agreeableness of Jim's theft is, perhaps, initially confined to the yumminess of the ice cream. But Janet's sense of propriety-agreeableness, by construction, simulates, as it were, *a Mary's* sense of the propriety: "Whatever judgment we can form concerning [our own sentiments]...must always bear some secret reference, either to what are, or to what, upon a certain condition, would be, or to what, we imagine, ought to be the judgment of others" (110.2). Whether Janet finds Jim's actions to be propriety-agreeable hinges in part on her assessment of whether she imagines that someone in Mary's position finds Jim's actions to be proper. So when Mary considers Janet's sense of the agreeableness of Jim's actions, she puts herself into Janet's situation. But Janet's situation, as pertains to discerning the overall agreeableness of Jim's actions, entails entering into *a Mary's* sense of the propriety of Jim's actions. In other words: Mary enters into Janet's entering into a Mary's situation.

Here we can readily see that, for moral attitudes within a society to get along, it is important that certain basic moral sensibilities be shared: Otherwise the Mary who enters into Janet's situation might be very different from the Mary that Janet conjures and relates to when judging Jim's action. To get along with one another and get on with the projects of life, society needs at least some basic grammar of morals.

The propriety-agreeable and otherwise-agreeable distinction high-

---

54. Here, consider useful-to-Janet: If Janet is starving, then we might say that the ice cream is to Janet not only agreeable but *useful*, serving the non-immediate purposes of self-preservation. Our chocolate ice cream example calls to mind Hume's treatment of exceptions to the rules of justice (EPM Appendix 3.7). Although it might, according to Hume, be agreeable to take money from a miser and give to the poor, Hume holds that we should disapprove of such redistribution on usefulness grounds: The rules of justice are useful in so far as they are all but universally and rigidly enforced. Smith might add to Hume's assessment that departures from the rules of justice are propriety-disagreeable.

lights important multidirectional sympathy between Mary and Janet in *Mary's* judging of Jim's action—multidirectional in the sense that the moments of sympathies vary in the matter of which of the two, Mary or Janet, is "the person principally concerned." In the micro-scene of Janet's pondering how Mary *judges* Jim's action, Mary is now the actor surveyed—by Janet. In that micro-scene of the drama, Mary is "the person principally concerned."

Elaborating propriety as it lives in lateral sympathies effectively subdivides Hume's conception of agreeableness into propriety-agreeableness and otherwise-agreeableness. But more significantly, Smith's account, in a sense, implies a breakdown of the Mary-Janet distinction. Remember, in our exposition of Hume, we said that Janet is a synecdoche for non-Jims. Well, Mary is a non-Jim. Thus, Mary and Janet are not necessarily mutually exclusive. But in Smith's account, Mary and Janet are more explicitly posited as distinct beings and more explicitly linked. Whereas in Hume, Mary sympathizes with Janet, in Smith, Mary sympathizes with Janet *and* Janet simultaneously sympathizes with *a* Mary (any spectator to Jim's conduct). A Mary's sense of the propriety of Jim's action informs Janet's sense of the propriety-agreeableness of Jim's action. The way 'Mary' now expands into a class of Marys might bring to mind what Smith writes about the pronoun *I*: "It may be said...to join in its signification the seemingly opposite qualities of the most precise individuality, and the most extensive generalization" (Smith, Language essay, LRBL 219).

Naturally the same goes for the relationship between Mary and Jim. Let's simplify the example: Suppose that Jim steals chocolate ice cream from Bob and eats it himself. Again, let's leave aside considerations of Bob. Jim's action might be, in some respects, otherwise-agreeable to himself, as he loves chocolate ice cream. But it might be propriety-disagreeable to himself in that he imagines a discord between his action and a Mary's sense of propriety. So Mary, in judging Jim's action on agreeableness-to-Jim grounds, enters into Jim's entering into a Mary's situation, once again. In this case, the Mary-Jim distinction blurs, as they enter into one another's situations. "When I endeavour to examine my own conduct...it is evident that I, the examiner and judge [Jim imagining himself as Mary], represent a different character from that other I [Jim], the person whose conduct is examined and judged of" (113.6).

At this point one wonders whether Smith's propriety phase is, after all, latent within Hume's four-factor account, for propriety was nestled within agreeableness all along. Hume, in EPM (8.12–14), in treating of agreeable qualities, in the space of just three paragraphs, uses "decency," "proper," "unsuitable," "decorum," "a MANNER, a grace, an ease, a genteelness, an I-know-not-what, which some men possess above others, which is very different from external beauty or comeliness." If Smith misrepresented Hume to rig the stage for his propriety-phase innovation, is that innovation, after all, just a repackaging of what is already in the true Hume?

The propriety phase is Mary's own

The propriety phase of moral approval is Mary's own in a way that lateral sympathy is not. In lateral sympathy, Mary tests Janet's or Jim's sentiments against her own. Mary sees whether they measure up. Such lateral sympathy does not necessarily entail much or even any self-assessment on Mary's part; she has little opportunity of further dialogue or excavation of Janet's or Jim's moral constitution, much less opportunity to reform those. But the propriety *phase* queries Mary as to the agreement of her immediate sentiments, her "clerk," her System 1 sentiments, as it were, with those of her deeper conscience, the institution behind the clerk.

Smith is aware that propriety is a species of agreeableness; his point is to open up the vertical dimension of moral judgment to conscious deliberation and comparison. In that vertical dimension Mary has an utterly unique and special position or office in relation to the sentiments on *both* sides of the sympathy in play: she uniquely resides in her immediate self (the clerk) and her conscience (the institution behind the clerk) (see TMS 113.6). The sympathy involved in moral approval within Mary is a complex procedure (Haakonssen 1981, 51–53). Her consciousness is an intricate concatenation of thoughts, ideas, sentiments, etc. She has knowledge of the intricate concatenation that no one else could possibly have. And she has control that, again, is utterly unique. Such knowledge and control spell an utterly unique power over her own conduct, a power called the will and socially recognized by way of focal points and emergent conventions regarding things constituting "her own" (*suum*, in Latin), including person, property, and promises due to her. She *owns* that will. It is her natural property.[55]

The will is a power, and with power comes responsibility. Because, says Smith, all moral judgment involves the propriety phase, and because you have an utterly unique knowledge and control over things at that phase, the responsibility for your moral judgment resides with you. By inserting the propriety phase, with its vertical sympathy, Smith tends to sacralize the office and responsibility of moral judgment.

Smith's emphasis on natural ownership in the process of moral approval, the conversation between Mary and her man within the breast, highlights indeterminateness in a way that Hume does not. In framing moral approval as involving a vertical sympathy, Smith moves to suggest that we actively seek to develop our conscience and scrupulously select exemplary interpretations and judgments to work from. The process of selecting exemplars and worthy interpretations necessarily has an element of indeterminateness, or bottomlessness. How are we to determine whom to select as exemplars? Who is judging our judgment of exemplary interpretation? There is no sure link between the propriety phase and the beneficialness phase. Things that we regard as improper and blameworthy, things that we condemn, might, when viewed from a different perspective, a higher level, be seen as proper, meritorious, and beautiful.

Indeed, Smith's main example of his propriety phase in TMS IV, the parable of the poor man's son, imparts indeterminateness.[56] The reader enters into the protagonist's youthful ambitions, which seem proper enough so long as he stays within the bounds of commutative justice. But at the end of his life, the poor man's son looks back and realizes that the true means to happiness were within him all along. "[H]e curses ambition, and vainly regrets the ease and indolence of his youth... Power and riches appear then to be, what they are, *enormous and operose machines*...ready...to crush in their ruins their unfortunate possessor" (182.8; italics added). But Smith brings us along further: "it is well that nature imposes upon us in this man-

---

55. David Friedman (1994) develops the idea of natural property and highlights how a locus of knowledge and control resides with the owner, and that that is socially focal.

56. On Smith's parable in relation to Hume's conclusion to Book I of the *Treatise*, see Matson and Doran (2017).

ner," rousing us to turn "the rude forests of nature into agreeable and fertile plains" (183.10). Smith concludes the parable on the view we take "in better health and in better humour" (183.9). He furnishes to youthful sons and daughters a parable of dual interpretations. By leaving us in enigmatic perplexity, the parable imparts the bottomlessness of our moral constitution, the indeterminateness of moral sentiment.

Smith's propriety phase, then, turns the propriety-agreeableness that is in Hume onto another species of acting—exercising moral judgment—and constructs beings so as to make applicable the concept of "agreement" or "sympathy" within the judger. The parable, furnished by Smith's hand, entreats us to not only to cultivate our faculty of judgment but to sacralize it. In so doing, he highlights the indeterminateness of judgment that vertical sympathy implies, and yet fortifies us to face that indeterminateness bravely. Operose machines are us.

Nonfoundationalism Illustrated

At the outset, we quotezd Hume's review of TMS. If Hume meant to say that "philosophy scarcely affords any thing more undeniable and conclusive" than Hume's own moral writings, should we agree? Does Smith merely rehash what is conclusively furnished by Hume? Indeed, as shown in Chapter 10 here, a protracted train of critics of TMS complained that it reasoned in circles and stooped to metaphor and allegory at the most crucial points, and thereby obscured the true foundations and fundamental demarcations of moral theory.

Figure 4.7 shows a spiral of moral judgment. Again, Mary judges Jim's conduct, but now not once, but repeatedly. We shall narrate a progression of multiple actions taken by Mary. Her actions unfold in a series of moments. We shall see that a loop-specific propriety phase begets a new understanding of propriety-agreeableness, which begets a new understanding of beneficialness, which begets a new propriety phase, which begets... With its unending begetting, moral judgment resembles the career of humankind.

FIGURE 4.7: THE SPIRAL OF MORAL JUDGMENT AND LOOP-SPECIFIC PROPRIETY PHASES

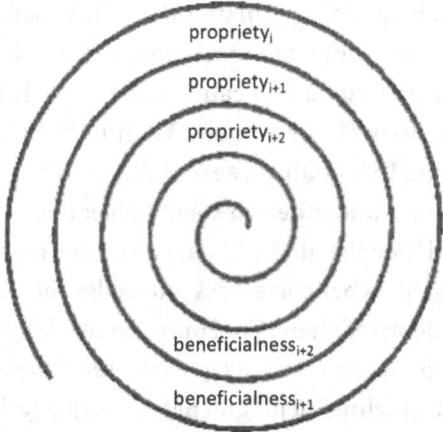

The progression winds clockwise, or inward. Supposing the progression good, think of inward as upward; the spiral rises up from the page.

Let's say Jim steals ice cream from Bob and gifts it to Janet. Mary is somehow apprised of Jim's action; perhaps she is witness to it, or perhaps she hears reports about it. The apprisal will feature subtleties relating to Jim's situation, Jim's motives, Jim's relationship to Bob, and to Janet, Bob's situation, Bob's reaction to the theft, Janet's situation, Janet's reaction, the established rules and expectations of such sorts of interaction, etc. In forming a moral sentiment regarding Jim's action, Mary in effect renders a moral judgment: She judges. The time-period of the act of judging is moment i.

Smith speaks of four sources of moral approval (326–327.16), which we do not here unfold, except to say that they immediately suggest four corresponding propriety clerks, who may be thought of as just one step removed from an overall clerk, the man at the counter who operates in the moment. Think of those four clerks as assistant clerks. One of the four assistant clerks is the assistant clerk that corresponds to the third source of moral approval—"the perception of the agreement or disagreement of any action to an established rule." That assistant clerk has assistants, and one of those is the assistant-assistant clerk who watches for violations of commutative justice violations, and, for the matter at hand (Jim's stealing of Bob's ice cream), that assistant-assistant clerk calls loudly (after "calls loudest," 84.2), "Commutative-justice violation!"

Hume's way of dissecting moment i is to say that up to moment i Mary had developed an understanding of matters like Jim's conduct: That understanding suggests a vague or inchoate set of aspects or effects of Jim's conduct, aspects or effects that can be categorized—if only by analysts like us—according to the four-factor account. Within the "agreeable" categories (that is, to Jim and to non-Jims), agreeableness takes the form of both propriety-agreeableness and otherwise-agreeableness.

The so-reckoned "beneficialness" would be subscripted with an i, making it beneficialness$_i$. This beneficialness antecedes the depictions in Figure 4.7 and so is *not* depicted there. For Hume, beneficialness$_i$ spells Mary's moral judgment in moment i; but, as we have seen, Hume by no means propounds that that "spelling" of judgment is necessarily determinate, nor speculative (in the sense of carefully reasoned out in moment i, or, indeed, carefully reasoned out at all); Mary's judgment in moment i is mediated by *her understanding* of all things that may pertain to a reckoning of the usefulness or agreeableness of Jim's conduct.

We have drawn Figure 4.7 so as to affirm Smith's contribution: In moment i there is an operation of the propriety phase. For Smith, there is, within Mary, an evolved understanding to moment i. But Smith's propriety phase spotlights Mary's operative sensibilities, the clerks of her evolved understanding. Such a clerk receives the apprisal of Jim's conduct and forms a moral sentiment—a judgment. That clerk is propriety$_i$ in Figure 4.7.

In the spiral, as we progress from propriety$_i$ the narrative transitions from moment i to the next moment, that is, moment $i+1$. Let's say that it is the next day, and Mary reflects on her moral sentiment of the day before. The experience she has had of judging Jim's conduct might enrich her reasoning about the aspects and effects of Jim's conduct. In our example, such enrichment could pull in several directions—we do not intend here any moralizing *of our own* about Jim's stealing of Bob's ice cream (even such violations of commutative justice have their rare warrant). Maybe Mary reconsiders the urgency of Janet's needs and desires and now feels more deeply the resentment of Bob. Or maybe the tendency is just the opposite: Maybe she now figures that Bob's resentment was just a momentary bother, insignificant to Bob, and that the violation of commutative justice is in this case more excusable than she had previously judged. Or yet, maybe her reasoning is enriched but not in a way that spells a different judgment. That is, maybe the moment $i+1$ judgment is basically the same as the moment i judgment, only the operation of a now more richly evolved moral constitution. What is significant here is that Mary's own propriety phase of the previous moment—a vertical sympathy with a clerk (or cleric) of the venerable institution that is her man within the breast—feeds into lateral sympathies, affecting her understanding of the propriety-agreeableness aspects of conduct such as Jim's. The experience of judging feeds into the next moment of her evolved understanding, and hence into the next generation of clerks—propriety$_{i+1}$. In this fashion, each of Mary's Smithian propriety phases relates to Humean propriety-agreeableness, first by reflecting her understanding of such up to the moment, and, second, by influencing her understanding of such after the moment and going forward.

Figure 4.7 highlights a correspondence between two notions of "good": (1) what is *good* conduct (propriety), and (2) what is good for the whole (beneficialness). A correspondence between the two goods is postulated in the way that Hume and Smith build out their systems of moral reasoning. In the four Scandinavian languages, *god* means good, and the word for God is *Gud* (in Icelandic, *Guð*).

Another aspect of Figure 4.7 is that of development of Mary herself, as she interacts moment by moment with the career of humankind. We see here that the individual's historicity has a place and standing *inside of* Smith's moral theory. As Griswold (2006, 185) put it, Smith develops a space for moral justification that "is neither free from historicity nor reducible to it" (see also Haakonssen 1981, 43–44). The diachronic development of self, and the importance of exemplars in the process, are features of Smith's theory that received rich expansion and elaboration in Ed. 6 of TMS.[57] In the spiral fashion, we get nuanced interpenetration of reason and tradition, of reason and sentiment, of theory and practice, of virtue and history, of

---

57. Smith's discussion of diachronic development beginning "A very young child has no self-command" and moving on to "a man of a little more firmness" and then "the wise and just man" (TMS 145.22–147.25) is new to Ed. 6, as is the entire "Of Self-command" section of the new Part VI, which contains much on the theme of diachronic development, as well as perhaps the most important moment on the theme of exemplars and independent judgment, namely the Parmenides-Plato tale (253.31).

nature and convention. Distinctions that some philosophers treat as foundational demarcations are humbled or even dissolved. With Ed. 6 Smith made the nonfoundationalism of TMS more elaborate and more apparent.

Odds and ends

Hume more than hints at vertical sympathy

Smith develops on Hume by staging his propriety phase and theorizing vertical sympathy. But, in fact, Hume's works show prelusions of vertical sympathy. In THN (3.2.1.12), he suggests our "relation to ourself" as the hinge of one's "love of mankind." In EPM (9.23), Hume says: "inward peace of mind, consciousness of integrity, a satisfactory review of our own conduct; these are circumstances very requisite to happiness." Or consider the wonderful words with which Hume concludes the same work (apart from the Appendixes):

> How little is requisite to supply the *necessities* of nature? And in a view to *pleasure*, what comparison between the unbought satisfaction of conversation, society, study, even health and the common beauties of nature, but above all the peaceful reflection on one's own conduct; what comparison, I say, between these and the feverish, empty amusements of luxury and expense? These natural pleasures, indeed, are really without price; both because they are below all price in their attainment, and above it in their enjoyment. (EPM 9.30)

Hume's general conception of the soul gives room for internal, vertical conversations and sympathies, and an evolving conception of the self:

> In this respect, I cannot compare the soul more properly to any thing than to a republic or commonwealth, in which the several members are united by the reciprocal ties of government and subordination, and give rise to other persons, who propagate the same republic in the incessant changes of its parts. And as the

same individual republic may not only change its members, but also its laws and constitutions; in like manner the same person may vary his character and disposition, as well as his impressions and ideas, without losing his identity. (T 1.4.6.19; see also "The Platonist," EMPL, 155)

Just as we have spoken of the human person as an institution, Hume suggests inward conversation and self-reflection. Such allegory resembles Smith's talk of the man within the breast. Hume writes: "You can never find it, till you turn your reflexion *into your own breast*, and find a sentiment of disapprobation, which arises *in you* towards this action" (T 3.1.1.26; emphasis added). He speaks of a "sympathetic motion in my breast" (T 2.2.9.14). Hume didn't elaborate on the vertical dimension of sympathy in his work. But he suggests that moral judgment of ourselves is a matter of a kind of vertical sympathy. We may add that in the Conclusion to Book I of the *Treatise*, Hume lives out before us a drama of self-disagreement, self-conversation, and conversion, a drama of vertical sympathy and "a progress of sentiments" (Baier 1991).

Why did Smith proceed as he did?

Assuming that all that we have said here would be agreeable to Adam Smith, we wonder: Why did he proceed as he did? We consider three hypotheses: (1) to distance himself from Hume in the public eye, (2) to set a stage for his propriety-phase innovation, and (3) to keep his nonfoundationalism enigmatic. Upon examination, these hypotheses are found to interrelate.

Smith may have wanted to appear to be critical of Hume, to allay suspicions. Hume was controversial—irreligious, irreverent, and irrepressibly inventive. Such traits made him unpopular with many Scots elites, particularly among the religious elite, and cost him university appointments. Associating with Hume was frowned upon in many circles. It was credibly reported that at Oxford the teenaged Smith was chided for secretly reading Hume's *Treatise* (Ross 2010, 71; Rasmussen 2017, 39). Hume candidly recognized his divisive effect in an April 1759 letter to Smith: "Scotland…is the Seat of my principal Friendships; but it is too narrow a Place for me, *and it mortifies me that I sometimes hurt my Friends*" (Corr. 44; italics added). In the same letter, as quoted earlier, Hume tells Smith he "profited" with TMS "by the Animosity against me," and just two months earlier told William Robertson the same in parallel fashion (Hume, *Letters*, 298). In 1776, Smith reports that his published praise of his departed friend "brought upon me ten times more abuse than the very violent attack I had made upon the whole commercial system of Great Britain" (Corr. 251; see Rasmussen 2017, 215f).

Perhaps Smith's misrepresentation of Hume's system as determinate, as speculative, and as lacking sympathy, and, Smith's obscuring of agreeableness, were moves of disassociation. He presented a somewhat suppressed and misleading version of Hume's moral philosophy so that he could present himself as a critic of Hume. People could then embrace and applaud TMS, despite its praises of Hume, as criticism of Hume.[58]

In TMS Ed. 6, published shortly before his death in 1790, Smith provides an important new sentence referring to Hume's four-factor account and the propriety phase. The sentence appears in the penultimate paragraph of the new Part VI: "In our approbation of all those virtues, *our sense* of their agreeableness, of their utility, either to the person who exercises them, or to some other person, *joins with our* sense of their propriety, and constitutes always a considerable, frequently the greater part of that approbation" (264.6; italics added). Here Smith interestingly seems to make "of their utility" an appositive of "of their agreeableness." But more importantly, he clearly maintains that Mary's judgment of Jim's action depends on her *sense of* things—twice using "our sense of" in the sentence. That phrasing tends to take back the connotation of determinateness he had originally ascribed to Hume: Propriety is not determinate but flows from our plexus of sensibilities. The passage, again, new to Ed. 6, communicates closeness to Hume. That closeness became more overt in later years—

---

58. It might be argued that something similar is done in WN (790–791.3–6). Smith presents Hume as an advocate for religious establishmentarianism: The quotation used by Smith is from the early part of Vol. III of Hume's *History of England*, treating early Tudor times. It is a bit hard to imagine Hume as a keen defender of religious establishmentarianism for the England of 1776 (much less its colonies), but Smith allows the reader to perceive him as such, and again uses Hume as a foil, now to his own discussion of religion policy upon the supposition "if politicks had never called in the aid of religion" (792.8). It must be acknowledged, however, that Smith (790.3) refers to Hume as "by far the most illustrious philosopher and historian of the present age." So maybe Smith's use of Hume here is more a reflection of Smith's tendency to create arch foils than of a need *in 1776* to distance himself from Hume.

for example, in 1776 Smith publishes his eulogy of Hume, the WN (790,3) description of Hume as "by far the most illustrious philosopher and historian of the present age,"59 and the deistic-sounding affirmation (793.8) of "that pure and rational religion" which antedates Christianity. The shift in Smith's posture toward organized religion, reflected in the eulogy, WN, and the changes to TMS Ed. 6, also conciliate toward the idea that Smith's true colors had all along been more Humean than he let on.

The second hypothesis to explain why Smith proceeded as he did is that Smith rigged the stage so as put into sharp relief his propriety phase, presented as an *innovation*. Indeed Smith says that the valuing of "fitness" (or propriety, for human conduct) is something that "has not, so far as I know, been yet taken notice of by any body" (180.3). But if Smith had used *beneficialness* and openly acknowledged that beneficialness entails both "utility" (as Hume used the term) and agreeableness, he would have had to address the relationship between propriety and the agreeableness entailed by beneficialness—we have seen how very abundantly Smith expresses propriety as a species of agreeableness (prompting the present paper to speak of propriety-agreeableness). Smith would have had to deal head-on with the intimate and complex relationship between propriety and agreeableness; he would have had to candidly admit that propriety is intimately connected to an understanding of the agreeableness of an action or character. Such matters would have been complicated. Maintaining a seemingly stark contrast between utility and propriety, then, gave dramatic effect to Smith's propriety-phase as an innovation.

Suppose that Smith had developed matters along the lines presented in this paper. He would have shown himself to be intricately linked and indebted to Hume. This link would exacerbate the first problem: the obvious likeness to Hume, indeed, the building upon Hume.

We may formulate a third hypothesis, which subsumes the first two: Smith was consciously quite nonfoundationalist, particularly in ethics and epistemology, but he sensed that nonfoundationalism was deeply disliked. The third hypothesis serves our interpretations because it helps us to

---

59. Note that "useful or agreeable" appears in the first sentence of the establishmentarian quotation Smith gives from Hume.

explain a passage that otherwise significantly upsets our interpretations.

In correspondence (Corr. 43), Hume, noting that a hospital is a scene of abundant sadness, suggested that Smith clarify the agreeableness of sympathy, and in the second edition Smith did so (46.9 n*), and we suspect that Hume was perfectly satisfied. Smith made more explicit several elements inhering in a sympathy (dissected by Haakonssen 1981, 51), which conforms neatly to a passage in Hume (T 2.2.5.21). Disagreeable thoughts evoke sadness, but in sharing the sadness there is consolation or commiseration, which is agreeable, and it too may be shared. There is an agreeableness in the agreement on the properness of disagreeable first-order sentiments. Smith's turn to the next-order sentiment regarding a sentiment's properness generates a recursivity.

Is our sense of properness proper? Every time the question is iterated, our account of ourselves becomes more difficult and perplexing. As we are trying to get our mind *around* things we usually swim *within*, we find that at those very high/deep levels our "clerks" are unseasoned, often feckless. But to close off the next iteration, to shut oneself off from such challenge, to declare "common sense" or "self-evidentness," is unhelpful, for each iteration asks of something more important than the preceding one. Such spirals of questioning and self-examination naturally frighten us. Smith's interpretation of our moral faculties embarrasses all who aspire to determinate, definitive answers in ethics; it especially challenges authorities who propound definitive answers or who sell simple answers to their followers. Smith encouraged us to press on nonetheless. He taught that we must try to handle each iteration by characterizing the being that would express the feelings of properness we incline toward defending. Such figures inevitably become figurative composites of exemplars, "the man within the breast." We think that Smith chose not to be upfront about the spiraling, nonfoundationalist, non-doctrinaire, non-demarcationist character of TMS's moral aesthetics.

That is how we explain a curious passage in TMS. In Part VII of TMS, Smith treats different systems of moral philosophy. He considers how different thinkers have treated of two questions. The first asks about the nature of virtue; the virtue-ness of conduct or character. The second asks about "the principle of approbation," or the operations or faculties within the judge by which virtue is apprehended and assessed. At the outset of the section about the second question, "Of the different Systems which have been formed concerning the Principle of Approbation," Smith writes:

> Before I proceed to give an account of those different systems, I must observe, that the determination of this second question, though of the greatest importance in speculation, is of none in practice. The question concerning the nature of virtue necessarily has some influence upon our notions of right and wrong in many particular cases. That concerning the principle of approbation can have no such effect. To examine from what contrivance or mechanism within, those different notions or sentiments arise, is a mere matter of philosophical curiosity. (315.5)

We reject the idea that our understanding of the faculties of approbation have no practical implications, and we reject the strong demarcating between "speculation" and "practice." Would it not be remarkable that "speculation" and "practice" are so fundamentally separable that a principle whose importance for practice is "none" holds in speculation "the greatest importance"? As Hume put it: "The end of all moral speculations is to... beget correspondent habits" (EPM 1.7). What great importance could a principle hold in speculation if it held none in any kind of practice?

That a matter of greatest importance in speculation holds no importance for practice goes directly against the whole pragmatist tendency of Hume and Smith,[60] as well as their whole tendency to keep philosophy in continual contact with the experience and sentiment of the talking and trading animal. Does not Smith, right in the first chapter of WN (21), present the "philosophers or men of speculation" as practicing a "business of a particular trade"? Indeed, something that we regard as a signal aspect of Smith's thought is the bringing of all human practice, from manufacturing pins to manufacturing self-judgment, under a general moral plexus. In our view, Hume and Smith tend to dissolve any dichotomy between theory and practice.

---

60. On the pragmatist facet of Smith, see Glaze (2017) and Shera (2022). For some general pragmatist/nonfoundationalist reading of Hume, see Shouse (1952) and Klein (2018).

On the supposition of a wise Smith, our interpretation leave us little choice but to invoke esotericism with respect to the passage. We suggest that Smith doesn't really mean what he says in the block quotation directly above, that he here deliberately puts out a red herring, one to obscure the nature and the importance of his own theory regarding the faculties of moral approval. His own theory—a signal feature of which is the organon that moral approval always involves a sympathy—is, again, spiraling, nonfoundationalist. That, it seems to us, is exactly why the critics of TMS sent it into oblivion, and kept it there, until such time that readers no longer held TMS's not being foundationalist against it (see Ch. 10). Smith was indeed proved right by subsequent history: He had great cause to make his nonfoundationalism obscure and enigmatic. Arthur Melzer (2014) explains four purposes or motives to esotericism and all four—defensive, protective, pedagogical, and political—might be enlisted to explain Smith's noble obscuring of nonfoundationalism.

Team Hume Smith

We reason that Hume quite whole-heartedly smiled on TMS. Yes, Smith had misrepresented Hume, and in several respects:

- Smith submerged agreeable into useful and into utility, thus altering, without any alert to the reader, the meaning of *useful* and *utility*.

- Smith creates a foil "Hume" for which the process of moral approving comes across as speculative ("thinking slow"), as opposed to immediate ("thinking fast").

- Also, and perhaps more importantly, Smith presents the foil "Hume" such that it makes moral conclusions rather determinate, as opposed to indeterminate.

In these respects, the foil is really quite misleading as a representation of Hume. But we suggest that Smith misrepresented Hume quite knowingly and deliberately, and that Hume understood his reasons for it, and didn't mind.

Smith proceeds to fashion the propriety phase, situated between moral approval and beneficialness, as a space to explore both the immediate and speculative sides of moral approval, and the indeterminateness of moral justification. He does so by proposing to elaborate the operations of moral approval in terms of the sympathy of the man within the breast, an organic composite of the exemplars within one's personal history. The excavation of one's moral approving, then, flows naturally into the world of social influence, including those focal figures meaningful to all parties of the conversation. This inner sympathy we have fashioned as vertical sympathy, in contrast to the lateral sympathy highlighted by Hume. But Hume too had hinted at vertical sympathy, so there, too, yet again, Smith shortchanged Hume. But we suspect that Hume was happy to let Smith keep the change, for it was reasonable to trust Smith's judgment that, among the practical alternatives, doing so best advanced universal benevolence. What was good for Smith was good for Hume, and for the whole.

CHAPTER 5

Adam Smith's Nonfoundationalism

[I was invited by Jonathan Imber, then editor of *Society*, to take part in a symposium on a target article by Amitai Etzioni (2016). I took the opportunity to expound on Smith's nonfoundationalism, using Etzioni's piece as a foil representing foundationalism. This chapter revises somewhat but preserves the original arrangement and symposium spirit, and the present tense even though, sadly, Etzioni passed away in 2023. But, first, I wish to clarify what it is that I am talking about: Nonfoundationalism is skeptical toward foundations for wisdom and virtue generally, that is, foundationalism in ethics and epistemology generally. My nonfoundationalist posture is not opposed to invocations of the metaphor of foundation within, say, dental hygiene, where one might say that that narrow virtue has a foundation in brushing and flossing, and likewise to some particular vein of knowledge or study. I do not wince over "the foundations of chemistry." I do suggest pausing over "the foundations of morality" or "the foundations of politics" or "the foundations of knowledge." There, the metaphor of foundation has, I think, proved a failure, as all the purported foundations have failed. In this book, it is true, I espouse Smithian organons, but I do not think it is apt to call those foundations; it would be more apt to call them dogmas, rather like how C. S. Lewis (2002, 727) calls the *Tao* a dogma.]

> [I]t is very seldom that one has a distinct notion of the foundation of their duties, but have merely a notion that they have such and such obligations.
>
> Smith (LJ 321)

Charles Griswold (1999, 165) describes Adam Smith's moral philosophy as "self-consciously nonfoundationalist," Samuel Fleischacker (2004) writes approvingly of it not being foundationalist (see 23-26), and Emma

Rothschild (2001, 231, 238; 2004, 152) notes that Smith is little concerned with "foundational or metaethical questions." These scholars do not fault Smith's TMS for being nonfoundationalist. Their agreeable attitude is rather different than the dominant opinion during a period of about 170 years, which faulted the book for not being foundationalist (see Ch. 10 here).

Nonfoundationalism is associated with philosophical pragmatism (William James, John Dewey, Richard Rorty), which is associated with postmodernism, which is associated with political leftism. I feel that nonfoundationalism dovetails with Smithian liberalism, centered on the principle of "allowing every man to pursue his own interest his own way, upon the liberal plan of equality, liberty and justice" (WN 664.3). The words "to pursue his own interest his own way" (which also appear in the "natural liberty" paragraph 687.51) highlight the particularism, moment by moment, of sentiment, interpretation, understanding, personal meaning, that ought to humble the selfhoods of happiness experts, health officials, busybodies, and meddlers, who often presume to know based on some quackish formulations. The words "the liberal plan of equality, liberty and justice" signify not so much a philosophical foundation as a political potentiality and a proposition. As for commutative justice, it is a social grammar, and grammar does not tell you what to write on your blank pages. Commutative justice is no foundation for ethics. For one thing, it cannot justify itself.

In apprehending the most important things, Smith saw, in the context of a stable polity, a presumption of liberty as one of the central options on the table. Smith's nonfoundationalism apprehends the options, sizes them up, and develops a nonfoundationalist case for any inclination for one over another. Shall we lean North, South, East, or West? Smith may be understood as expressing liberal sensibilities and as mounting a nonfoundationalist case in their favor.

A brief on Smith's nonfoundationalism is pertinent to Amitai Etzioni's article "Happiness Is the Wrong Metric" (2016). Its main idea is susceptible to criticism of a nonfoundationalist flavor.

In the article we learn that, while many researchers maintain that "pleasure" or "satisfaction" is what motivates people, Etzioni sees that "people are motivated in part by their quest to live up to their moral commitments." Such motivation, he holds, "cannot be reconstituted as another source of satisfaction." The insight that "both pleasure and moral commitments significantly influence human behavior" heralds a new understanding of human preferences, and brave new opportunities for "changing cultures and social and political structures, which shape preferences." Etzioni concludes by calling for "a social movement...to withdraw the legitimacy of an old regime and invest the freed legitimation in the formation of a new one." To make such a call inspired by his dual-motivation insight, Etzioni must think that the distinction is solid and deep.

But the distinction is not solid and deep. Sure, in the moment, we might use such a distinction. Consider an example offered by Etzioni:

> To illustrate this point very briefly, if one states that "I would LIKE to go to a movie but OUGHT to visit a friend in the hospital" and reads this as not different from "I would like to go to a movie or a dinner," one has lost half of what social science needs to study.

It's not that I disagree (though I doubt that many would regard the two statements as not different). The problem is that Etzioni is thinking in terms of two pillars—a pillar of "pleasure"/"satisfaction" and a pillar of doing-duty.[61] Upon these two pillars, researchers, regulators, experts, nudgers, and uplifters shall develop an accurate understanding of preference formation and promulgate a new and improved polity.

"Pillar" serves as a nice metaphor for *foundationalism*. Indeed, the term foundationalism suggests a foundation of a building, a solid, uniform, unchanging, immovable block, much like a pillar, upon which a description or understanding stands and claims its soundness.

---

61. The expression "doing-duty" seems apt for the motivation highlighted by Amitai. He describes it as "the sense one has after doing something considered to be a moral duty," and "attempting to live up to moral commitments." He proceeds to give as appellation for such motivation "affirmation." It seems to me that doing one's duty, avoiding disappointment, is what Etzioni describes; it would be yet another step (though, admittedly, a small, natural step) to reflecting on one's duty and doing-duty to experience affirmation (see Klein 2012, 270-271). So I refrain from using Amitai's appellation ("affirmation") and instead use "doing-duty."

Understanding of Preference Formation		
Pleasure/ Satisfaction Motivation		Doing-duty Motivation

To the nonfoundationalist, however, such an image of understanding is suspect, particularly in moral philosophy. If an image serves as non-foundationalism's metaphor, it is a spiral. Unlike a block-like structure or movement along a straight line, a spiral shows interdependence or movement from a top to a bottom and then back to a top; thus each top depends on a bottom, and that bottom on a preceding top. A spiral depicts distinct loops (which a simple circle or cycle does not), such that the top at one loop may be somewhat different than the top at the next, and similarly for the bottoms. Within each loop, we have, as it were, a distinct subscript on "top" and "bottom."

The spiral works differently than the one in *The Wizard of Oz*. Dorothy landed in Oz, learned of the yellow-brick road, and decided to follow it.

That spiral started at a definite point in Dorothy's world, and at a definite time in Dorothy's experience. Man's spiral, however, has no start and no end, and living it is not a matter of decision.

Dorothy's journey wound outward, but man's journey is to find a cohesive center of consciousness, to make his doings coherent. His spiral winds inward. As he passes from moment i to moment i+1 he winds deeper into the spiral.

Yet, as he winds further along, arriving at moment i+1, he finds the road widening and opening up new scenes of strange and wondrous objects:

> *Cattle in the marketplace*
> *Scatterlings and orphanages*
> *He looks around, around*
> *He sees angels in the architecture*
> *Spinning in infinity*
> *He says Amen! and Hallelujah![62]*

In 1757, Edmund Burke (1990, 67) wrote: "Infinity has a tendency to fill the mind with that sort of delightful horror, which is the most genuine effect, and truest test of the sublime."

Amitai's two motivations, satisfaction and doing-duty, recur as we circumnavigate the spiral's loops (or layers or levels). Let us associate "going to the movie" with satisfaction$_i$:

---

62. Paul Simon, "You Can Call Me Al," 1986.

Think of a spiral winding upward from the page. We see that satisfaction$_i$ relates, on either side, to doing-duty:

$$... \text{doing-duty}_{i-1} - \text{satisfaction}_i - \text{doing-duty}_i ...$$

On the one side, in doing-duty$_{i-1}$, we have duties such as that of not disappointing one's expectations of seeing the movie, of rewarding oneself after a hard week, of staying conversant with modern culture, of stimulating one's mind, of *resisting* other iniquitous activities, and of who knows what else. Also, in considering any manner of occupying oneself, there is the abiding duty of minding the cost, what would be forgone. On the other side, in doing-duty$_i$, we have the continuance of things at the preceding loop, but man reviews and revises, though usually only in small ways. Perhaps the movie sparks new perspectives and sentiments, which affect some of his abiding duties. Also, it might lead to new transitory duties: "I must post about it on Facebook."

Likewise, if we associate "I ought to visit my friend in the hospital," with doing-duty$_i$, we can easily think that it relates to satisfaction on either side. The word *ought* derives from *owe*. One might then look for the source of the obligation, such as the convalescent friend's sympathy, kindness, and companionship, and one's memories thereof. And, looking forward, there is the expectation of the friend's gratitude for the visit, and, most importantly, the satisfaction that comes with doing one's duty, the pleasure in the approval of the man within the breast. Or, the avoidance of his disapproval: "it is this inmate who, in the evening, calls us to an account for all those omissions and violations, and his reproaches often make us blush inwardly both for our folly and inattention to our own happiness, and for our still greater indifference and inattention, perhaps, to that of other people" (262.1).

Etzioni recognizes that one can identify a satisfaction associated with doing-duty, but he shoos us from of doing so: "it seems best to separate the quests for self-satisfaction from efforts to adhere to one's value." He says that "Understanding what makes some societies more self-oriented and pleasure seeking and others more dedicated to affirmation [or doing-duty] is a major subject for...public discourse *and policy*. Collapsing the two kinds of pursuits into one means losing the conceptual tools this kind of analysis requires" (my italics). Thus, Etzioni suggests that we must either collapse the two kinds or pursuits into one or keep them separate. But the spiral approach affords a subtle approach in which the two kinds of pursuits are neither collapsed into one nor kept separate. Contrary to his insistence that duty-doing "cannot be reconstituted as another source of satisfaction," instances of duty-doing may indeed be usefully construed that way. In my view, students of comparative culture or ethnology ought to be prepared to enter into the individual's spiral, to pass from satisfaction to duty and back again. In comparing one society with another, the difference in the importance that people place on doing-duty might be less illuminating than differences in *what it is* their duties demand.

Some people have understood Smith to be saying that what is right for an individual simply conforms to that individual's sentiment: Each individual has his own set of moral faculties; those faculties produce sentiments regarding human conduct; and those moral sentiments determine what is right for that individual. Smith's theory, they say, finds no basis for moral judgment; it collapses into "relativism." They add that Smith says that the individual is not alone, that the individual gets his moral sensibilities from the community or society, as though such was monolithic or had a monolithic set of moral sensibilities, and then "relativism" simply reemerges at the level of the community or society.[63]

But Smith develops an outlook that lends itself to considering humankind as a single whole. Within the spiral of the whole, we explore what *our* moral faculties are: We do not know what they are. Our interpretations of them emerge from the school of life. What does our schooling tell us? What is it that we *have been schooled to*—or, *should*—do? Smith presupposes that each of us is engaged in a journey, a diachronic self-conversation about what "my" moral faculties are and what they tell me: Plato and Aristotle countenanced infanticide: Is it right of me to criticize them for that (as Smith

---

63. The error of treating social influences as monolithic to the individual is confuted by DelliSanti (2023). Cropsey (2001, 21) holds, wrongly, that "Adam Smith's explicit doctrine is that each man will act virtuously when he wins the approbation of his conscience, of 'the man within the breast.'" Melzer (2001, 153) criticizes Smith's nonfoundationalism, saying that Smith's theory "tries to use the principle of manners to explain morals." Chapter 10 here surveys numerous foundationalist critics of TMS.

does at 210.15)? Smith's outlook bypasses talk of "relativism" versus "absolutism," and is nonfoundationalist.

Suppose Jill is the daughter of Anne. Smith proposes that in any case of Jill's judgment (or approval or moral sentiment) regarding the doings of Ted the judgment is connected to a sympathy with a spectator, such as Anne, who also observes and morally reacts to Ted's doings. That is, in all instances of judging Ted, moral approval is connected to, perhaps determined in or confirmed in, a sympathy or fellow-feeling in the matter of judging Ted. The organon of Adam Smith is that approval always relates to a sympathy. In the example, the organon points to a Jill-Anne sympathy, not a Jill-Ted sympathy (though that too plays a role). Smith shows us that, in speaking of the moral sentiments of Jill, we may sustain the organon everywhere and always, by resorting to the man within Jill's breast as the being with whom Jill finds sympathy.

As for one's judging of one's own conduct, Smith writes:

> When I endeavour to examine my own conduct, when I endeavour to pass sentence upon it, and either to approve or condemn it, it is evident that, in all such cases, I divide myself, as it were, into two persons; and that I, the examiner and judge, represent a different character from that other I, the person whose conduct is examined into and judged of. (113.6)

And the procedure repeats: Smith proceeds to divide the judge. After all, judging is a form of conduct, and the procedure may be applied again, producing a judge of the judge, and again, iteratively, spiral style. If we are spiral savvy, we understand that there is no lexical ordering of judge and judgee, and that, in any particular parable or homily, wherever we pick up the story, judge and judgee tacitly relate to one another, that the doors in either direction are open to us, that there is no absolute starting point.[64]

We create a judge of our actions by "endeavouring to view them with the eyes of other people, or as other people are likely to view them" (110.2).

---

64. For discussion on lexical ordering, see Griswold (1999, 82) and Forman-Barzilai (2010, 172, 174).

But it is not "other people" in undifferentiated, proximate mass. As we go, there are certain other people, certain individuals, who evoke wonder and admiration, and inspire emulation (20.3, 48.14, 75.3, 114.3, 117.9, 159.7, 192.11, 247.25, 323.10, 335–336.23–24); influenced by such exemplars, the man within the breast develops. Jim's man within the breast is Jim's own; it evolves in Jim's individuated process of experience and discrimination; it is product and warden of Jim's judgment. That judgment can make itself independent of any particular pressure toward conformity, though not of all such pressures—from the organon, that would be nonsensical.

The man within the breast cultivates principles or "general rules." Smith contrasted the cultivation process, as he saw it, with a view he rejected, namely, deduction from "ultimate foundations":

> When these general rules, indeed, have been formed, when they are universally acknowledged and established, by the concurring sentiments of mankind, we frequently appeal to them as to the standards of judgment.... They are upon these occasions commonly cited as the ultimate foundations of what is just and unjust in human conduct; and this circumstance seems to have misled several very eminent authors, to draw up their systems in such a manner, as if they had supposed that the original judgments of mankind with regard to right and wrong, were formed like the decisions of a court of judicatory, by considering first the general rule, and then, secondly, whether the particular action under consideration fell properly within its comprehension. (160.11)

Smith sought to straighten the rod by bending it the other way, namely, toward "induction" from sentiments experienced:

> [The general rules of morality] are ultimately founded upon experience of what, in particular instances, our moral faculties, our natural sense of merit and propriety, approve, or disapprove of. We do not originally approve or condemn particular actions; because, upon examination, they appear to be agreeable or inconsistent with a certain general rule. The general rule,

on the contrary, is formed, by finding from experience, that all actions of a certain kind, or circumstanced in a certain manner, are approved or disapproved of. (159.8)

The general maxims of morality are formed, like all other general maxims, from experience and induction. We observe in a great variety of particular cases what pleases or displeases our moral faculties, what these approve or disapprove of, and, by induction from this experience, we establish those general rules. (319.6)

We just quoted Smith saying that the general rules are "ultimately founded" on our moral data in particular instances, but of course he would agree that each moral datum, each moral sentiment, of the instant, is influenced by the moral rules we had cultivated up to then. In the two passages just drawn from (159–160.8–11, 319–320.5–7), Smith emphasizes the "induction" direction of cultivation, but I hold that Smith does not mean to place "induction" over "deduction," but rather to show that our moral reasoning evolves in a back-and-forth manner, or spiral style. The editors of TMS say that Smith's "own habits of reasoning include both deduction and induction, as one would expect" (Raphael and Macfie 1976, 22). As for the notion that, in the moment, Jim's entire history of moral data is the foundation of his moral rules, that manner of speaking fails because, contrary to the "foundation" metaphor, there is no such clear "entire history," no time zero, and any history is not only Jim-specific, but diffuse and mysterious, even to Jim. Indeed, it is misleading of me to speak of Jim's moral "data."

Smith introduces the word "induction" only near the end of TMS, in addressing whether reason is "the principle of approbation," that is, the process or faculty that generates moral judgment. He notes that "induction is always regarded as one of the operations of reason," and he affirms that "virtue may very properly be said to consist in a conformity to reason, and so far this faculty may be considered as the source and principle of approbation and disapprobation" (320.6). But, Smith continues, the "first perceptions, as well as all other experiments upon which any general rules are founded, cannot be the object of reason, but of immediate sense and feeling," and, "reason cannot render any particular object either agreeable or disagreeable to the mind for its own sake" (320.7). Smith rejects the notion that reason alone is the generator of moral judgment.

I think Smith tended toward the view that reason, on any signification of the term, could hardly be regarded as foundational. First, reasoning proceeds upon premises, but are they sound? Should the premises be *believed in*? Second, as a flat computer-like logical processor of information, reason might present limits to which virtue must conform, but the limits are weak; such reason leaves virtue underdetermined. Third, as a wider, richer, imaginative, creative faculty—performing what C. S. Pierce termed abductive reasoning, to arrive at new insights, connections, formulations, or interpretations—, reason is far too vague, open-ended, unruly to be thought of as foundational. Rather, it is a spiral, of which each loop features a set of "particular instances" of moral experience and a set of sensibilities of general rules, each set with its own subscript corresponding to the loop. One side of the spiral shows moral experience affecting rules (when challenged, "we generally cast about for other arguments," 89.8); the other side shows rules affecting moral experience.

The set of rules reflect the man within the breast, or conscience; either way, the set of rules too bears a subscript, even if it changes little from loop to loop. In explaining why a man of humanity in Europe would not visit upon China a great earthquake to prevent the loss of his pinky, Smith says: "It is reason, principle, conscience, the inhabitant of the breast, the man within, the great judge and arbiter of our conduct" (137.4).

By speaking of Jim's conscience as Jim's "man within the breast," Smith leads us into a spiral, for the figure naturally invites iteration, that is, to ask after *that* man's conscience, that is, Jim's conscience's conscience. And to iterate yet again: Jim's conscience's conscience's conscience.

Jim's conscience calls Jim to mind his larger, more enduring interests, which include benevolent interests (noted in TMS's first sentence) and the love of those we live with. Conscience causes Jim's mindfulness to take up conduct and habits that effectively extend Jim's care further into the future and farther in social consequences. Iterating part-whole, Jim graduates from whole to whole, each with a different subscript:

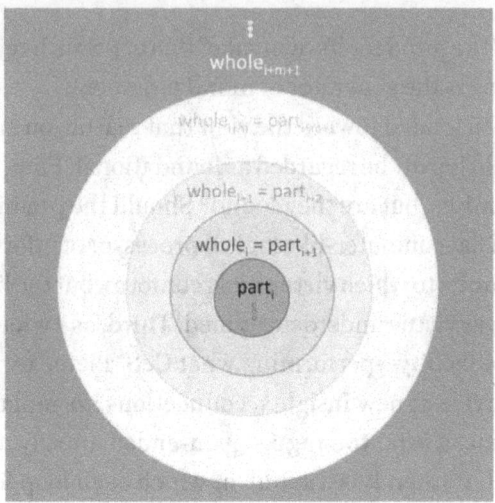

Division, Burke wrote in 1757, "must be infinite as well as addition; because the idea of a perfect unity can no more be arrived at, than that of a compleat whole to which nothing may be added" (Burke 1990, 66).

From the Paleolithic success of solidarity in the family and band, perhaps, and the genes so selected, humankind evolved the creed and conviction of the holiness of the whole, effervescent tribal manifestations of which are described by Emile Durkheim in *The Elementary Forms of Religious Life*. It wasn't until the 15th century that the noun *whole* was written with the w-. The words *holy* and *whole* came from common Nordic, Germanic, and Old English "hel-" and "hal-" roots, and both relate etymologically to *heal* and *health*.[65] Griswold (1999, 135) speaks of the impartial spectator as "the personification of the public."

Jim's conscience realizes that the larger, more enduring interests of Jim that Jim tends to neglect generally move with the good of larger wholes, so it drifts toward counseling Jim toward just such considerations. Long ago, that idea, serving the larger whole, caught on as lovely, agreeable, becoming. Smith counsels us to regard the pursuit of wisdom and virtue as the best game in town, better than games of fame, wealth, or political power; he mounts the case partly by arguing that the alternatives are actually pretty

---

65. The common roots of *holy* and *whole* remain clear in Swedish today: One would translate "the holiness of the whole" as *heligheten av det hela* or *helhetens helighet*.

lame. We don't have anything better to do.

But even if Jim is such a votary, that by no means ensures that Smith would think that Jim's conscience is doing a good job. The drift of the conscience, the man within the breast, is usually toward virtue, but the drift may be quite defective and erroneous, and it might be weak. Asking, now, after the man-within-Jim's-breast's conscience, we say, again, that *that* conscience drifts toward virtue, toward larger beneficialness, and towards the correction and overcoming of preceding-order defects and errors. It looks "to interrogate and sometimes to subvert the *very measure* by which he [Jim] has become accustomed to judging himself and the world" (Forman-Barzilai 2010, 177). But it again is weak and still somewhat defective. The higher-order consciences might lack traction in getting Jim to behave more virtuously, but we can say that they readily exist, if only in our imagination, or as allegory.

If virtue and serving the whole are mutually constitutive, then in pursuing virtue you admire exemplars who serve the whole; you spurn those who hurt or neglect the whole by favoring only a part or party. You spurn the partial. Those who care beyond any particular part or party, and serve the whole, are impartial.

In TMS, Smith introduces impartial spectators as actual people who happen to be present, to be spectating, and to have "no particular connexion" to any of the parties, and hence, presumptively, to be partial to none of the parties (135.3). But Smith takes the idea further, into theism or allegory, and arrives at the impartial spectator that beholds the largest ethically relevant whole—say, humankind, including future generations[66]—and is "well informed,"[67] a superhuman, super-knowledgeable being—which I call, as in preceding chapters, God/Joy.

The man within the breast is a "representative" of God/Joy (215.11). As representative, he is, again, defective and weak. But Jim's only path toward virtue is by way of the man within the breast.

Now iterating, the man within the man within Jim's breast is yet closer

---

66. Going beyond humankind certainly makes sense; Smith speaks of "all rational and sensible beings" (237.6).

67. Smith speaks of an impartial spectator being well informed at 130.32 and 294.94.

to God/Joy. On such construction, the iteration would lead to God/Joy. We might think of it as analogous to a sequence that converges to God/Joy in the limit:

Jim's conscience's conscience's conscience's...conscience = God/ Joy.

As written there ("= God/Joy"), the ellipsis represents infinite iteration. In finite terms we say that, for any given arbitrarily small epsilon, there is a finite conscience-iteration length N such that for every "Jim's ... conscience" sequence greater than N the difference between it and God/ Joy is less than epsilon.

Our construction displays universalism in three ways. Suppose that Amitai Etzioni and I, Dan Klein, are discussing Jim's conduct. We express and partly articulate the rules or standards by which we approve or disapprove of Jim's conduct.

1. The first universalism is that the rules and standards go not only for Jim but for anyone; yes, there are quite particularistic things about Jim and his situation that bear on the matter, but those things correspond to complications in the rules; they are not a basis for invoking Jim-rules as opposed to some other set of rules. Maybe we approve of Jim stealing the bread, but, if so, it is because at that particular node on that particular branch of the universal tree, as it were, we approve of "human" stealing the bread.

2. As Etzioni and I both adhere to the principle of having virtue or praiseworthiness correspond to advancing God/Joy's pleasure in beholding the whole, we both, in reckoning the consequences of Jim's conduct, regard the consequences for everyone among humankind, including people far off and far away. Universal benevolence is universal in its beholding; it considers "the total effect" (Coase 1960, 44).

3. Even if Etzioni and I differ sharply in our judgments about Jim's conduct, we have faith that Amitai's conscience's... conscience and Dan's conscience's...conscience converge

toward a common standpoint or sensibility (Haakonssen
1981, 58).

Each, Amitai and Dan, has, in the moment, his own standpoint, but
both need a notion of a common standpoint to search for something that
adjudicates over both standpoints, a search that leads to the next loop in
a spiral. The notion of a common standpoint goes, not just for Amitai and
Dan, but for all human judges. God/Joy's standpoint would represent a sort
of universal standard for adjudicating human standpoints.

One may object: But the framework is empty, it begs the question of
what sorts of behavior are virtuous. Where I said, "think of the spiral winding upward," one may object: How do we know what is upward? Such a
question has no good foundationalist answers. Each of us, including those
who think they have good foundational answers, develops sensibilities and
carries on. Whether one recognizes it or not, one relies heavily on his or
her exemplars. Our exemplars may help mediate our disagreements. True,
the bare framework does not inform us on virtue. We recur to exemplars,
to traditions of thought, in discussing important worldly matters. Smith
gave us not only organons but explorations of moral experience, public policy, and more, expressing judgments throughout. There is plenty of meat
on the bones.

God/Joy does not provide a foundation. God/Joy is universal in beholding, but we don't see what He/she sees, and we do see as He/she sees. We do
not have foundational access to God/Joy. Many theists say that we do not
have foundational access to God (even those who believe that scripture is
the word of God might feel that there is no foundational way to adjudicate
interpretations of scripture, nor interpretations of "scripture is the word of
God"). The framework is a way of thinking, and the case for embracing it is
nonfoundational. We may discuss whether it is better than the alternatives.

To illustrate our nonfoundationalist reading of Smith, let me treat four
topics in TMS, each very briefly.

I. Smith suggests that in estimating Jim's conduct we compare it to
two standards, perfection and propriety. Perfection is only a vague idea,
not foundational; it is something "no human conduct ever did, or ever can
come up to" (26.9; see also 247–248). Propriety is a sort of average performance within our community or reference group (25.7, 26.9). This "ordi-

nary degree itself seems neither blamable nor praise-worthy" (80.6), but it separates praiseworthiness and blameworthiness (26.9, 80.6). And Smith proceeds to distinguish one level of propriety from another. The admiration we feel for great actions, he says, arises from our perception of "the great, the noble, the *exalted propriety* of such actions" (192.11; italics added; see also 240.9). The individual, at the start, is accustomed to his community's propriety, and then apprehends an "exalted propriety." The individual may enter a new more exalted group. Elsewhere, Smith considers two kinds of self-restraint, one from a "vulgar prudence" and another from "the sense of propriety," and says the former constitute "a propriety and virtue of a much inferior order" to the latter (263.5). Smith implies a sort of ladder of propri-eties (see 247–248). One can think of a spiral, each loop of which showing a "propriety" and a "moral experience and reflection," each with a subscript.

II. It is similar with prudence. When we speak of Jim in a simple con-text, we will attribute contextual considerations to be objects of his imme-diate prudence. But we can also ponder Jim's more enduring moral and spiritual context, in which the doing of what had previously been aspi-rational duties has been routinized and become an object of his self-in-terest. Thus, Smith speaks of a "superior prudence," which is a prudence "combined with many greater and more splendid virtues, with valour, with extensive and strong benevolence, with a sacred regard to the rules of jus-tice, and all these supported by a proper degree of self-command" (216.15). From the spiral spirit, we may reason that Jim's virtuousness is chiefly the matter of what it is that Jim makes his self-interest.

III. Smith treats (in TMS Part IV) the relationship between moral approval and "utility." He suggests that moral approval and utility, when properly understood and reckoned, do coincide (188.3). He insists, how-ever, that, in the moment, moral judgments spring from a sense of over-all propriety,[68] not impressions concerning utility. The move points to a diachronic spiral process involving moral approval, overall propriety, and impressions concerning utility, each with a subscript corresponding to the

---

68. I write overall propriety because, it seems to me, Smith uses *propriety* both with respect to an aspect of one's conduct and with respect all aspects considered more holistically. The latter, described by Smith at 202.5, is what I mean by overall propriety, and it seems to be the sense Smith means in Part IV.

loop of the spiral. It is here that Smith proceeds to speak of an "exalted propriety" (192.11).

IV. Early in TMS, Smith develops "two different sets of virtues," the amiable and the respectable (23.1). Later we find that "The person best fitted by nature for acquiring the former of those two sets of virtues, is likewise best fitted for acquiring the latter.... The man of the most exquisite humanity, is naturally the most capable of acquiring the highest degree of self-command" (152.36). Smith suggests a diachronic personal development in which the amiable faculties of one loop feed into the respectable faculties of the next, and vice versa. Moral improvement is a yin-yang of amiable and respectable, a vital, humbling affair that makes one kindly toward others who manifestly have not yet gotten very far (248.25).

There are other topics in TMS that lend themselves to a nonfoundationalist spiral approach (for example, the third sense of justice at 270.10, such that each loop would feature "object" and "estimation," or that each estimation then becomes an object of estimation). Likewise, I think of knowledge as a spiral of information, interpretation, and judgment (Klein 2012, 145-147). We might also consider sentiment and reason (see Matson 2017a, 2017b; Forman-Barzilai 2010, 179).

The spiral approach does not dissolve or dispense with the distinctions used within a loop. In the loop, in a given context, the distinctions can certainly be useful, as in the context of a man deciding between going to a movie (satisfaction) and visiting a friend in the hospital (duty-doing). Our discourse is contextual, both in that we refer to things in their context and in that our own discourse is situational or contextual. Sometimes an instance of behavior will be usefully treated as satisfaction, sometimes as duty-doing. Indeed, I think the various virtues, as Smith describes them, may be understood as different sets of lenses, such that the very same behavior can variously be treated in terms of prudence, temperance, courage, generosity, benevolence, and so on (Klein 2023a, ch. 19).

Some might feel that nonfoundationalism subverts ethics by turning it into murky spiral soup. But, it seems to me, embracing nonfoundationalism highlights the specialness and the importance of those merely grammar-like rules of conduct, rules that Smith describes as "precise and accurate" (175.10–11, 327.1; see also 340.34). Those rules provide nothing like a foundation for the ethics of what you ought to do with your stuff; they merely sanction you against using it to mess with another's stuff. A political ethic that puts a premium on extending such principle to public policy, such that the sanction against messing goes also, at least presumptively, for the jural superior, making what Smith called the liberal plan, is an option on the table, and the case for it is nonfoundational.

Competence in nonfoundational thinking will help one to tangle with the purported blocks and pillars that so often accompany contrary options. Justifications for governmentalizing social affairs often involve a pretense of knowledge (Hayek 1989), a pretense dressed in a foundationalist, unduly demarcationist distinguishing of concepts. Smith (WN 687.51) said that those who assume a duty to superintend the affairs of private society expose themselves to "innumerable delusions." Such delusions are often propped up by quackish foundations.

Think of nonfoundationalism as a kind of apophatic knowledge: Knowledge of what ethics (and hence epistemology) is not.

Ought Is an Is regarding What Is Owed to God/Joy: On the Positive-Normative Distinction

> We should resent more from a sense of the propriety of resentment, from a sense that mankind expect and require it of us, than because we feel in ourselves the furies of that disagreeable passion. There is no passion, of which the human mind is capable, concerning whose justness we ought to be so doubtful, concerning whose indulgence we ought so carefully to consult our natural sense of propriety, or so diligently to consider what will be the sentiments of the cool and impartial spectator.
>
> Adam Smith (TMS 38.8)

Virgil Storr generously arranged a symposium on a book of mine (Klein 2012). One of the commentaries is by Solomon Stein (2014), "Coordination: Descriptive or Normative?" It knocks my book for neglecting the supposedly meaningful and important distinction between "positive" and "normative." It is thoughtful, meticulous, and well written. I asked whether it would be okay for me to take this opportunity to write on the positive-normative distinction, and Storr said yes. What I offer here is a meditation that relates to Stein's commentary only, and even there is not specific to his commentary.

For me, the positive-normative distinction is a dominated alternative

Stein's commentary is a critique, a careful, thoughtful, stern, and fair critique. According to Stein, my book faults "modern economists...for their dishonesty or delusion in claiming to be engaged in a positive project when they are 'really' engaged in a normative one" (49). Stein says that my book is an "attempt to combine the positive and normative into a single approach" (42). He says, "intermingling between positive and normative approaches weakens, rather than improves, the quality of both" (42). He suggests that such intermingling "comes at a high cost" (53).

When a critic says, "Our author does X and X is bad," one response, however uncommon, is for the author to accept the criticism and retract doing X. It is more common for the author to object to the criticism. In objecting to the criticism, the author's defense usually takes one of two forms: either he says, "No, I do *not* do that bad thing X," or he says, "Yes, I do X, but X *isn't* bad; it's good."

My reply takes a form that is perhaps different than any of those. I object, but neither by asserting that I do not do X nor by asserting that X is good. Rather, I say that X is not a worthy formulation. My counterattack is that Stein errs at a point that precedes, as it were, the first word of his piece. He errs in adopting the positive-normative distinction.

I do not employ the positive-normative distinction in the book. In fact, I never talk that way. For me, the positive-normative distinction is always and everywhere a dominated alternative.

Often the distinction is beaten by some other distinction. Figure 6.1 shows six distinctions. I remark only on the first in the list. The wording comes from Adam Smith's distinction between two kinds of rules. In the matter of moral rules (or the rules of the virtues), he says that for all the virtues except one the rules are "loose, vague, and indeterminate;" the one exception is commutative justice, the rules of which are "precise and accurate" (TMS 174–75.8–11, 327.1–2). Smith draws a parallel to the rules of writing, saying that aesthetic rules of writing are loose, vague, and indeterminate, while those of grammar are precise and accurate. For our purposes, the distinction can be thought of as pertaining to the sentence or to the business of judging or assessing the sentence (that is, assessing its truth, validity, soundness, worthiness, merit). For example, if someone says, "Raising the minimum wage by $1.65 an hour will make society better off," we might be inclined to say that the sentence is rather loose, vague, and indeterminate, because the idea of society being better off is. Or we might say that *assessing* the sentence is a business that is rather loose, vague, and indeterminate. Perhaps this distinction (that is, between the sentence and the business of assessing the sentence) is rather empty, but I draw it here nonetheless because doing so might help show the ways to apply the first row of Figure 6.1.

FIGURE 6.1: DISTINCTIONS THAT SOMETIMES BEAT THE POSITIVE-NORMATIVE DISTINCTION

1.	precise and accurate	loose, vague, and indeterminate
2.	reserved	outspoken
3.	unassuming; tactful	declamatory; strident; overbearing; emphatic; fervent
4.	uncontroversial	controversial
5.	conventional	unconventional
6.	centrist; establishment or status-quo oriented	socialist/progressive/libertarian/ etc., etc. (as the case may be)

It has been my experience, on encountering talk of positive-normative, that the sentences in question can be improved upon. It is not that the speaker means nothing when he talks "positive/normative." It is that what he means can be clarified, sharpened, by instead using one or more other distinctions, such as those in Figure 6.1 (which is not a complete list). John Searle (1964, 58) points out that distinction 1 in the Figure and the distinction between "different kinds of illocutionary force" (which may be associate with distinction 2 or distinction 3 in the Figure) are not the same, even though they are often conflated.

In 1756, Adam Smith remarked upon the *Encyclopédie*, saying that "the style of some of them [the entries] is more *declamatory*, than is proper for a Dictionary; in which *not only declamation, but any loose composition*, is, more than any where, out of its place" (EPS 247; italics added). It is easy to imagine that commentators today would say "normative" rather than "declamatory." But is that an improvement? Notice, too, that Smith here implies a distinction between declamation and looseness; today's sorry commentators are apt to use "normative" for either.

Besides replacing positive-normative talk, sometimes simply deleting such talk, without replacement, is an improvement. I suggest that such talk is always dominated. If it is in your vocabulary, perhaps you should expunge it.

Is and *Ought*

In the first sentence of his famous essay "The Methodology of Positive Economics," Milton Friedman quotes John Neville Keynes distinguishing between positive and normative. The first edition of Keynes's book *The Scope and Method of Political Economy* appeared in 1891, and it may have helped start "normative" talk (see Figure 6.2; by the way, "positive science" starts around 1800).

FIGURE 6.2: N-GRAM FIGURE FOR "NORMATIVE," 1880–2008 (ENG. CORPUS, 1-YR SMOOTHING)

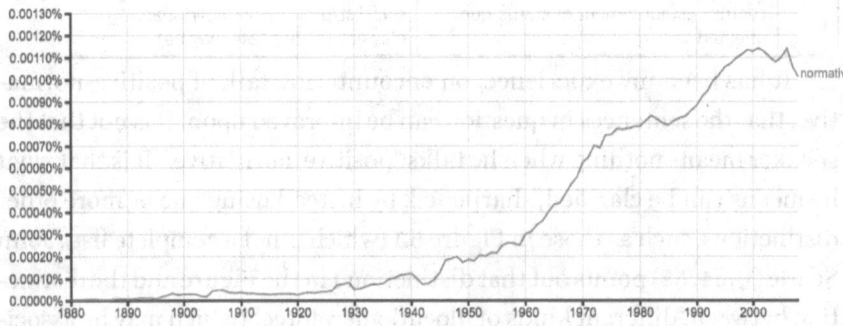

Source: Google's Ngram Viewer

J. Neville Keynes distinguishes "*a positive science*...[,] a body of systematized knowledge concerning what is; a *normative* or *regulative science*...[,] a body of systematized knowledge discussing criteria of what ought to be...." (Keynes as quoted by Friedman 1953, 3). Friedman also quotes Keynes saying that confusion between the two "has been the source of many mischievous errors," and urging the importance of "recognizing a distinct positive science of political economy."[69] Friedman endorses all of

---

69. The Keynes quotations, including the brackets within the first one, are here exactly as reproduced in Friedman, who, in the last one, Americanized "recognising" and dropped italics; the quotations appear in Keynes (1904, 3–35, 46).

this, saying: "Positive economics is in principle independent of any partic- ular ethical position or normative judgments. As Keynes says, it deals with "what is," not with "what ought to be" (Friedman 1953, 4).

It is common for those like Keynes and Friedman who affirm posi- tive-normative talk to do so on the basis of a distinction between *is* and *ought*. But is the distinction between is and ought an important, useful dis- tinction? Are *is* sentences, as a category, substantively different from *ought* sentences? I will suggest that: (1) it is easy to recast any *ought* sentence as an is sentence, and vice versa; (2) every is sentence can be understood as conveying tacit "oughts;" (3) every *ought* can be understood as an *is*.

Recasting an *ought* sentence as an *is* sentence, and vice versa

Say X is some policy reform, and consider the sentence: "The government ought to do X." That sentence, it seems to me, is substantively the same as, practically equivalent to, any of the following:

"The government's doing X would increase overall social well-being."
"The government's doing X is desirable."
"Reform X is good."
"It is desirable/good that the government do X."

There is a simpler, more universal way to recast an *ought* sentence as an *is* sentence. The is/ought dichotomy refers, I presume, to the main clause of a sentence. Thus, "The government ought to do X" is an *ought* sentence while "I think the government ought to do X" is an *is* sentence. By insert- ing "I think" at the start of any *ought* sentence you make an *is* sentence.

Also, one can recast "The government ought to do X" as "Wisdom holds that the government ought to do X." John Neville Keynes advises us to use the term *science* narrowly, to denote some distinct positive science of eco- nomics. He informs us: "The best recent authorities, however, at any rate in this country, use the term in the narrower sense" (1904, 35 fn 2). Is there a substantive difference between saying, "You ought to use the term *science* narrowly," and saying, "The best authorities think you ought to use the term narrowly"? I hardly think so.

Here, by the way, Keynes was differentiating his standpoint from that of "Adam Smith and his contemporaries, as well as some modern economists," who "mean by a science any systematic body of knowledge, whether consisting of theoretical propositions, or of practical rules of action" (ibid.).

As for recasting an *is* sentence as an *ought* sentence, first, we should understand that many of our words plain connote a moral sentiment: "There are certain terms in every language, which import blame, and others praise" (Hume, EMPL, 227). But we may make the point much more universally, seeing an *ought* in every *is*. We can recast "Richmond is the capital of Virginia" as "You ought to think/believe Richmond is the capital of Virginia." As Michael Polanyi (1966) put it: "To claim validity for a statement merely declares that it *ought* to be accepted by all" (78).

Is as conveying tacit "oughts"

Besides seeing a tacit "You ought to believe that" at the start of every *is* sentence, there is another sense in which one can see tacit "oughts" in an *is* sentence. Every instance of our discourse is embedded in a situation of human purposes. In his first sentence Milton Friedman signals the purpose of avoiding "mischievous errors." Friedman writes of "the *importance* of" recognizing a distinct positive science (italics added).

Importance has a ubiquity that is important here. Again, every sentence takes place in a discourse situation, embedded in human purposes. And human purposes are embedded in judgments about what are the most important things. The most important things include the questions to examine, and sometimes they are made explicit. For example, one section of TMS is called, "Of the Questions which ought to be examined in a Theory of Moral Sentiments" (Smith 1790, 265). But it is folly, and out of step with Michael Polanyi and Friedrich Hayek, to think that all of the important things can be made explicit. The most important things include the most important aspects of human betterment, the most important interpretations to employ in addressing such matters, the most important problems, troubles, or challenges, the most important formulations of a particular issue, the most important positions on the issue, the most important arguments for a position, the most important grounds or evidence for an argument, and so on. Every "most important" refers to what is most important among the whole universe of things to consider, so a judgment of what is most important, and how things stack up, relates to the judge's wide knowledge of things. All such judgments are made in service to purposes involved in any *is* sentence.

When someone reports what the trend of joblessness *is*, he might also be saying: "We ought not focus so much on what the official *unemployment* rate is." When someone says that black markets and reductions in quality and safety *are* consequences of drug prohibition or of rent control, he might also be saying we ought not flatten our analysis down to a simple supply-and-demand diagram (which eclipses those consequences). When someone says that a policy reform will tend to have certain dynamic political or policy consequences, or moral and cultural consequences, he might again be saying what things our account of important consequences ought to include.

Also, when someone formulates an *is* sentence, he is suggesting how we ought to formulate matters. When someone says that one of the benefits of raising the tax on cigarettes is that it will reduce smoking, he is also saying that we ought to think of such a consequence as a benefit. Hume suggested the moral significance inheres in the very coining of words: "That people, who invented the word charity, and used it in a good sense, inculcated more clearly and much more efficaciously, the precept, be charitable, than any pretended legislator or prophet, who should insert such a maxim in his writings" (EMPL, 229).

Indeed, an *is* sentence is an affirmation of the words used in the sentence. Where Adam Smith (1776) says, "The division of labour is limited by the extent of the market" (31), he is in effect saying that you ought to embrace expressing thinking in terms of "the division of labour," and in terms of "the extent of the market." Where he says, "To hinder, besides, the farmer from sending his goods at all times to the best market, is evidently to sacrifice the ordinary laws of justice to an idea of public utility...." (539), he is in effect saying that you ought to embrace expressing thinking in terms of "the ordinary laws of justice." Where he says, "To remove a man who has committed no misdemeanour from the parish where he chuses to reside, is an evident violation of natural liberty and justice" (157), he is in effect saying that you ought to embrace expressing thinking in terms of "natural liberty."

Where Solomon Stein says that I intermingle "positive and normative approaches," he is in effect saying you ought to embrace expressing thinking in terms of "positive and normative"—and it is that "ought" that I here take issue with.

Where Milton Friedman says, "John Neville Keynes distinguishes...," he is in effect saying that in these matters you ought to regard Keynes as high authority. Every such invocation of authority in effect carries such an "ought." Indeed, in everything an author says, he is in effect saying, "you ought to consider thinking about the matter as I do." Every author is saying, in effect, "I have thought carefully and scrupulously about the matter, so you ought to regard me as something of an authority on it."

The key point, here, is that in the situation of writing or saying the sentence, there is no clear, upper-most, final framework that sets the terms and standards with which judgments of importance are then determined. I grant that, if there were two realms of human matters, two realms clearly different and separated by a bright, shining line, then some kind of distinction fitting that line, a distinction between two realms, would presumably be in order. Proponents of the positive-normative distinction typically write as though there is some such pair of realms. They speak of means versus ends (sometimes "given" ends). They speak of facts versus values (sometimes "ultimate" values). Such talk is practiced by John Neville Keynes, Milton Friedman, and Solomon Stein.[70] It is practiced by E.M. Zemach, who, in rejecting John Searles's 1964 paper "How to Derive an 'Ought' from an 'Is'" and related thoughts in Searle (1969), says: "What we need here is the "absolute" kind of obligation, which is meaningless and void outside the game boundaries" (Zemach 1971, 62).[71] I say we need only to sense the layers of obligation about us, and to see that, wherever we are able to talk intelligibly, such layers will be about us. Traversing layers, refocusing the conversation from one layer to next looser, vaguer, more indeterminate layer, might be very difficult. The first steps in such a refocusing often begin clumsily. Thomas Paine (1795) said: "One step above the sublime makes the ridiculous, and one step above the ridiculous makes the sublime again." But there

70. Such dichotomizing is pervasive in J. N. Keynes's book and Friedman's writing. As for Stein, one example is when he writes of "the distinction between the descriptive and the moral project" as "two distinct levels of analysis" (48).

71. Zemach (1971) treats, in addition to Searle (1964), Searle (1969).

is no definitive ending. There is no absolute, ultimate, upper-most layer.

I do not mean to suggest that speaking of means versus ends, or facts versus values, is never useful. But to propose to organize discourse—striving to keep one sort of discourse separate or distinct from some other sort—on the basis of some such distinction is like proposing to do that on the basis of up versus down, right versus left, or beginning versus ending. All of these notions find their meaning within the discourse situation. What to me, in my apartment, is up is down to my upstairs neighbors. What is an ending here is a beginning there. What in one conversation is an end is a means (or potential means) in another conversation. What in one conversation is a value is a fact (perhaps a factual potentiality) in another conversation. It seems to me that the whole positive-normative aspiration entails a denial that we are always, continually, ineluctably contesting, exploring, correcting, modifying, and revising our judgments about what things—be they words, interpretations, formulations, interests, human experiences, issues, positions, arguments, forms of evidence, and so on—*ought* to be regarded as most important or most worthwhile. Until that great shining demarcation line in the sky is discovered and jointly beheld, we should expect to sense tacit "oughts" in every *is* sentence.

And, by the way, since we do (and should) become committed, to one degree or another, to judgments about the most important things, we necessarily have and use sentiments in doing our science. (Sentiments include both passions, which have a tendency to impel action, and emotions, which may be only passive.) For example, it has been argued that a sentiment of regret is essential to the concept of error (Klein 2012, 344). Other sentiments are essential in correcting or overcoming error. If such claims are right, and if an essential part of science is correcting error, then it is nonsensical to try to wring sentiment out of science. The passion to separate science, reason, analysis, and logic from sentiment is a bad one.

Ought as an *is*

In spoken English, instead of using "ought to," people will often use "supposed to." A mother tells her toddler, "When someone gives you something, you are supposed to say 'thank you.'" Before getting to "ought," and then "should," let me begin with "supposed to."

Suppose an elderly couple have invited their son and his fiancée for dinner at home. During the day the father telephones the son, "We are out of wine. Can you pick up a bottle on your way over?" The son says, "Sure, I'll do that." Later the young couple approach the home in their car, and the fiancée says, "Honey, weren't we supposed to pick up a bottle of wine?" The sentence "We are supposed to pick up wine" is an *is* sentence.

Return to the mother saying to the toddler, "When someone gives you something, you are supposed to say 'thank you.'" That too is an *is* sentence; it is looser and vaguer in its associated task of assessment: Who is supposing that the toddler will say thank you? Are we so sure that that being supposes that the toddler will say "thank you"? People know, after all, that toddlers are still learning their manners. The mother's "supposed to" is looser, vaguer, than the fiancée's, but both are *is* statements.

After dinner the son and his fiancée arrive back home, and he grows affectionate. "Stop," she says, "we're supposed to wait till after the wedding." That is another *is* sentence, again loose and vague. If one were to ask her, "Who is supposing?," she might say God. Sentences about what God supposes are *is* sentences. Sentences about what a fictitious character, such as Shrek, supposes, wants, or does are *is* sentences. "John F. Kennedy is turning over in his grave" is an *is* sentence. And so is "America wants new leadership."

Or, when asked, "Who is supposing?," the fiancée might say, "I am the one supposing." That makes sense. We understand the statement to her fiancé to be saying that some larger, more enduring, more central, more sacred part of herself expects and depends on their waiting till after the wedding. As Adam Smith might say, her "man in the breast" is supposing. Another *is* sentence.

Suppose a man named Hutcheson lends ten pounds to a man named Smith. Then we might say, "Smith owes Hutcheson ten pounds." Suppose that Hutcheson also teaches and aids Smith. Then we might say, "Smith owes Hutcheson gratitude/esteem/love." Beyond Hutcheson, Smith might feel that he has been taught and aided by humankind generally, and Smith might say, "I owe humankind love." These are all *is* sentences.

Adam Smith himself says:

If I *owe* a man ten pounds, justice requires that I should precisely pay him ten pounds, either at the time agreed upon, or when he demands it. What I *ought* to perform, how much I *ought* to perform, when and where I *ought* to perform it, the whole nature and circumstances of the action prescribed, are all of them precisely fixt and determined. (Smith 1790, 175; italics added)

Here Smith goes naturally from "owe" to "ought." That *ought* derives etymologically from *owe* is confirmed by both the *Oxford English Dictionary* and the *Online Etymological Dictionary*. The latter, in the *ought* entry, says that *ought* came from the Old English word *agan*, meaning "to own, possess, owe." Specifically, *ought* comes from its past tense, which is *ahte*. In fact, in the *owe* entry, it indicates that until the 15ᵗʰ century the past tense of *owe* was *oughte*, which then was replaced by *owed*, while *oughte* developed into *ought*. Further, in the *ought* entry, it says that *ought* "has been detached from *owe* since 17c., though *he aught me ten pounds* is recorded as active in East Anglian dialect from c.1825."

I imagine the following dialog between an Interviewer and Adam Smith:

Interviewer: You say you ought to pay Hutcheson ten pounds. What do you mean by that?

Smith: I owe him ten pounds, and so I have a duty to him.

Interviewer: Yes. But where is the *ought*?

Smith: Well, to say that I have a duty to him implies that, unless other and greater duties say otherwise, I ought to meet that duty.

Interviewer: But what does it mean to say that you *ought* to meet your duties?

Smith: Well, I owe it to myself to meet the duty to Hutcheson, and so I have a duty to myself.

Interviewer: Fine. But what does it mean to say that you ought to meet the duty to yourself.

Smith: Well, I owe it to myself to meet *that* duty, and so I have a duty to meet that duty.

Interviewer: Fine! But what does it mean to say you ought to meet the duty to meeting that duty?

Smith: Well, we have supplied a spiral without end.

Interviewer: I see that. And that means we haven't gotten to the bottom of it—in fact, that we *won't get to the bottom.*

Smith: I should only counsel that you make yourself accustomed to that. Should it trouble you so?

Interviewer: Well, in my schooling, I learned that *ought* statements are different than *is* statements. I recognize that your "owe" statements are *is* statements, so I am trying to find the differences in *ought* statements.

Smith: I see no necessary difference between some two sets of statements so characterized. What sort of schooling is practiced where you come from?

Interviewer: I have attended the best universities of my times and been taught by the best authorities. What's more, I have studied the best authorities from the time of John Neville Keynes. And they all seem to agree on this matter.

Smith: I see. Well. One authority of your times, McCloskey, says: "Economists do not pay enough heed to moral questions, hiding behind the sophomore philosophy of normative/positive" (1995, 553). Is not she, or any of the many authorities she shows, saying much the same, one of the best?

Interviewer: No, she's not. The best authorities find her provocative, but disagree with her on many things.

Smith: Allow me another stroke to gratify your animus against "ought." Where I write:

Nature, accordingly, has endowed [man], not only with a desire of being approved of, but with a desire of being what ought to be approved of; or of being what he himself approves of in other men. (117)

I am saying each of us, such as James, is endowed with one or both of the following: (a) a desire of being of such character that he perform what is owed to God or to a God-like allegorical being that some call Joy; (b) a desire of being of such character that would be socially approved of in a society in which people owed to themselves duties like those of which James approves. (Let me point out that, while (a) and (b) are distinct, they go naturally together, since the only way James has to approach God/Joy is by heeding what he himself approves of in other men.)

Now I have expelled "ought" and instead use "owe," which you allow is an *is*. There is no important difference between the passage from page 117 of my book and the exposition that follows, though the first is more natural.

Interviewer (showing wonder and surprise): Hmmm. You say some provocative things—that I can say positively. But I ought to let you go. Thank you, Dr. Smith.

Smith: Maybe you ought or maybe you oughtn't. In any case, thank you for your visit.

Finally, let's turn to *should*. I again use the *Online Etymological Dictionary*. At the *should* entry, it says: "c.1200, from Old English *sceolde*, past tense of *sceal* (see shall)." At the shall entry, the first and main paragraph is as follows:

shall (v.) Old English *sceal*, Northumbrian *scule* "I owe/he owes, will have to, ought to, must" (infinitive *sculan*, past tense *sceolde*), a common Germanic preterite-present verb (along with *can, may, will*), from Proto-Germanic **skal-* (cf. Old Saxon *sculan*,

Old Frisian *skil*, Old Norse and Swedish *skola*, Middle Dutch *sullen*, Old High German *solan*, German *sollen*, Gothic *skulan* "to owe, be under obligation;" related via past tense form to Old English *scyld* "guilt," German *Schuld* "guilt, debt;" also Old Norse *Skuld*, name of one of the Norns), from PIE root **skel-* (2) "to be under an obligation." (Online Etymological Dictionary entry for *shall*)

The immediately foregoing block quotation suggests that *should*, like *ought*, derives from words that mean "to owe." But I want to remark on something else about the foregoing. It mentions the Swedish infinitive verb *skola*, which, by the way, is the infinitive verb for the word today of ordinary Swedish *skulle*, meaning "would" or "should." Well, *skola*, today, is also the noun for "school." In fact, many of the words in the foregoing are close to words for "school" in the respective language. In its *school* entry, the *Online Etymological Dictionary* says:

school (n.1) "place of instruction," Old English *scol*, from Latin *schola*... The Latin word was widely borrowed, cf. Old French *escole*, French *école*, Spanish *escuela*, Italian *scuola*, Old High German *scuola*, German *Schule*, Swedish *skola*, Gaelic *sgiol*, Welsh *ysgol*, Russian *shkola*. (Online Etymological Dictionary entry for *school*)

Compare these old and varied origins of the noun *school* with the old and varied origins with the verb *should* (through *shall*). It seems pretty clear that they are related. Heck, to turn "schooled" into "should," just drop the *c*, change the second *o* into an *u*, and drop the *e*. The relation might be that *should* evolved from *schooled*, or that they co-evolved from related origins.

I suggest that, besides seeing *should* as being, like *ought*, a loose, vague, and indeterminate form of "to owe," we may see it as a loose, vague, and indeterminate form of "to be schooled to"—or, more elaborately, of "to be schooled, even if only in a wide metaphorical sense, to." One form is present perfect, as in, "have been schooled to." Another is a future perfect, "will have been schooled to [once I explain the reasons]." Another is a conditional: "would be schooled to [if I explained the reasons]." For some *should* talk we will need to go even further. Thus, "It should be sunny tomorrow" may be read as "You would be schooled to believe that it will be sunny tomorrow if I explained why I say it will be sunny tomorrow."

One might say that there is a narrowness to "to be schooled to" that makes what I am suggesting untenable. Nonetheless I press on with the suggestion, namely, that "to be schooled to" can be thought of widely so as to permit us to read every "should" as a form of "to be schooled to."

Smith writes: "A very young child has no self-command; but, whatever are its emotions, whether fear, or grief, or anger, it endeavours always, by the violence of its outcries, to alarm, as much as it can, the attention of its nurse, or of its parents" (TMS 145.22). And as long as it remains at home in the care of its "partial protectors," the child is indulged. But venturing beyond home advances the child's schooling:

> When it is old enough to go to *school*, or to mix with its equals, it soon finds that they have no such indulgent partiality. It naturally wishes to gain their favour, and to avoid their hatred or contempt. Regard even to its own safety teaches it to do so; and it soon finds that it can do so in no other way than by moderating, not only its anger, but all its other passions, to the degree which its play-fellows and companions are likely to be pleased with. It thus enters into *the great school of self-command*, it studies to be more and more master of it*self*, and begins to exercise over its own feelings a discipline which the practice of the longest life is very seldom sufficient to bring to complete perfection. (1790, 145; italics added)

Smith is speaking of belonging to society as a form of schooling. Indeed, Smith offers a full, eloquent paragraph describing the "man of real constancy and firmness, the wise and just man." At the heart of the paragraph Smith writes: "He has never dared to forget for one moment the judgment which the impartial spectator would pass upon his sentiments and conduct. He has never dared to suffer the man within the breast to be absent one moment from his attention. With the eyes of this great inmate he has always been accustomed to regard whatever relates to himself." This man, he says, "has been thoroughly bred in *the great school of self-command*, in the bustle and business of the world, exposed, perhaps, to the violence and injustice of faction, and to the hardships and hazards of war" (146; italics added).

Thus, when Smith writes "should," for example in the opening quotation of this chapter—"We should resent more from a sense of the propriety of resentment, from a sense that mankind expect and require it of us..."—we may recast it: "We have been schooled to resent more from a sense of the propriety of resentment, from a sense that mankind expect and require it of us...." Figure 6.3 provides samples recasting "should" as "have been schooled to."

FIGURE 6.3: RECASTING "SHOULD" AS "HAVE BEEN SCHOOLED TO"

You should capitalize the first word of a sentence.	You have been schooled to capitalize the first word of a sentence.
You should keep your promises.	You have been schooled to keep your promises.
You should help your neighbor.	You have been schooled to help your neighbor.
You should be honest with yourself.	You have been schooled to be honest with yourself.

All of the "schooled to" sentences are *is* sentence. They may be loose, vague, and indeterminate, they be sound or unsound, but they are *is* sentences.

Conclusion

I have treated the positive-normative distinction in terms of the is-ought distinction. I have shown that it is easy to recast any *ought* sentence as an *is* sentence, and vice versa, that every *is* sentence, in fact, in the discourse situation, conveys tacit "oughts," and that we can understand "ought" and "should" generally as a form of "owe," and "should" also as a form of "to be schooled to," both of which are *ises*.

Ought is an *is*.

God/Joy is special, and what we owe to God/Joy is special. So *ought* is a special *is*.

But, again, it is an *is*.

The diminishment of the is-ought distinction has been offered as part of a broader suggestion, namely that, perhaps, for you, as for me, positive-normative talk is always and everywhere a dominated alternative. The better alternative may be other words, such as the menu offered in Figure 6.1, or the better alternative may be silence. Such diminishment forms only a part of the case for the suggestion. A large part untreated here is the unhappy consequences of positive-normative talk. Also untreated here is explanation for commitments to positive-normative talk.

Coda 1: Relating what I say in this chapter to John R. Searle's "How to Derive 'Ought' from 'Is'" (1964):

I think what I say is in the same vein and spirit as what Searle says. Here are a few remarks:

- Searle focuses entirely on deriving an *ought* from a set of *ises*. My main message is that *ought* is an *is*. If I am right, then to derive an *ought* from *ises* is to derive an *is* from *ises*. Now, it might seem that if we establish that *ought* is an *is*, there is no need to show that we can derive an *ought* from *ises*, since we all know that we can derive an *is* from *ises*. However, *ought* is a kind of *is*, just as "created" is a kind of *is*, and to show persuasively that that kind of *is* can be derived from a set of other *ises* is often a valuable thing to do. Hence, my contention that *ought* is an *is* does not obviate concern for deriving an *ought* from other *ises*.

- After providing a baseball example (56) in which the umpire calls a player out at second base and we then derive that that player ought to leave the field, Searle elaborates a bit on what he calls "institutional facts." He relates the baseball example to a promise to pay back a loan, suggesting that the promising, like the baseball playing, involves institutional facts. Searle doesn't say much, however, about the "institution" in question. Searle never writes of God, an allegorical being, the conscience, or anything of the sort. Above, I confected an exchange between Smith and an Interviewer. What I have Smith saying there is a step in the direction of identifying the "institution" in question. Just as we speak of *oughts* in baseball with regard to players who appear on that field, we speak of *oughts* in social life with regard to people who appear on that field.

• As already noted, Searle (1964, 58) points out that distinctions like those in my Figure 6.1 are often conflated.

Coda 2: About David Hume's is-ought paragraph in *A Treatise of Human Nature* (T: 3.1.27):

That paragraph is probably one of the reasons that Hume disavowed the *Treatise*. The paragraph is lamentable, not so much for what Hume is driving at, but rather for how recklessly he drove at it. Here is one way to interpret what the paragraph drives at:

In many of the books that I [Hume] have read, the author makes (explicitly or implicitly) claims—100 claims, let's say—about various objects and then proceeds to state or imply two more claims about his own sentiment. The 101st claim is about the existence and nature of his own sentiment. The 102nd claim—and here is the rub—is about that sentiment's relation with yet another object, namely the good of the whole. That is, the author asserts or implies a superior connection or correspondence between his sentiment and our better aligning our own thought and other conduct to serving the good of the whole. (That is, the author implies that his sentiment is a superior sign or indication of what we owe to God/Joy and hence of what we *ought* to do.) This last claim, of connection or correspondence, cannot be deduced from the author's preceding 100 claims. [Hume's "some new relation or affirmation" is that connection or correspondence, or affirmation of his sentiment being a superior sign; such correspondence is shown in expression (*) on page 200 below.] And when it comes to "vulgar systems of morality," we especially doubt the correspondence between their authors' sentiment and what we owe God/Joy, and in that sense their *oughts* are not satisfactorily founded on their preceding *ises*. That is, at the end of their

discourses they assert, if only implicitly, that their moral sentiment is a superior sign, but they do so without having given reasonable grounds for granting such superiority. We might believe
the author's 100 claims but not believe *in* the author. The author
has not provided adequate grounds for his 102nd claim.

Again, Hume's is-ought paragraph is lamentable. But the simplistic
understanding of it—what Geoffrey Hunter (1962) mocked as the "Brief
Guide interpretation"—is wrongheaded. In his 1962 paper, Hunter wrote,
"Hume makes *ought*-propositions a sub-class of *is*-proposition" (p. 149), a
statement that dovetails with what I have argued here, viz., that *ought* is an
is. (Hunter improved upon his own 1962 interpretation in Hunter 1963.)

CHAPTER 7

The Circumstantiality of Bivariate Relationships in TMS

> Philosophy...accustoms [the soul] to consider the general Essence of things only...*to abstract from all their particular and sensible circumstances....*
>
> [It] was, upon this account, regarded as the great purifier of the soul.
>
> Adam Smith (EPS 124.4; italics added)

> Great Britain should...endeavour to accommodate her future views and designs to the real mediocrity of her circumstances.
>
> Adam Smith (WN 947.92)

> [A]cquired wisdom and experience only...teach incredulity...,
> and they very seldom teach it enough.
>
> Adam Smith (TMS 335–6.23)

In TMS, Adam Smith offers many reasonings about how a change in one thing, A, is attended by a change in another thing, B. Uppercase delta (Δ) signifies "difference" or "change in." Thus, ΔA means change in A. In this paper I explore features of TMS's reasonings about how ΔB attends ΔA.

In proffering a lesson on such bivariate relationships, Smith sometimes seems to go out of his way to posit a state of the world in which the lesson would break down. That feature suggests an irony about knowing how ΔB attends ΔA. We might think we understand the bivariate relationship. The claimed relationship, however, holds only for certain states of the world.

The relationship is circumstanced.

If the professor presents a relationship about how ΔB attends ΔA, and then expounds also on the circumstantiality of that relationship, the students might be discouraged and disappointed. The professor's authority depends on a supposed superior grasp of system knowledge, of knowledge not too confined to particular circumstances or certain states of the world. The student's motivation lies in the aspiration of gaining knowledge with power in its degree of generalizability. The lead epigraph to this chapter suggests that people look to philosophy to purify the soul by learning generalization and abstracting away from circumstantiality. Such aspiration is discouraged by emphasizing circumstantiality. Extreme circumstantiality rebuffs generalizability, disappoints the student, and embarrasses authority.

Isn't science more than a hodgepodge of relationships, each pegged to a separate and disjointed set of circumstances? And if it were such a hodgepodge, we might suspect that even the hodgepodge is incomplete, "upon account of the still greater variety of possible circumstances" (339.33).

Economists sometimes speak of the analysis of relationships within a system as "comparative statics." The term "comparative statics" speaks of a comparison between two equilibrium states. Comparative statics address the question: From a given set of values and holding certain parameters (or "exogenous" variables) constant, how does a change in A affect the level of B, once the change has worked its way through the system (that is, through the system's "endogenous" variables)? Glory Liu and Barry Weingast (2020) explain that Smith often uses comparative statics.

FIGURE 7.1: A MONOTONICALLY INCREASING FUNCTION

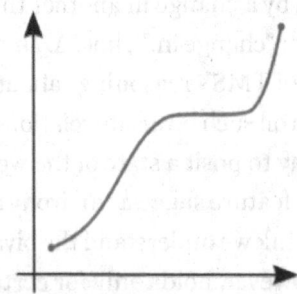

If we are sitting in a room of 70 degrees Fahrenheit and an experimenter then raises it to 80 degrees, what will be, fifteen minutes hence, the Δper-$spiration$? For the relationships treated in this paper, Smith is concerned to teach us that, under certain conditions, the relationship is monotonic, such that, either, as A increases, B generally increases, or as A decreases, B generally decreases (as in Figure 7.1).

Smith aims to teach us more than monotonic relationships. He also aims to teach us that those relationships hold only under certain conditions or circumstances. Thus, there are qualifiers or preconditions or presuppositions. One sort of qualification is that the monotonic relationship holds only within a certain domain of the variables. If the room temperature is increased by ten degrees so as to bring it up to 180 degrees, how much more will we perspire?

Only in a certain domain does the monotonic relationship hold. Outside that domain, the relationship breaks down. Perhaps the relationship reverses. Perhaps it flatlines: perhaps B would be dead, as we would be dead in conditions of 170 and of 180 degrees (hence, $\Delta perspiration$ = 0). Or, perhaps most importantly, "the relationship breaks down" could mean that we can no longer talk intelligibly about A, or B, or a relationship between them. Perhaps the words stop making sense in those outer circumstances.

Using the letter m from "monotonic," let the notation $A\underline{\ m\ }B$ mean that A qualifiedly has (*usually* has, *potentially* has, *tends to* have, etc.) a monotonic relationship with B. Put differently, $A\underline{\ m\ }B$ means that a positive ΔB is expected to attend a positive ΔA, and a negative ΔB is expected to attend a negative ΔA.

Socrates is famous for posing questions rather than asserting conclusions. Smith expresses high regard for the "Socratick method," "the smoothest and most engaging manner," "bringing on the audience by slow and imperceptible degrees" (LRBL 145, 146). Sometimes Smith leaves us to find not only the answers but also the questions.

On a few occasions, in teaching $A\underline{\ m\ }B$, Smith posits *zero A*.

At the beginning of Part III of TMS, Smith says that previously he had treated our judgments concerning the conduct of others; now he treats our judgments concerning the conduct of ourselves. The principle is the same: We consider what a "fair and impartial spectator" would feel upon viewing the conduct and sympathize with that "supposed equitable judge" (110.2). Smith then exposits the following relationship: One's experience in society $\underline{m}$ one's adeptness in judging one's own conduct.

To illustrate, Smith posits a "human creature" who had grown "up to manhood in some solitary place, *without any* communication with his own species" (110.3; italics added). Here, A is the individual's total to-date lifetime experience of communication with the human species. Smith posits zero A—he says "without any." Such a creature would have no sense of sympathizing with a fair and impartial spectator of his conduct, and hence he could not judge his own conduct. By telling us that zero A would lead to zero B, Smith means to illustrate the $A \underline{m} B$ under discussion.

But is it possible for someone to grow up to adulthood without ever having had human contact? The thought is horrifying, but if a newborn were left alone in some solitary place, he would not survive two days, much less grow up to adulthood. Smith, in fact, writes: "*Were it possible* that a human creature could grow up to manhood in some solitary place, *without any* communication with his own species...." (110.3; italics added). And later: "*If it was possible*...that a person should grow up to manhood *without any* communication with society...." (192.12; italics added). Notice the repetition of "without any."

It is odd that Smith would teach $A \underline{m} B$ with such an impossibility. Smith could have posited a feral child, like Peter the Wild Boy, a youngster lost to the wilderness, and thereafter showing *little* adeptness at judging his own conduct. When we read Smith's illustration, what enters our mind is a feral child story. Why not avoid our having to make the adjustment? Why push the illustration to zero A?

Another example comes in Smith's section "Of Justice and Beneficence" (78–91), where he examines the roles those two virtues play in enabling society to subsist and prosper. The justice spoken of here is "mere" or commutative justice, "abstaining from what is another's (269.10). As for beneficence, it is elsewhere termed distributive justice and consists in "the becoming use of what is our own" (269–70.10).

The $A \underline{m} B$ here is: Holding the level of commutative justice constant (among neighbors and other jural equals), as distributive justice declines, so does the warmth and loveliness within "the immense fabric of human society" (86.4).

Before expositing that relationship, Smith first gives another state of the world, evidently a small, simple prelapsarian community: All social assistance "is reciprocally afforded from love, from gratitude, from friendship, and esteem, the society flourishes and is happy. All the different members of it are bound together by the agreeable bands of love and affection, and are, as it were, drawn to one common centre of mutual good offices" (85.1).

Then Smith posits a second case in which commutative justice is maintained but there is "*no* mutual love and affection." No man, he supposes, "should owe *any* obligation, or be bound in gratitude to *any* other." And again he says the society functions "*without any* mutual love or affection" (86.2; italics added), again using "without any." That society, Smith teaches, "though less happy and agreeable, will not necessarily be dissolved. Society may subsist among different men, as among different merchants" (85-6.2).

But can a decent level of commutative justice be maintained *without any* distributive justice? The answer is no. Smith also teaches that "the duties of justice, of truth, of chastity, of fidelity" would falter without regard to distributive justice such as "the general rules of civility and hospitality" (163.2). Smith says that a "sacred and religious regard" for the rules of commutative justice "can scarce ever fail to be accompanied with many other virtues, with great feeling for other people, with great humanity and great benevolence" (218.2).

Smith has again posited an impossibility: If distributive justice were zero, not only would loveliness be absent, but commutative justice would collapse! The maintenance of commutative justice depends on the becoming virtues. To use Smith's writing analogy (175.11, 327.1): Grammar cannot be maintained among writers destitute of aesthetic sense.

Smith then proceeds to the third case, a setting without commutative justice. The "prevalence of injustice must utterly destroy" society. The fabric of human society must "crumble into atoms" (86.3-4). But the second case joins the third case in crumbling into atoms. Indeed, when Smith teaches the dependence of commutative justice on distributive justice (163.2), he echoes "crumble into atoms" with "crumble into nothing." At 163.2 and 218.2 he tells us that the story at 85–86.2 is an impossibility.

And thus we see something misleading in paragraph 86.4. He says commutative justice "is the main pillar that upholds the whole edifice," while distributive justice "is the ornament that embellishes" (86.4). An edifice, upon its main pillar, may stand secure, all devoid of ornament and embellishment. But commutative cannot stand without distributive justice. Distributive justice does indeed comprise the ornaments of life. It does indeed embellish. But, also, it, along with Smith's third sense of justice, coalesces the soil *beneath the pillar* and, with gravitational pull, steadies the pillar on the soil. An edifice devoid of ornament may stand, but a society devoid of distributive justice cannot. Smith's edifice metaphor is incomplete and even misleading in the primacy it seems to give to commutative justice. This upholding pillar presupposes some degree of societal terra firma.

In the example of a newborn left alone in an isolated place, our mind adjusted to a youngster who becomes a feral child. In the present example, we adjust to thinking of, not zero, but *low* distributive justice—but not so low as to undo a decent level of commutative justice. On some such circumstances we can see that incrementally higher distributive justice (A) is attended by incrementally higher loveliness (B).

FIGURE 7.2: B'S CIRCUMSTANCED DEPENDENCE ON A

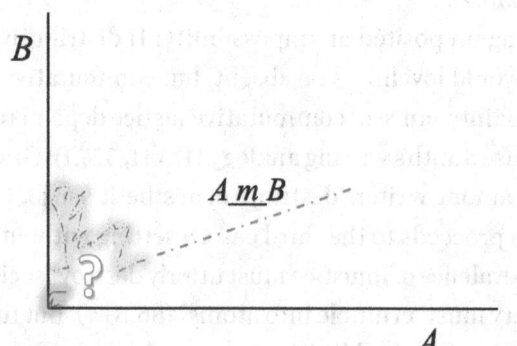

Figure 7.2 represents aspects of the foregoing examples. $A\underline{m}B$ holds well enough within a certain domain, but not elsewhere. Why not say that? Why, in both cases, did Smith say "without any," thus positing cases *outside of* that domain? Why posit cases in which his lesson does not hold?

Perhaps Smith presents us with cases of $A = 0$ to get us to see what $A\underline{m}B$ is not. Perhaps he prompts us to see that $A\underline{m}B$ is *not* a tractable monotonic relationship radiating from $A = 0$. For $A = 0$, we don't know what to make of $A\underline{m}B$, but we might see what *not to* make of it.

Does knowing what something is not count as knowledge?

Suppose that we awaken in our house to find that it snowed during the night, and we see footprints in the snow showing that someone had walked up to the front door. Would knowing that the mysterious person was *not* Tim count as knowledge about the world? Yes, indeed. *Apophatic knowledge* is knowledge about what something is not. Knowing that the trackmaker wasn't Tim might be important.

Perhaps Smith is educating us in apophatic knowledge, knowledge about what $A\underline{m}B$ is not. Smith inspires us to see that our claims about the world should be reconstrued as claims about certain phases of the world, certain domains or states of the world, or certain *circumstances*. Perhaps our understandings are always circumstanced. I suggest that Smith posits $A = 0$ to get us to ponder qualifications on $A\underline{m}B$ understandings. He teaches us the circumstantiality of bivariate relationships. Smith would concur with C. S. Lewis (2002, 730): "There are progressions in which the last step is *sui generis*—incommensurable with the others—and in which to go the whole way is to undo all the labour of your previous journey."

Bivariate relationships of this circumstanced type are also relevant for our understanding of Smith's views in *The Wealth of Nations*. We may relate Figure 7.1 to "allowing every man to pursue his own interest his own way" within the bounds of commutative justice (WN 664). Smith generally teaches that liberty $\underline{m}$ social wellbeing (although he makes exceptions). Yet we naturally wonder: Would maximal well-being obtain under zero government initiation of coercion? Consider David Hume's conservative-liberal adage: "[L]iberty is the perfection of civil society; but still authority must be acknowledged essential to its very existence" (EMPL, 41). If one were to take the liberty principle, in its direct sense, to its logical conclusion, that would imply zero governmental initiation of coercion and, since such initiation is an essential feature of government, zero government. There would remain no government authority. But Hume's adage says that such authority is essential for liberty. To quote C. S. Lewis (2002, 726) on something perhaps related: "This is one of the many instances where to carry a principle to what seems its logical conclusion produces absurdity."

Smith intends for us to understand that liberty _m_ social well-being is a circumstanced relationship. Under certain civilizational circumstances it makes a worthy precept or maxim, in which case it should then carry a presumption, vital to our civil affairs. But, *under certain civilizational circumstances*. Not only is the maxim defeasible but the exceptions are circumstantial. Smith seemed to advocate the full institutional degovernmentalization of religion for circumstances like those in North America, but did he advocate the same for Great Britain?

Yet societal circumstantiality generally points in favor of "the liberal plan of equality, liberty, and justice" (WN 664). When "Philosophy descended" from the Heavens to the Earth, it treated objects that "were more apt, when they came to be attended to, to embarrass and perplex it, by the variety of their species, and the intricacy and seeming irregularity of the laws or orders of their succession" (EPS 106). Friedrich Hayek (1978, 181) noted that science pursues discovery of "regularities of events," while "economic competition" excels in discovering particularly circumstanced opportunities for social betterment. If by nature social life is highly circumstantial, maybe the book of nature's most important exegetes are not scientists, but neighbors, entrepreneurs, and others operating through processes that Smith and Hayek say are comparatively autocorrective. This line of reasoning is not popular with progressives, pretenders to progressive research programs, and supposed experts. "The expertise required to repeat, in every situation, 'Let the market decide'... is not great" (Menand 2001, 302). Smith favors keeping social affairs voluntary and decentralized, that people may recognize and appreciate the circumstances, including the intricacies of consciousness and sentiment, and correct errors (Mueller 2020). Espouse a presumption against governmentalizing social affairs, Smith teaches.

Another lesson might be that Smith's liberalism maintains a conservative attitude about reformations to the polity (Klein 2023b, ch. 5). Appreciation of societal circumstantiality brings some adages to mind:

- Better the devil you know than the devil you don't know.
- The best is the enemy of the good.
- If it ain't (terribly) broke, don't fix it.

Let us turn to Section III of Part II of TMS: "Of the Influence of Fortune upon the Sentiments of Mankind, with regard to the Merit or Demerit of Actions."

An individual, Jim, takes some action, and we estimate the merit or demerit of his having done so. Smith discusses factors that influence our judgment of Jim's merit. The title of the section calls our attention to the role of chance, or fortune. Sitting between Jim's acting and the results is fortune:

$$Jim's\ acting\ (or\ Jim's\ will) - fortune - results$$

Our estimation of Jim's merit is influenced by fortune—for example, whether Jim was unlucky in prosecuting his intentions. Sheer luck affects our estimation of Jim's merit.

Smith gives an example: A loud noise—sheer bad luck—causes Jim's horse to take fright and run down someone in the street (104.10). Jim may then face some legal liability, as well as some downgrading of his merit as assessed by the community. But Jim may have been perfectly innocent and done nothing to deserve such downgrading.

Here again we have a monotonic relationship between two variables. A is the goodness level of the results. B is people's estimation of Jim's merit. Here, our expression $A\,\underline{m}\,B$ means that better results (positive ΔA) tend to be attended by higher estimations of merit (positive ΔB).

Smith's treatment is puzzling in the way it proceeds. He begins by saying that "[w]hatever praise or blame can be due to any action, must belong... to the intention or affection of the heart." Closely related to intention or affection of the heart are "the external action or movement of the body, which this affection gives occasion to." It "is abundantly clear," he says at the outset, that "the good or bad consequences, which actually, and in fact, proceed from it" "cannot be the foundation of any praise or blame." He sums up: "To the intention or affection of the heart, therefore, to the propriety or impropriety, to the beneficence or hurtfulness of the design, all praise or blame, all approbation or disapprobation of any kind, which can justly be bestowed upon any action, must ultimately belong" (92–93.1–2). And he says we all agree: "When this maxim is thus proposed, in abstract and general terms, there is nobody who does not agree to it" (93.4 and Smith repeats the point at 105.1). Thus, Smith starts by saying that we all agree that fortune *should not* influence our estimation of Jim's merit.

But it does! "[T]he actual consequences which happen to proceed from any action, have a very great effect upon our sentiments concerning its merit or demerit, and almost always either enhance or diminish our sense of both" (93.5; see also LRBL 129). He calls this influence of fortune an "irregularity of sentiment" (93.6, 97.2, 100.4, 104–108).

Smith taxonomically illustrates the supposed irregularity:

    i.   fortune arresting intended beneficial consequences (97–99.2–3),

    ii.   fortune arresting intended hurtful consequences (99–101.4–5),

   iii. fortune giving rise to unintended beneficial consequences (101–102.6),

   iv. fortune giving rise to unintended hurtful consequences (101–104.6–10).

In all cases, Jim comes in for either more blame or more praise than, "in abstract and general terms," he deserves.

In the section's last chapter Smith resolves the paradox: But we *don't know* intention! We don't know what Jim willed. We don't know his actions minutely. In the *Treatise*, Hume had said that moral judgment "must look within to find the moral quality," but, "This we cannot do directly; and therefore fix our attention on actions, as on external signs"—signs of motive (Hume 2007, 307)—and Smith plainly knew it: "Sentiments, designs, affections...are placed by the great Judge of hearts beyond the limits of every human jurisdiction, and are reserved for the cognizance of his own unerring tribunal" (105.2). When knowledge of Jim's intention is deficient, therefore, we *should* let the results—one kind of "sign"—play a role, even though results flow in part from a roll of the dice. Today's social results are more verifiable and clearly observable than Jim's quondam intentions and minute bodily movements. As they say in comedy, timing is everything.

Smith's "abstract and general terms" make sense, it turns out, only under a strong knowledge assumption. That assumption reaches beyond one, such as Mary, who pronounces on Jim's conduct. Suppose Mary *witnessed* Jim's evil deed. Mary knows quite minutely and with high certainty Jim's action. But if there is no way for that intelligence to become a matter of common knowledge—"her word against his"—then Mary may have to refrain from insisting publicly on Jim's impropriety. For everyone to judge solely on the basis of intention and action, it may not be sufficient that only some know the truth.[72] Indeed, even if Jim feels certain of his own innocence, he himself feels piacular for any hurt he inadvertently caused (104.10, 107.4); such a feeling may arise in Jim from his awareness that his own innocence cannot be common knowledge among the community, and, even if it can be, from the shared social habit of the influence of fortune, by way of results.

Having the knowledge required for the "abstract and general" principle would be a circumstance that is abnormal—if A is deficiency of our knowledge, it is like $A = 0$. Outside of that abnormal circumstance, we must get used to letting fortune, by way of results, influence our moral sentiments. We try to adjust accordingly (108.6), but fortune must have some influence. We fully eradicate the influence of fortune "scarce in any one instance" of actual life (105.1).

The pattern we notice in TMS is not adequately described as simply the assuming of the fantastical. Another fantastic assumption is that a man of humanity in Europe could cause an earthquake in China by evading a pinky amputation (137.4). Fine, let's run with that. Likewise, Smith posits a circumstance of zero uncertainty of the permanence of a situation (149.31). Fine. But the pattern we are noticing is the positing of circumstances in

---

72. It is important to have honest courts, honest government, honest science, honest journalism, and honest friends, family, and "those we live with" (116.5, etc.).

which the very lesson being taught breaks down. By positing at the outset of the "Influence of Fortune" section, and sustaining to the last chapter, a premise in which fortune's influence *would not exist*, Smith makes us puzzle. He has posited a case in which the $A \underline{m} B$ elaborated does not make sense. That's how he passes it off as an "irregularity of sentiment." Once we get beyond that extreme assumption, we see in the influence of fortune not an irregularity but a regularity, since the regular state of the world is that we are and remain highly deficient in our knowledge of Jim's intentions, will, and actions.

Implied within Smith's analysis is a monotonic relationship: Fortune's influence on our moral sentiments will move with the deficiency of knowledge. If our knowledge of Jim's action and intention is highly deficient, we will be more influenced by fortune, by way of results; if our knowledge of Jim's action is highly exact and certain and common to us all, we will be less influenced by fortune. If Jim is my personal friend who confides frankly and openly to me, I will be influenced less by fortune. That is a tacit lesson of Smith's discussion, a lesson about the circumstantiality of fortune's influence on our moral sentiments.

⬦

We have seen instances in which Smith posits impossible circumstances or presupposes abnormal circumstances. Now we turn to Smith attributing such to "Stoics," and knocking them for it.

Smith's representations of other thinkers are not to be trusted. Smith uses "Stoic" for his own purposes. He himself signals doubts about his descriptions of the Stoics (291.41). In what follows I mean Stoic as presented by Smith.

He sums up the moral attitude: "This contempt of life and death... and...the most entire submission to the order of Providence—the most complete contentment with every event which the current of human affairs could possibly cast up, may be considered as the two fundamental doctrines upon which rested the whole fabric of Stoical morality" (288.35). Stoicism "endeavours to render us altogether indifferent and unconcerned in the success or miscarriage of every thing which nature has prescribed to us as the proper business and occupation of our lives" (292.46).

There are things about Stoicism that Smith likes: the monotheistic universal benevolence; the composure advised when suffering blows to your own health, fortune, or reputation (143.16); perhaps the contempt of death.

However, "[t]he plan and system which nature has sketched out for our conduct seems to be altogether different from that of the Stoical philosophy" (292.43). Smith dislikes the "the most complete contentment with every event." Smith dislikes the suggestion that, come what may, the occasion for serenity is at hand. Smith represents the Stoical attitude as follows:

> All that I had to do is done already. The directors of my conduct never command me to be miserable, to be anxious, desponding, or afraid. Whether we are to be drowned, or to come to a harbour, is the business of Jupiter, not mine. (277.29)

A prayer of Reinhold Niebuhr comes to mind:

> God, grant me the serenity to accept the things I cannot change, courage to change the things I can, and wisdom to know the difference.

Wisdom to know the difference is the key. The knowing of the difference is a business perennially unfinished. We may always change our beliefs, sentiments, and actions. Such a change affects the world, if only because those beliefs, sentiments, and actions make part of it. Almost always we can improve. However, we are never sure what to improve, how to improve.

Smith, then, is constructing a Stoical moral attitude that presupposes a circumstance that rarely obtains. Rarely do we know exactly, as though it were a matter of correcting a child's grammar; people naturally advance to more challenging and indeterminate circumstances. A conceit of knowing or having known all that at the time was knowable engenders an unjust blamelessness, serenity, or apathy. Smith knocks the Stoical moral attitude for not fessing up to the abnormality of the circumstance it supposes. When we see that, we see that the Stoical moral attitude can be too self-flattering and too self-pardoning. Smith regards "complete contentment" an abstract fancy in most circumstances of actual life. The Stoical counsel is specious.

Complete contentment kills upward vitality.

Now drop the Stoic presupposition, and let's return to Jim. We can all relate to the experience Jim has when he arrives, at last, to the results of his conduct and then realizes that some part of him was up to something of which he hadn't been consciously aware, something that even belies reports he had made about his own intentions and motives. Moreover, even if Jim were to know all that moves him, even if he knows the elephant in his brain, others do not and hence do not necessarily accept his report though it be quite true. The results of action, on top of supposed knowledge of intentions and actions, will testify to praiseworthiness and blameworthiness even when it is a matter of you judging you, and fortune is bound to play a role in the matter.

Smith relishes the sharing of sentiment, and hence the expressing of sentiment, such as the grief that attends the death of one's child. "The stoical apathy is, in such cases, never agreeable, and all the metaphysical sophisms by which it is supported can seldom serve any other purpose than to blow up the hard insensibility of a coxcomb to ten times its native impertinence" (143.14). Smith believes in sociable sentiments socially expressed. He believes in hoping, and in rejoicing when fortune goes your way, and in aching a bit when it does not. Life is for the tasting. Indeed, the "most complete indulgence" of that "most furious of all the passions" is, at least when between certain persons, acknowledged "to be perfectly innocent," says Smith, "by all laws, both human and divine" (28.2).

And tasting brings learning. Smith believes in learning from "the bustle and business of the world" (146.25). Activeness brings better knowledge of how to improve. "Man was made for action"; he should "call forth the whole vigour of his soul, and strain every nerve, in order to produce those ends which it is the purpose of his being to advance" (106.3). Since activeness helps us fulfill duty, activeness becomes a duty. Smith speaks well of assiduity (41.1, 83.1, 173.6, 181.8, 213.6).

Smith's Stoics recognize that one must "discharge his own duty" properly, that one must not commit any false strokes, which would bring regret and mortification (277. 21, 279.24). But to the Stoical "wise man...the exact observation of this propriety was equally easy upon all occasions" (278.23). "The events of human life can never find him unprepared, or at a loss how to maintain that propriety of sentiment and conduct which, in his own apprehension, constitutes at once his glory and his happiness" (278.23; see also 290.39). The Stoical moral attitude professes that one can obtain a full confidence of never making false strokes, of never erring. In that full confidence, the Stoical moral attitude enjoys an "entire resignation" to the vicissitudes of fortune (277.21).

It might be said that Smith is unfair to use "Stoic" as he does. The unfairness abates the more we see what Smith is up to. After caricaturing them as he does, Smith suggests that the self-arrogated full confidence and pretension of complete contentment flowed from their circumstances. "[A] Grecian patriot or hero could not avoid frequently employing his thoughts in considering what he ought both to suffer and to do in banishment, in captivity, when reduced to slavery, when put to the torture, when brought to the scaffold" (282.28). "It was impossible…that a Grecian patriot or hero should not familiarize his imagination with all the different calamities to which he was sensible his situation must frequently, or rather constantly, expose him" (282.28). Likewise, Smith says that, from a life of abuse and jeopardy, Epictetus "could preserve his tranquility only by fostering in his mind the most sovereign contempt of human life" (288.36). The pretended confidence and complete contentment with which Smith has characterized the Stoical wise man was a refuge from the surrounding tumult and precariousness. Smith at least provides them with an excuse for the folly he pins on them.

In the highest sense of the term, the impartial spectator is for theists God and for some others an allegorical being called Joy. To coalesce all such votaries, I refer to the supreme impartial spectator as God/Joy.

Smith speaks of the conscience as *the man within the breast*, which I abbreviate as MwB.

Smith says that Jim's MwB is a representative of God/Joy (215.11). The same goes for yours, mine, and everyone else's. That's one sense in which God/Joy is universal. Given the evident diversity of all the MwBs, they cannot all be good representatives, and in God/Joy's eyes perhaps none rises much above the common.

Speaking of MwB, Smith goes so far as to say: "If we place ourselves completely in his situation, if we really view ourselves with his eyes and as he views us, and listen with diligent and reverential attention to what he suggests to us, his voice will never deceive us" (227.22). Even if we have a quarrel with Jim's MwB, we could hardly say that Jim has a duty to defy his own MwB. As Obi-Wan Kenobi said to Luke Skywalker: "You must do what you feel is right, of course." Or Martin Luther: "It is neither safe nor right to go against conscience" (1999, 32:112).

Now we come to the following expression of a bivariate relationship, referred to as expression (*):

God/Joy's approval of Jim's conduct _m_ Jim's MwB's approval of Jim's conduct   (*)

And we come to the matter of the circumstantiality of expression (*).

Surely, Smith encourages us to make our conduct in common life more in keeping with what our MwB approves of. Surely there is a supposition that, usually, expression (*) holds, that MwB's approval attends God/Joy's approval. Smith wants us to heed MwB and augment approval from him. If MwB's approval attends God/Joy's approval then it also attends universal beneficialness, since there is a built-in correspondence between that and God/Joy's approval.[73]

Smith encourages us to heed our MwB, often over against what princes or elites or majorities approve of. Smith tells us to choose praiseworthiness when praiseworthiness and praise appear to be at odds and to love true glory (that is, praise for what is praiseworthy) more than mere fame or popular praise. Even above the love of true glory, Smith exalts "the love of virtue, the noblest and the best passion of human nature" (309.8). "The man who acts solely from a regard to what is right and fit to be done, from a regard to what is the proper object of esteem and approbation, though these sentiments should never be bestowed upon him, acts from the most sublime and

---

73. In God/Joy's eyes, there can, because of the role of fortune, be daylight between beneficialness and His/her approval, but humans are not to allow daylight between God/Joy's approval and their most perfect understandings of such universal beneficialness.

godlike motive which human nature is even capable of conceiving" (311.10).

He encourages our MwB to be, not independent of all social influences, but a unique composite of influences so as to be ready to be independent of any particular social influence, such as a parent, a clan, a teacher, a cleric, a church, a pundit, a political party, or an author such as Smith or Marx. Our MwB is our entrepreneurial innovation in the sphere of competing moral outlooks (DelliSanti 2023).

But does expression (*) hold in all circumstances? When Jim feels very sure of having complete MwB approval of his conduct, does that enhance *our confidence* in God/Joy's approval of his conduct? Or do we tend to think that expression (*) holds up only within a limited range?

Smith discusses one's "love...of applause" (238.3), both one's passion to regard himself highly and one's passion to have others regard him highly (246.22–262.53). The proud man wants others to estimate him as he estimates himself but he estimates himself too highly (255.35). The vain man estimates himself more or less accurately, perhaps, but he wants others to estimate him higher than he estimates himself (255.36). Each, in different ways, wants others to estimate him higher than he deserves (or corresponding to God/Joy's estimation). The solicitations of these two passions, for self-approbation and for approbation from others, are "continual and almost incessant." These two passions "are, in the course of a life, very apt to mislead into great deviation" (237.2). Like the love of ease and of pleasure, these passions call for self-command in the form of "temperance, decency, modesty, and moderation" (238.3).

Smith says we have a desire for the approval of our MwB. We have a passion for self-approbation. When other approbation misdirects, we must use that passion to correct our passion for other approbation. Smith encourages our ability to use self-approbation to correct or conquer that other passion: "the irascible part of our nature is...called in to assist the rational against the concupiscible" (268.7).

But self-approbation flows from our MwB, and our MwB is not necessarily a good representative of God/Joy; there is danger in the passion for self-approbation, as well. Just as an indifference to the results of one's action and the role of fortune attends a self-flattering and self-pardoning "Stoical" complacency, an indifference to public disapprobation, particularly in young adults, forebodes "a most improper insensibility to real honour and infamy" (145.19).

Let us look at another passage in which Smith speaks of the love of virtue:

> The love of just fame, of true glory, even for its own sake, and independent of any advantage which he can derive from it, is not unworthy even of *a wise man*. He sometimes, however, neglects, and even despises it; and he is never more apt to do so than when he has *the most perfect* assurance of *the perfect propriety of every part* of his own conduct. His self-approbation, in this case, stands in need of no confirmation from the approbation of other men. It is alone sufficient, and he is contented with it. This self-approbation, if *not the only*, is at least *the principal object*, about which he can or ought to be anxious. The love of it is the love of virtue. (117.8; italics added)

Shall we agree that when a wise man feels "the most perfect assurance of the perfect propriety of every part of his conduct," he "stands in need of no confirmation from the approbation of other men"? Hmmm. Do I smell the man grown up in the wilderness without any human contact? Or the society with commutative but without any distributive justice? Or perfect and complete knowledge of another man's intentions and minute bodily movements? Or a society with zero government initiation of coercion?

There is plenty in Smith suggesting that a wise man never feels "the most perfect assurance of the perfect propriety of every part of his conduct":

> The wise and virtuous man...imitates the work of a divine artist, *which can never be equalled*. He...*feels so well his own imperfection*, he knows so well the difficulty with which he attained his own distant approximation to rectitude.... His whole mind, in short, is deeply impressed, his whole behaviour and deportment are distinctly stamped with the character of real modesty; with that of a very moderate estimation of his own merit, and, at the same time, of a full sense of the merit of other people. (247–8.25; italics added)

Or consider this:

> [The wise and virtuous man] remembers, *with concern and humiliation,* how *often,* from *want of attention, from want of judgment, from want of temper,* he has, both in words and actions, both in conduct and conversation, *violated the exact rules of perfect propriety,* and has *so far departed* from that model, according to which he wished to fashion his own character and conduct. (TMS 247–48.25; italics added)

In editions 2 through 5 Smith wrote that Stoics "teach us to aim at a perfection *altogether beyond the reach of human nature*" (60n.c-c; italics added; see also 26.9). Yes, it seems that, once again, Smith has posited something of which he teaches the impossibility.

In the 117.8 block quotation given above, Smith affirms that wisdom's chief object of anxiety is self-approbation, thus propounding expression (*). But right there he suggests that it is "not the only" object. It is the "principal object." Approbation from others remains an important object of anxiety for the wise person. A wise man "stands in need of no confirmation from the approbation of other men" never.

Some tend to think that our passion for praiseworthiness derives from our passion for praise from others, but Smith teaches that our passion for praise from others derives in large measure from our passion for praiseworthiness or, at least, for self-approbation. "Our uncertainty concerning our own merit, and our anxiety to think favourably of it, should together naturally enough make us desirous to know the opinion of other people concerning it; to be more than ordinarily elevated when that opinion is favourable, and to be more than ordinarily mortified when it is otherwise" (126.24). The praise of others is not express in expression (*), but the expression's righthand side, featuring Jim's MwB's approval, is bound to relate to the praise of others.

Now suppose there were a Jim who felt he had "the most perfect assurance of the perfect propriety of every part of his own conduct." What do we say about such a Jim? With reference to expression (*), there are at least two ways to go. One is to say that, although the empirical Jim—the walking, talking Jim—*felt* that he had the entire approval of his own MwB, he does not. Jim's MwB may be sound enough, but not getting through to the empirical Jim. Perhaps the voice of MwB is weak, or perhaps Jim is not listening carefully; perhaps Jim is misunderstanding MwB. Another way to go is to say that Jim *does* have the entire approval of MwB, but that MwB is faulty. Again, MwB is not necessarily a good representative of God/Joy. Smith suggests that it is possible for Jim's violent passions to cow MwB into "mak[ing] a report very different from what the real circumstances of the case are capable of authorizing" (157.1). Whichever way we construe this self-assured Jim, we are left doubting that Jim is "[t]he wise and virtuous man" (247–8.25).

Perhaps MwB does not have the approval of the man within *his* breast. MwB is a composite cultivated through time, diachronically, and stands perennially in need of improvement. The righthand side of expression (*) speaks of Jim's conscience, but beyond that would be Jim's conscience's conscience. *That* man, we postulate, is a better representative of God/Joy, but, again, still not necessarily a very good one.

⌖

But does it make sense to talk of expression (*) as a bivariate relationship? Such talk would seem to *presuppose a dataset*. Only then do we speak of a relationship between the two variables. Expression (*)'s two variables, however, are MwB's approval and God/Joy's approval. Each data point would consist of a pair of values, one for MwB's approval and one for God/Joy's approval. Suppose we grant that Jim has data on MwB's approval. Do we believe he has collected data on God/Joy's approval? Has anyone collected data on that? "No," I hear someone say frankly, and I concur. I suppose that everyone in the God/Joy coalition would concur. Scriptural revelation of God's laws does not make a data series of God's approval of Jim's actions. It's for Jim to figure out whether God approves of his action. Think of it as a challenge in interpreting and applying those laws.

Well, are we to throw out expression (*), and anything like it, and throw up our hands? Don't we go through life pretending that our conduct and conscience relate to some notion of societal betterment, conduct that if beheld by a great beholder would earn us her approval for conducing to the good? Doesn't every one of us have an interest in being praiseworthy, even if it is not a predominating interest?

You and I maintain that we have some feeling for God/Joy's approval. It is like goodness of movies. We don't have a definition of a good movie, but we watch and discuss movies as though we know something about movie goodness. In similar fashion, we cannot do without something like expression (*).

Perhaps we should rewrite expression (*), replacing God/Joy's approval with MwB's MwB's approval. That would be somewhat more empirical than God/Joy's approval. Still, think how circumstantial remains Jim's reading of the lefthand-side value of his wannabe datapoints. In the collecting of each datapoint, the value recorded into his dataset will depend on intricacies of mind and breast. Is Jim's reading of the data steady and scrupulous, or is it wavering? No wonder Smith hat-tips Aristotle on virtue as something regular and habitual, something embedded within Jim's life among those he lives with (272.14).

We have arrived at a place of fear and trembling: First, our discussion considered the circumstantiality of an (A, B) datapoint: Does that (A, B) datapoint belong to conditions that make it part of a pattern showing an A $\underline{m} B$ monotonic relationship, or does that particular (A, B) datapoint occur under confounding circumstances? But now we are asking: Under what circumstances can we find confidence in even knowing the (A, B) datapoint? That is, do we know the report of our conscience, and is that report aligned with the good? We are talking about the data of our own moral self-estimation. What are the rules for such confidence, and how are those rules limited by circumstances?

I don't think Smith has easy answers to that difficult question, about the rules for data collection for one's own moral self-estimation. Smith says: how far one's conduct may have been influenced by the desire to do praiseworthy action and how far by the desire for praise "may frequently be unknown even to himself" (126.26). Jim has virtues "which he himself could scarce be sure that he possessed, and for which even the man within the breast could scarce venture to afford him any distinct and clear testimony" (132.33).

In our search for guidance and confidence, let's listen to Smith on virtue, friendship, frankness, and openness:

> [O]f all attachments to an individual, that which is founded altogether upon esteem and approbation of his good conduct and behaviour, confirmed by much experience and long acquaintance, is by far the most respectable. Such friendships, arising not from a constrained sympathy, not from a sympathy which has been assumed and rendered habitual for the sake of convenience and accommodation, but from a natural sympathy, from an involuntary feeling that the persons to whom we attach ourselves are the natural and proper objects of esteem and approbation, can exist only among men of virtue. Men of virtue only can feel that entire confidence in the conduct and behaviour of one another, which can at all times assure them that they can never either offend or be offended by one another. Vice is always capricious—**virtue only is regular and orderly**. The attachment which is founded upon the love of virtue, as it is certainly of all attachments the most virtuous, so it is likewise the happiest, as well as the most permanent and secure. Such friendships need not be confined to a single person, but may safely embrace all the wise and virtuous with whom we have been long and intimately acquainted, and upon whose wisdom and virtue we can upon that account entirely depend. (224-5.18; boldface added)

Here Smith says true friends commune in virtue "regular and orderly." It's a lovely ideal. Circumstances will at times challenge, complicate, and confuse friendship. Friends, I suppose, share a sense of *more* regular and orderly and of *less* regular and orderly, of upward and downward, and they help each other correct errors. The faltering of a friendship is marked by incidents of capriciousness, unclarity, concealment, and dismissiveness. "Reserve and concealment...call forth diffidence. We are afraid to follow the man who is going we do not know where." "Frankness and openness conciliate confidence" (337.28). Frankness and openness, it seems to me, are things to cherish and venerate.

Most of the quotations about ineluctable failure and regret, even in the wise and virtuous man, and his dependence on frank and open friendship (coming from 126.26, 132.33, 224-5.18, 247–48.25, and 337.28) were new to Ed. 6 of 1790, and then there is also the new discussion of "the superior stations"—"the courts of princes, the drawing-rooms of the great"—lacking virtue (63–65). "In many governments the candidates for the highest stations are above the law" (64.8). At the end of his life, Smith dwelled on the importance of friendship, frankness, and openness to one's sense of God/ Joy's approval. In circumstances in which those conditions are wanting, the bivariate relationship shown in expression (*) may not amount to much.

I said circumstantiality saps coherence from a subject matter and dampens the will to study the subject. Circumstantiality upsets system knowledge and embarrasses authority. "Things of so fleeting a nature can never be the objects of science, or of any steady or permanent judgment" (EPS 121.2). If the rules of virtue depend greatly on circumstances—that is, if the set of rules itself varies greatly with circumstances—we will be less interested in trying to learn any supposed rules of virtue. In a cosmos of supreme circumstantiality, we could scarcely sustain a notion of the good of the whole and of means of advancing it, and hence a notion of virtue.

And the perception of high generalizability tends to inspire the will to study. The more generalizable the rules of virtue seem to be, the more inclined are we to study those rules. Here we have another $A \underline{m} B$. Smith cautions us against the temptation to over-estimate generalizability. If we oversimplify the world, we tout oversimplified rules of virtue. Our study of true virtue will be correspondingly amiss. Smith points out the perennial hazards of hubris, conceit, and vanity. Also perennial is the hazard of self-deceit and delusion. Each person faces hazards of moral deterioration. Somewhere between the extremes of perfect irregularity and perfect regularity we seek a world worth believing in, worth being upwardly vital within.

Our discussion arrived at doubt about the most important bivariate relationship—that between MwB's approval and doing good. Smith seems to suggest that a person, Jim, can best know the relationship between his MwB's approval and his doing good under circumstances of his having frank and open friendships. Outside of those circumstances, do not expect Jim to show much upward vitality. The implication for politics is that we want that kind of government that best conduces to frank and open friendships (Mueller 2021).

Perhaps Smith found a way—by puzzles, curious illustration, Stoical foils, and other means—to hide circumstantiality from tyros and to teach it to proud readers of the book of virtues. Few relish the implications of the intricacy of consciousness and the still more mysterious complexities beyond.

CHAPTER 8

In a Word or Two, Placed in the Middle

By Daniel Klein and Brandon Lucas

I n reading *The Wealth of Nations* you may have noticed that the 6-gram "led by an invisible hand to" comes quite near the physical center of the work. In *The Theory of Moral Sentiments*, the 6-gram appears, but it comes some way past the physical center.

But from the third edition of *The Theory of Moral Sentiments*, Smith appended his language essay—an appendage not appearing in the Glasgow/OUP/LF edition. Figure 8.1 shows the placement of the 6-gram in the original tomes under Smith's control.

FIGURE 8.1: IH % OFFSET FROM CENTER, BY LEAF-COUNT, TMS AND WN, BY EDITION.

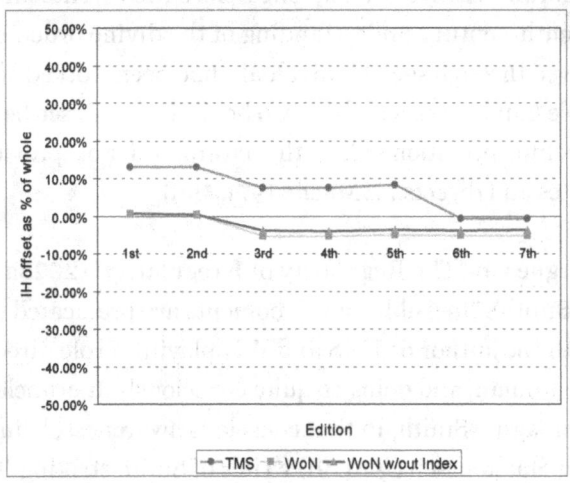

Source: Leaf-counts from inspection of the editions.[74]

---

74. Online Appendix: Complete explanation and record of measurements and leaf counts for the six editions (two of TMS, four of WN) examined physically at the Library of Congress, and the other eight editions accessed electronically (leaf counts only): http://econfaculty.gmu.edu/klein/Assets/Appendix_IH_TMSandWN.xls.

The Figure will be reproduced and explained later in this chapter. Here we contemplate Adam Smith's intentionality in locating his famous phrase about intentionality. We contend that the physical centrality of "invisible hand" was the art of an invisible hand.

The phrase "invisible hand" was very special to Smith. Alec Macfie (1971) wrote:

> Smith's central endeavor throughout all his writings was indeed to explore and build into his system of thought the inclusive scope and manifold interrelations of this system of "Nature." ... *The "invisible hand of Jupiter" has in the books become the energizing power of the whole system.* (Macfie 1971, 598–99; italics added)

Macfie argues that "the invisible hand of Jupiter" was thought by Romans to be the cause of lightning, and the "invisible hand" of TMS and WN are not so different:

> [T]here is no inconsistency. The explanation is the view of history typical of the Enlightenment. In the Essay Jupiter represents the ignorant "savage's" view, long before the seventeenth- and eighteenth-century understanding of the divine order, mainly preserved through social individuals, had been worked out. The invisible hand passages of the two books in fact describe Adam Smith's interpretation of how the natural order of "providence" animates and directs.... (Macfie 1971, 596)

Klein argues in "The Regularity of Irregularity" (2023a, ch. 6) that all three of Smith's "invisible hand" moments are predicated on an irregularity—with the author of TMS and WN playing a role directly parallel to the crude Roman, and doing so quite consciously. It is unclear whether one should imagine Smith, in that conscious awareness, being devout or ironic. Knud Haakonssen (1981, 91) writes of Smith striking "that perfect equipoise between irony and encomium which is so typical of him." Something striking about "invisible hand" in WN is that it is virtually the only moment in WN where Smith emanates theism.

In his article "Adam Smith's Invisible Hands," Peter Minowitz (2004) suggests that Smith was aware that what people take to have been the product of nature's or God's authorship would be greatly affected by the authorship of leading cultural figures—or authorities. Minowitz writes: "Only *Moral Sentiments* attributes an Author to nature, and some of the differences between the two books may signal that Smith has used 'invisible' authorial skills to 'lead' his readers, especially when he appeals to God or nature as *authorities*" (409). In a footnote to the article, Minowitz makes the following observation:

> The two discussions [with "invisible hand," in *TMS* and *WN*], furthermore, are similarly located in their respective works: Book IV of *WN* and Part IV of *TMS* (*TMS* is divided into parts rather than books). The account of feudalism occupies the central book of *WN*, and is followed quickly by the invisible hand, which lies roughly in the middle of *WN*, page-wise. In *TMS*, similarly, the invisible hand appears in the central part. (Minowitz 2004, 404)

What Smith said about Thucydides

In the student-transcribed notes of his 1762–63 lectures on rhetoric and belles letters, Smith says:

> There is no author who has more distinctly explained the causes of events than Thucydides. He is in this respect far superior to Polybius, who is at such great pains in minutely explaining all the externall causes of any event that *his labour appears visibly* in his works and is not only tiresome but at the same time is less pleasant by the constraint the author seems to have been in. Thucydides *on the other hand often expresses all that he labours so much in a word or two, sometimes placed in the middle of the narration* but in such a manner as not in the least to confound it. (LRBL 95; italics added)

Notice how Smith says of Polybius that his "labour appears visibly," suggesting that, "on the other hand," the labour of Thucydides' hand remains invisible. Smith speaks of Thucydides with only high admiration and even defends him against critics (LRBL 6–7, 86–88, 95, 99, 106–10, 141, 169).

This LRBL passage, which has not previously been noted, shows that Smith was mindful of expressing special ideas in special ways: "in a word or two" and "placed in the middle." The passage is remarkable, and not least for the word "often," as it reveals that Smith perceived Thucydides to have employed the particular practice not just incidentally, but often. Smith is referring to a practice employed by Thucydides within a narration which is among the many narrations constituting *The Peloponnesian War*, and not specifically for the entire set of tomes, as here pursued with respect to TMS and WN.

The quoted passage contrasting Thucydides and Polybius comes in Smith's discoursing on the writing of histories or narratives. Smith treats the writing of narrative separately from writing to "prove some proposition" (LRBL 89; see also 62). Argumentation to prove some proposition he subdivides into the didactic and the rhetorical/oratorical (62, 89). If we were to place Smith's own works within this system, both TMS and WN would be in the didactic-argumentation category. Still, we do not think it at all irregular to suggest that Smith would see a device noted by him in Thucydides' narrative writing to be potentially suitable in didactical argumentation.

Kiddushin 30a

Professor Russell Roberts has apprised us of a deep tradition in classical Hebrew scholarship. A prime example is the following passage written some 2000 years ago, here reproduced directly from an English translation of the *Talmud Bavli* (Schottenstein 1992) but inserting ellipse where Hebrew text was retained in Schottenstein (1992):

> … the Early Sages were called *sofrim* ("those who count"),…for they counted all the letters of the Torah…. The letter *vav* of the word *gachon*…represents the half-way point of the letters of a Torah scroll…. The words *darosh darash*…represent the half-

way point of the Torah's words.... The verse that begins with the word *vehisgalach*... represents the half way point of the Torah's verses.... In the passage *y'charsemenah chazir miya'ar*...the letter ayin of the word *ya'ar*, is the half-way point of the Book of Psalms.... The verse, *vehu rachum yechaper avon* ...represents the half way point of the verses in *Psalms*. (Schottenstein Edition of *Talmud Bavli* 1992, *Kiddushin* 30a)

In *Kiddushin* 30a, following the words just quoted, there is further commentary about midpoints. The Talmud itself, then, talks about midpoints in the Torah.

The passage shows that midpoint analysis existed long before Adam Smith's times. It is possible that Adam Smith was aware of such textual analysis and devices, beyond what he observed in Thucydides, and that he was aware that others were aware of it, which can help to make midpoint devices focal. And even if Smith was unaware of such traditions, the *Kiddushin* passage suggests that midpoints have a focalness that is natural or universal.

In pondering Smith's intentionality, many questions bubble up:

- Were midpoint-type traditions alive in Smith's setting? Even if not, was anyone aware of their former life? Were documents representing such traditions accessible to Smith at Balliol? Did any eighteenth-century writer, aside from Smith, ever speak of middle-placement or such devices?

- Would an author with a lengthy work going to press, such as the 1st edition of WN, where "led by an invisible hand" is dead center, even have means to ascertain where the midpoint of the forthcoming work would be?

Our method raises such questions, but we do not address them here.

"Spectator" bookending in WN

The expression most associated with Smith is "invisible hand." What would be second? Surely, "impartial spectator."

"Spectator" appears twice in WN, at the beginning and at the end—specifically, in the second paragraph of the first chapter ("the view of the spectator") and in the antepenultimate paragraph of the last chapter ("impartial spectators of the conduct of all"). That "spectator" bookending in WN suggests intentionality about the physical placement of key words in the work. Midway in the 1776 WN, within a few leaves of the exact midpoint, between the two occurrences of "spectator" sits "led by an invisible hand." It would be apt to connect "spectator" and "invisible hand," since the impartial spectator, in the highest sense, is, on a providential view, that very being whose hand is invisible.

The importance of the middle, the center

In the present section we elaborate evidence pertaining to the importance of middle/center in Smith's thinking. When quoting Smith, we put *middle* and *center* in all-caps (MIDDLE, CENTER).

For a great many objects, such as a building, a garden, a painting, or a human body, the center is special. As for a book, the center is special in several respects. The front and the back are the first places one looks for an author's gist or "punchline." They would also be the places first examined by a censor, and the censor's monitors. But diving into the middle of a book often means diving into the middle of an argument, and one often cannot understand the middle in isolation (cf. Strauss 1952, 24-25).

The middle has charms apart from the need to conceal. An author might make what is central ideationally also central physically. What do Smith's ideas center around? An invisible hand. What phrase is at the center of his masterworks? "led by an invisible hand."

Thomas Schelling's *The Strategy of Conflict* explores the properties that make something focal. One property mentioned repeatedly is symmetry or middle-ness (Schelling 1960, 57, 96, 104, 108 n., 114, 117–18, 232, 279, 283, 284, 289, 294). The center is uniquely equidistant from the ends. In the lectures on rhetoric and belles lettres, Smith remarked on focal and aesthetic properties of middle-ness. Discussing the proper number of subordinate propositions to develop in one's argument, he says:

In the number 3 there is as it were a MIDDLE and two extremes; but in two or four there is no MIDDLE on which the attention can be so fixt as that each part seems somewhat connected with it. The Rule is in this matter the same as in Architecture.... (LRBL 143)

In TMS he gives an architectural illustration:

The conveniency of a house gives pleasure to the spectator as well as its regularity, and he is as much hurt when he observes the contrary defect, as when he sees the correspondent windows of different forms, or the door not placed exactly in the MIDDLE of the building. (TMS 179)

Aesthetic connotations arise in Smith's discussion of music and states of mind. After treating the brisk and lively state of mind associated with being gay and cheerful, and the slow brooding state of mind associated with melancholy, he turns to a middle state: "What may be called the natural state of the mind, the state in which we are neither elated nor dejected, the state of sedateness, tranquillity, and composure, holds a sort of MIDDLE place between those two opposite extremes" (EPS 197). He repeats:

We all readily distinguish the cheerful, the gay, and the spright-ly Music, from the melancholy, the plaintive, and the affecting; and both these from what holds a sort of MIDDLE place between them, the sedate, the tranquil, and the composing. And we are all sensible that, in the natural and ordinary state of the mind, Music can, by a sort of incantation, sooth and charm us into some degree of that particular mood or disposition which accords with its own character and temper. (EPS 197)

Is it plausible that, while he was in a "composing," "middle," "natural" state of mind, Smith composed at the middle of a work on the laws of nature a phrase of special significance?

The center or middle may also have ethical connotations. Being equidistant from the ends, it gives rise to equal portions, and thus has an egalitarian connotation. It also connotes balance. Such balance relates to Smith's "two different sets of virtues," the amiable and the respectable, and his call to balance "the great law of Christianity," "to love our neighbor as we love ourselves," and "the great precept of nature to love ourselves only as we love our neighbor" (TMS 23, 25). In "perfect virtue," Smith suggests, "the propriety of our own sentiments and feelings seems to be EXACTLY IN PROPORTION TO the vivacity and force with which we enter into and conceive [another's] sentiments and feelings" (TMS 152). And when Smith wrote publicly of the man who approached "as nearly to the idea of a perfectly wise and virtuous man, as perhaps the nature of human frailty will permit," namely, David Hume, he said: "His temper, indeed, seemed to be more happily BALANCED, if I may be allowed such an expression, than that perhaps of any other man I have ever known" (Corr. 221).

Discussing the virtue ethics of Aristotle, Smith explains: "Every particular virtue, according to him, lies in a kind of MIDDLE between two opposite vices, of which the one offends from being too much, the other from being too little affected by a particular species of objects" (TMS 270). Fortitude "lies in the MIDDLE" between cowardice and presumptuous rashness, frugality "lies in the MIDDLE" between avarice and profusion, magnanimity "lies in the MIDDLE" between arrogance and pusillanimity. Smith affirms that in this respect Aristotle's take "corresponds...pretty exactly" to his own (271; see also 40, 172, 198–99, 201).

Yet, on a wider view, in the first paragraph in the review of ethical systems, Part VII of TMS, Smith says that all foregoing systems "coincide with some part or other" of his ethical plexus, but many of them "are derived from a partial or imperfect view of nature," and therefore "are many of them too in some respects in the wrong" (265). That is, foregoing ethicists often took their system too far. In a fashion parallel to what Smith says about Newton in relation to foregoing systems of natural philosophy (EPS 104-05), Smith incorporates the valuable and makes a well-centered, well-balanced plexus. Smith's admonitions against system may be seen as a call for a virtuous complex center.

Indeed, an analogy would be the center of a celestial system. A search on "center" and "central" in Smith's *Essays on Philosophical Subjects*, which contains both the Astronomy essay and the Ancient Physics essay, shows Smith's fascination with central forces and the periodical revolutions about them. Also, in a solar system, the center is occupied by a source of light and heat. Some early readers of TMS suggested that Smith was presenting a kind of moral Newtonianism (Ross 1995, xxi).

Smith discussed the force field, if you will, of sympathy and benevolence, and again we see centrality holding special importance. At the center is the individual's relation with himself or herself. The "sympathetic gradient" (Peart and Levy 2005) ranges outward, to one's family, friendships, neighborhoods, colleagues, "orders and societies," the nation, and finally "universal benevolence" or humanity (TMS 219-37). Smith's social-distance theory parallels gravitational theory of physics, and he says we can hardly imagine it being otherwise:

> The [gravitational] law too, by which it is supposed to diminish as it recedes from its CENTRE, is the same which takes place in all other qualities which are propagated in rays from a CENTRE, in light, and in every thing else of the same kind. It is such, that we not only find that it does take place in all such qualities, but we are necessarily determined to conceive that, from the nature of the thing, it must take place. (EPS 104)

In Book I of WN there is a short paragraph—a paragraph combining nature, centrality, and gravitation—that any reader should sense as a moment of taking stock and receiving the learning of what Smith is teaching:

> The natural price, therefore, is, as it were, the CENTRAL price, to which the prices of all commodities are continually gravitating. Different accidents may sometimes keep them suspended a good deal above it, and sometimes force them down even somewhat below it. But whatever may be the obstacles which hinder them from settling in this CENTER of repose and continuance, they are constantly tending towards it. (WN 75.15)

Finally, we note that Hume (EMPL, 545ff) eulogized the "middle station in life," and Smith said that virtue and fortune were best aligned in the "MIDDLING and inferior stations of life" (TMS 63).

To sum-up this section, we have noted a number of ways in which the center or middle may have appealed to Smith as a place to put something special:

- The ancient idea of burying something special at the center of a work.

- The center as a Schelling point, making what is ideationally central also physically central.

- The aesthetic appeal of the center, as with a door "placed exactly in the middle of the building" (TMS 179).

- The center as a point of balance, symmetry, and equality; this relates to Smith's call to balance our love or ourselves and our love of our neighbors.

- A "middle" or "natural" state of mind—"the sedate, the tranquil, and the composing"—as a psychic state between the "sprightly" and the "melancholy" (EPS 197).

- The Aristotelian idea of the virtuous center found "between two opposite vices" (TMS 270).

- The Newtonian or celestial analogy of a center about which the rest of the system turns, with the center radiating warmth and light (EPS 104).

- The center as a position of "repose and continuance," a place towards which things gravitate (WN 75).

- We shall also suggest the middle as "one common centre of mutual good offices" (TMS 85), a place where people come together.

Such points may have aroused a fancy to express all that one labours in a word or two, placed at the midpoint. Such conjecture would explain what is shown in Figure 8.1.

The location of IH in TMS and WN

In the first edition of TMS, "invisible hand" (abbreviated IH) comes somewhat past the midpoint of the book. From the third edition, however,
Smith's essay on the first formation of languages was appended following
the text of TMS, thus putting IH closer to the center of the whole. With
changes in the final edition, IH was dead center. As for WN, IH was dead
center in the first two editions, and always near the center.

In 2009, Klein (277) aired the conjecture that it was intentional centrality, and the conjecture was derogated by Gavin Kennedy (2009b, 378)
and J. Bradford DeLong (2009). Klein then recruited Brandon Lucas to
look into the matter carefully. We have confined our investigation to editions printed in London by Millar/Strahan/Cadell, thus neglecting the
Dublin and Philadelphia editions. We have investigated original editions
of both TMS and WN through 1793. For each of the two works there are sev-
en editions through that date, but in both cases the 7th edition is extremely close to the 6th. We include the 7th editions because doing so makes the
placement of IH in the final editions more visible in Figure 8.1, and because
the Library of Congress contains only the 1st and 7th TMS editions, and the
1st, 3rd, 5th, and 7th WN editions.

Our chief method of quantification—the method represented in Figure
8.1—is counting leaves of the set. (A "leaf" contains two pages, one on each
of its sides.) We counted the leaves manually for the six sets available at the
Library of Congress, and from scanned electronic copies for the other eight.
On online appendix contains the data and details of our methods (http://
econfaculty.gmu.edu/klein/Assets/Appendix_IH_TMSandWN.xls).

Figure 8.1 (repeated below) shows the percentage by which IH is offset from the center for all editions. Along the horizontal axis are the seven
editions of each work. Along the vertical is the percentage offset. Suppose,
for example, IH had appeared on the first leaf of the work; then it would
be offset from the center by -50 percent, and would be charted at the bottom of the Figure. Alternatively, if IH had appeared on the last leaf of the
work, then it would be offset from the center by 50 percent of the whole,
and would be charted at the top of the Figure.

FIGURE 8.1 (REPEATED): IH % OFFSET FROM CENTER, BY LEAF-COUNT, TMS AND WN, BY EDITION.

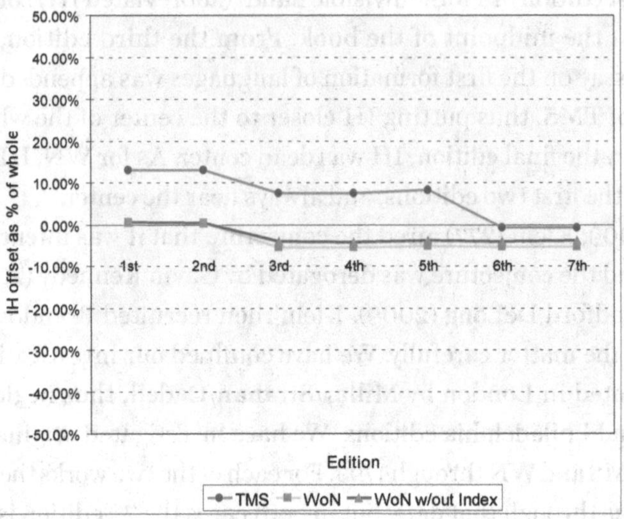

Source: Leaf-counts from inspection of the editions.

The Theory of Moral Sentiments

The 1st edition of TMS, 1759, consisting of a single volume, has IH quite a bit beyond the midpoint. Subsequent changes, however, brought the IH passage toward the center of the tomes that contained TMS, and ultimately extremely close. Beginning with the 3rd edition (1767), Smith appended the language essay (which had been published 1761). Later, with the 6th edition (1790), Smith made significant changes that put IH at the center of the set. That edition was essentially identical to the "7th edition" published in 1792, which we were able to examine physically. Figure 8.2 shows the location of the IH passage (a credit card sits at the IH page). Counting all leaves (including even the blank spacer leaves at the front and end of each volume), we find that the two volumes of the 7th edition of TMS contain 492 leaves. The midpoint would be leaf 246. IH appears on back of leaf 242. The offset is 3.5 leaves. The offset as a portion of entire set of leaves (492) equals 0.0071.

FIGURE 8.2: *THE THEORY OF MORAL SENTIMENTS*, "7ᵗʰ EDITION," 1792.

The Wealth of Nations

Figure 8.3 shows a photograph of the 1ˢᵗ edition of WN, 1776. The two volumes of WN 1st edition contain 562 leaves in the entire set of two volumes. The midpoint would be between leaf 281 and leaf 282. IH appears on leaf 285. Counting the offset at 4 leaves (as opposed 3 leaves), the offset as a portion of the entire set of leaves (562) equals 0.0071. (If we were to omit the title page and the table of contents, which we do *not* do in Figure 8.1, the offset goes down to a single leaf, or a portion of the entire equaling 0.0018.)

FIGURE 8.3: *THE WEALTH OF NATIONS*, 1ˢᵀ ED., 1776.

The 2nd edition was very close to the 1st (Campbell and Skinner 1976, 62), but with WN's 3rd edition, appearing 1784, IH drifts a bit, now a bit shy of the midpoint. There were two reasons for this. One is that at the end an index is introduced. The other is that Smith found need to make additions, and as he says in a letter to Strahan (22 May 1783), "the Principal additions are to the second Volume" (Corr. 266; likewise see letter to Cadell, p. 263). But even with the changes, IH remains close to the midpoint throughout the remaining editions.

The three volumes of the 7th edition of WN contain 796 leaves. The midpoint would be leaf 398. IH appears on leaf 357. The offset would then be 41 leaves. The offset as a portion of entire set of leaves (796) equals 0.0515. If we were to omit the index (25 leaves), the total leaf count goes down to 771, and the offset goes down to 28.5 leaves, or a portion of the entire equaling 0.037. IH, then, never moves far from the center of WN.

In Figure 8.1, the top (red) line shows that, in TMS, IH starts with an offset beyond the center equaling about 13 percent of the whole, and then it falls to the dead center in the chief two steps just mentioned. The lower (light blue) line shows that, in WN, IH starts in the dead center and then, from the 3rd edition, drifts a bit beyond the center, with the introduction of the index and additions. We also include a dark blue line that removes the index from the calculation, reducing the offset in WN's later editions.

Contending with Rousseau

According to Dennis C. Rasmussen (2008), Nicholas Phillipson (2010, 145–57), and others, Smith was contending with Rousseau over the moral character of commercial society and related ethical and political issues. If so, that preoccupation may well point to a *third* feature that is common to the two paragraphs that contain "led by an invisible hand": they both hark back to the Rousseau passages that Smith had translated and provided in his article in *The Edinburgh Review* in 1756.

As already noted, Smith's first publication was a sly review of Johnson's dictionary, published in *The Edinburgh Review*. The next year he published in that journal a lengthy letter on literature that dwells peculiarly on Rousseau and offers translation by Smith of passages from Rous-

seau's *Discours sur l'origine de l'inégalité*. We read the piece as another
sly dig, this time against Rousseau. Smith registers his disdain of "Mr.
Rousseau of Geneva" (EPS 254) by satirically esteeming Rousseau's effu-
sive dedication to Geneva, which is entirely incongruous with the quoted
passages about society's endemic deceit. The dig is doubly ironic because
Smith is knocking the doctrine of endemic deceit in a manner that is itself
satirical. (But one satire does not a deceitful civilization make.)

Smith also knocked "Mr. Rousseau of Geneva"[75] in his essay Of the Imitative Arts, saying he is "more capable of feeling strongly than of analising
accurately" (EPS 198), and in a letter to Hume, speaking of Rousseau as
being "as great a Rascal as you, and as every man here believes him to be,"
as well as an "hypocritical Pedant" (Corr. 112–13).

TMS's invisible-hand paragraph probably constitutes the primary
moment in the book's answer to Rousseau. As noted by TMS editors D.
D. Raphael and A. L. Macfie (TMS 183, n. 5), in the very same paragraph
Smith writes that industrious improvements "have turned the rude forests
of nature into agreeable and fertile plains" (183), while Rousseau had written in Discours: "and the vast forests of nature were changed into agreeable plains"—this translation is Smith's, for the passage is among the few
provided in Smith's 1756 piece in *The Edinburgh Review*.

But, as noted by others,[76] the connection goes far beyond that noted by
Raphael and Macfie. Consider the entire sentence in the Rousseau passage:

> But from the instant in which one man had occasion for the
> assistance of another, from the moment that he perceived that
> it could be advantageous to a single person to have the provi-
> sions for two, equality disappeared, property was introduced,
> labour became necessary, and the vast forests of nature were
> changed into agreeable plains, which must be watered with the
> sweat of mankind, and in which the world beheld slavery and

---

75. In three different works Smith referred to him as "Mr. Rousseau of Geneva" (see EPS 198, 250,
254; Language essay (in LRBL 205)).

76. Rasmussen (2008) traces other hints left by Smith and makes clear that Smith saw himself as
responding to Rousseau. Rasmussen refers to work by Pierre Force, Michael Ignatieff, and Ryan
Hanley, among several others. See especially pp. 6, 81–82, 88–89, and 126–27.

wretchedness begin to grow up and blossom with the harvest. (Rousseau translated and quoted by Smith, EPS 252)

TMS offers direct counterpoint:

[Nature's] deception...rouses and keeps in continual motion the industry of mankind. It is this which first prompted them to cultivate the ground, to build houses, to found cities and commonwealths, and to invent and improve all the sciences and arts, which ennoble and embellish human life; which have entirely changed the whole face of the globe, have turned the rude forests of nature into agreeable and fertile plains.... The earth by these labours of mankind has been obliged to redouble her natural fertility, and to maintain a greater multitude of inhabitants.... The produce of the soil maintains at all times nearly that number of inhabitants which it is capable of maintaining. The rich...divide with the poor the produce of all their improvements. They are led by an invisible hand to make nearly the same distribution of the necessaries of life, which would have been made, had the earth been divided into equal portions among all its inhabitants, and thus without intending it, without knowing it, advance the interest of the society, and afford means to the multiplication of the species. (TMS 183–84)

Now to the next pair of paragraphs. The next Rousseau paragraph translated and provided by in Smith's 1756 letter contains the following:

[Man] obliged therefore to endeavour to interest them in his situation, and to make them find, either in reality or in appearance, their advantage in labouring for his. It is this which renders him false and artificial with some, imperious and unfeeling with others, and lays him under a necessity of deceiving all those for whom he has occasion, when he cannot terrify them, and does not find it for his interest to serve them in reality. To conclude, an insatiable ambition, an ardor to raise his relative fortune, not so much from any real necessity, as to set himself above others, inspires all men with a direful propensity to hurt one another; with a secret jealousy, so much the more dangerous, as to strike its blow more surely, it often assumes the mask of good will; in short, with concurrence and rivalship on one side; on the other, with opposition of interest; and always with the concealed desire of making profit at the expence of some other person: All these evils are the first effects of property, and the inseparable attendants of beginning inequality. (Rousseau translated and quoted by Smith, EPS 252–53)

WN responds:

[E]very individual necessarily labours to render the annual revenue of the society as great as he can. He generally, indeed, neither intends to promote the public interest, nor knows how much he is promoting it. By preferring the support of domestic to that of foreign industry, he intends only his own security; and by directing that industry in such a manner as its produce may be of the greatest value, he intends only his own gain, and he is in this, as in many other cases, led by an invisible hand to promote an end which was no part of his intention. Nor is it always the worse for the society that it was no part of it. By pursuing his own interest he frequently promotes that of the society more effectually than when he really intends to promote it. I have never known much good done by those who affected to trade for the public good. It is an affectation, indeed, not very common among merchants.... (WN 456)

In point-counterpoint fashion, the two pairs of paragraphs capture the core of the whole debate: Where Rousseau sees dependence and subordination, Smith sees interdependence and reciprocity among equals; where Rousseau see endemic deceit, Smith sees a candid self-interest within just rules; where Rousseau sees exploitation and immiseration, Smith sees a concatenation of voluntary agreements yielding widespread benefits and the development of the becoming virtues.

Thus, the TMS paragraph IV.I.10 and the WN paragraph IV.ii.9 have *three* remarkable features in common: (1) they both contain "led by an invisible hand"; (2) they both occur well-nigh dead-center in certain editions of the work; and (3) they both hark back to, and respond to, the Rousseau passages that Smith had translated and provided in 1756.

Specific speculation, on the assumption of intentional centrality

The centrality represented by Figure 8.1 was probably intentional. Now, *on an assumption* of the truth of the general conjecture, it is useful to proceed to a more specific conjecture that best fits what we have learned.

Smith put "led by an invisible hand to" into the first edition of TMS without, let us say, intending centrality—in that edition it is not very central. Though affecting, the phrase is not exceptionally out of the ordinary in TMS, and by no means original with Smith. Although we are inclined to think that from the very first edition Smith regarded TMS's "led by an invisible hand" as quite special, it may be that physical centrality was not initially a part of his intentions.

Our specific conjecture is that by some time in the 1760s, and necessarily by 1776, Smith had become intent on centrality. Appending the language essay to TMS, first occurring in the 3rd edition of 1767, would fit that story. This part of the conjecture raises the question of whether Smith would have had other good reasons for appending the language essay to TMS. Indeed, we see affinities between it and TMS (Klein 2023a, ch. 22).

The repetition of "led by an invisible hand to" in WN is, of itself, striking, if only because WN is so largely devoid of theistic affirmation. Notions of "the great Conductor" and so on, frequent in TMS, otherwise disappeared in WN. As Minowitz (2004, 408) points out, the only exception, apart from "invisible hand," in WN, and it is a mild one, involving "the wisdom of nature" making society resilient and robust (WN 674).

Moreover, it occurs well-nigh at the exact center of the 1st edition of WN. The specific conjecture would say that this centrality was decided and intentional. Continuing forward, the conjecture would then have Smith reworking TMS towards its final edition and making intentional efforts to move the phrase even closer to the center—and indeed in the final set of TMS it is well-nigh dead-center.

Meanwhile, in the subsequent editions of WN, the phrase drifts somewhat from the center, but only a little, and partly due to the addition from 1784 of an index. Smith may have figured that the index doesn't "count," that he had achieved sufficient centrality, and was not concerned with maintaining precise centrality. Smith found that he needed to make some additions, and, as stated in his letters, they came mainly in the second half of the work (Corr. 266, 263).

Was it intended by Smith? Was it intended by no one? Was it intended by God? Once again, something about Smith leaves us wondering.

CHAPTER 9

Smith's Attitude Toward Rousseau

This chapter is a review essay of: Dennis C. Rasmussen, *The Problems and Promise of Commercial Society: Adam Smith's Response to Rousseau* (University Park: Pennsylvania State University Press), 2008 xi, 193.

> Thus you see, he is a Composition of Whim, Affectation, Wickedness, Vanity, and Inquietude, with a very small, if any Ingredient of Madness.... The ruling Qualities abovementioned, together with Ingratitude, Ferocity, and Lying, I need not mention, Eloquence and Invention, form the whole of the Composition.
>
> David Hume, letter to Adam Smith, Oct. 8, 1767 (Corr. 135)

The contents of Professor Rasmussen's book are well described by the title, *The Problems and Promise of Commercial Society: Adam Smith's Response to Rousseau*. The author summarizes Rousseau's condemnations of commercial society and then explores Smith's sympathy with the criticisms and then his response. With an introduction and conclusion, the whole makes a neat treatment of a perennial discussion, focused on two of humankind's principal voices. The book is lucid, learned, and instructive. I highly recommend it.

I have differences with some of Rasmussen's interpretations. But the differences are ones that would merely alter some of the attitudes of the reader who travels through Rasmussen's excellent study. They are not differences that would bring down what he has constructed, for they do not question the solid foundation, viz., that Smith took Rousseau seriously and learned from him, and that Smith's works, at profound moments, are very plausibly seen as contending directly with Rousseau.

My differences follow a pattern. In my Hayekian conservative liberalism, I am, compared to Rasmussen, more inclined to view Rousseau as dishonest, fundamentally foolish, and baleful, particularly in the sense that his works tend to embolden illiberal morals and anti-liberal movements; and more inclined to view Smith as tending toward this view of Rousseau.

Rasmussen motivates the study:

> Rousseau's critique of commercial society was one of the earliest philosophic critiques of this kind of society, and even today it remains among the most comprehensive such critiques ever offered. Indeed,...most of the serious arguments made today against commercial society were anticipated to some degree by Rousseau.... [A]nyone who hopes to make a persuasive defense of this kind of society will have to take all of the many different aspects of Rousseau's critique into account. And Smith... attempted to do precisely that. (Rasmussen 2008, 5)

Rasmussen treats of Rousseau's ideas in a single meaty chapter. He provides a rich yet efficient review of Rousseau's criticisms. I will not treat them and instead let his own summary move us along:

> Rousseau sees the commercial society that the *philosophes* so lauded as an unmitigated disaster. The division of labor produces great inequalities and makes people weak and ignorant, thereby undermining citizenship. Dependence on the opinions of others encourages a great deal of role-playing, ostentation, deception, and immorality. And the expansion of people's desires results in endless toil, constant postponement of gratification, and misery. Commercial society, in short, produces people who are good neither for themselves nor for others. According to Rousseau, we have procured prosperity at the cost of our goodness and our happiness. (Rasmussen 2008, 40)

To help us understand Rousseau's appeal, it might be useful to consider Hayek's atavism thesis: that our genes and instincts are still basically Upper

Paleolithic, that we are fish out of water, that the mentality and ethos of the small band find foolish expression in modern political notions (Hayek 1967, 120; 1976, esp. ch. 11; 1978; 1979: 153–176; 1988, esp. ch. 1). Also, I see congruence between such Hayekian ideas and Smith's, a congruence explored by Brandon Lucas (2010). It might be fruitful to bring such ideas to bear in treating Rousseau.

After reviewing the criticisms, Rasmussen reads Rousseau's works for possible remedies or escapes from the problems of commercial society: "*The Social Contract* and Rousseau's other political works show how to surmount these problems through citizenship in a virtuous republic; his autobiographical works show how to escape them through a life of solitary reverie and contemplation; and *Emile* shows how to retain a measure of natural goodness through the proper kind of education" (41). Rasmussen concludes that "even Rousseau himself ultimately seems to hold out little hope that any of these solutions are truly possible in the modern world" (41). He sums up Rousseau's conclusion: "Escape is impossible and the misery of commercial society is our fate" (48).

A sensible reader of Rousseau knows that he fails to address responsibly how we might better accommodate ourselves to our fate. Yet Rousseau's irresponsibility is often over-indulged, and doing so is probably conducive to one's success as a Rousseau scholar. Even though Rasmussen comes down with Smith in favor of commercial society, he is indulgent toward Rousseau. As Smith might have put it (TMS 270), Rasmussen does Rousseau more than justice.

As he turns to Smith, Rasmussen devotes a chapter to Smith's sympathy with Rousseau's criticisms, and then two to Smith's response. Again, the treatment is instructive, but I have some differences. Here I use much of my allotted space to consider Smith's attitude toward Rousseau.

John Rae (1895, 196) surmised that Smith and Rousseau likely met during the December 1765 fortnight they were both in Paris. Rasmussen revisits the question and concludes otherwise (p. 54). I suspect that Smith would not have wanted to meet Rousseau.

Although Smith never refers to Rousseau in TMS or WN, he does, first, and most importantly, in his 1756 letter to *The Edinburgh Review* (EPS 246, 250–4), in the 1761 language essay (which was appended to TMS from the

1767 third edition onward) (LRBL 205), in the *Lectures on Rhetoric and Belles Lettres* (LRBL 9), in the essay on the imitative arts (EPS 198–99), and in three letters addressed to Hume (Corr. 112-14, 125, 132).

After bringing out two issues (in August 1755 and March 1756) *The Edinburgh Review* shut down, "due to a violent outcry from narrow church-men over the theological views contained in notices of religious works" (Bryce 1980, 229–30; see also Mackintosh 1818, xii–xvi). Edited by Smith's friend Alexander Wedderburn, the *Review* contained much sly writing. The first issue contains Smith's waggish review of Samuel Johnson's dictionary; I cannot relate the joke here, but the pinch comes with "but by which the determination is rendered easy" (EPS 241).

"A Letter to the Authors of the *Edinburgh Review*" is the second and only other contribution known to have been authored by Smith (in Mackin-tosh's reprint of 1818, which is available in cheap paperback, he leaves eight items anonymous; see 26–27, 45–49, 67–68, 71–78, 95–96). In the Letter, Smith encourages the *Review* to expand its coverage and then makes mean-dering comments about literature in several countries, but dwells especial-ly and peculiarly on Rousseau's *Discourse on Inequality*. Smith translates three passages, filling nearly three pages. Then he writes:

> I shall only add, that the dedication to the republic of Geneva, of which Mr. Rousseau has the honour of being a citizen, is an agreeable, animated, and I believe too, a just panegyric; and expresses that ardent and passionate esteem which it becomes a good citizen to entertain for the government of his country and the character of his countrymen. (EPS 254)

Rasmussen rightly puts great importance on the Letter. The passag-es that Smith translated contain challenges that Smith later responded to, and, in at least two instances, phrasings in TMS hark back to phrasings in the translated passages and thus constitute subtle allusion to Rousseau.

But I think Rasmussen misreads Smith's Letter. Rasmussen says that the Letter is "on the whole respectful and at times admiring" (56; see also 60). Of Smith's praise for Rousseau's dedication to Geneva, Rasmussen writes: "While most of Smith's statements on Rousseau are relatively neutral, this final comment adopts a much more admiring tone" (66). Further: "Perhaps, then, Smith praises Rousseau's dedication so highly because while the *Discourse* as a whole might seem to endorse revolutionary change (given its radical critique of all existing societies), the dedication tempers this appearance by adopting a much more moderate stance...." (68).

I'm sorry, but I feel little doubt that Smith's praise for Rousseau's dedication is satirical. It comes after three long and lurid passages about the wretchedness and deceit of our social world. In the final quoted sentence, the sentence which directly precedes Smith's praise, Rousseau holds that "...in the midst of so much philosophy, so much humanity, so much politeness, and so many sublime maxims we have nothing but a deceitful and frivolous exterior...." (EPS 253–54). With those words ringing in your ears, move directly to Smith's praise. And reread Rousseau's dedication, "which some readers have considered suspiciously fulsome" (Cranston 1984, 9).

Seeing the praise as satirical makes understandable, indeed amusing, what is otherwise oddly desultory, just as does seeing the joke in the review of Johnson.

After praising the dedication, Smith resumes with but one final paragraph, which soon says that "Mr. Voltaire, the most universal genius perhaps which France has ever produced, is acknowledged to be, in almost every species of writing, nearly upon a level with the greatest authors of the last age, who applied themselves chiefly to one" (EPS 254). Smith then works in a mention of Voltaire's "letter to Mr. Rousseau of Geneva," which had been published in France. In that August 30, 1755, letter, thanking Rousseau for sending the *Discourse on Inequality*, Voltaire jovially criticizes the work and to some extent chastises Rousseau. It seems to me that here, in championing Voltaire and bringing up Voltaire's letter, Smith is digging in against Rousseau. Other features of the Letter not treated here also support reading the praise as satirical.

Rasmussen sees the possibility that Smith's Letter is aimed against Rousseau. He offers insightful comments about Smith's "philosophical chemistry" remark; he mentions that some scholars (most notably Hundert 1994, 220) regard the Letter as an attack on Rousseau; and he says that Pierre Force "drastically overestimates" (65) Smith's agreement with Rousseau. But, still, I think Rasmussen's reading is off. On the matter of whether Smith's praise is satirical, I admit that, after checking most of the English-language secondary literature cited by Rasmussen, I have not found that specific interpretation on offer. But, in peculiar remarks, James Mackintosh calls "Smith's commendation of Rousseau's eloquent dedication" "an instance of the seeming exaggeration of just principles...." (1818, x).

Rasmussen also mishandles some of Smith's other references to Rousseau. Smith frequently calls Rousseau "eloquent," and Rasmussen seems to overrate the significance of that. As related at the head of this piece, Hume, too, noted Rousseau's "Eloquence." In TMS, Smith says that Mandeville's "eloquence...enabled him to impose upon his readers" (TMS 310). In the language essay, Smith speaks of Rousseau as "ingenious and eloquent" (LRBL 205), and, in the 1756 Letter, of the Cartesian system as "ingenious and elegant, tho' fallacious" (EPS 244). Many remarks in *LRBL* (esp. 106, 144–45, 138, 196) make clear that Smith does not necessarily endorse those he deems eloquent. Edmund Burke (1999a, 272) said "eloquence may exist without a proportionable degree of wisdom."

Rasmussen notes that, in a letter to Hume, Smith calls Rousseau a "Rascal" and a "hypocritical Pedant," but, in treating Smith's published references to Rousseau, he underplays the critical element. In the language essay, "M. Rousseau of Geneva," though "ingenious and eloquent" fails to see something quite obvious (LRBL 205; cf. Rasmussen, 56). In the essay on imitative arts, Smith writes that "Mr. Rousseau of Geneva" is "more capable of feeling strongly than analising accurately" (quoted by Rasmussen, 56) and then quotes and criticizes Rousseau's contention that music "imitates, however, everything, even those objects which are perceivable by sight only" (EPS 198–99). Nelson Lund (2022) treats Smith's treatment of Rousseau and argues that Smith consistently treated Rousseau unjustly; I agree with much, if not all, of Lund's criticisms of Smith, but the larger point is that Smith is consistently unfriendly toward Rousseau.

Rasmussen quotes Smith writing to Hume, "I am thoroughly convinced that Rousseau is as great as a Rascal as you, and as every man here believes him to be," but he does not consider the possibility that here Smith chides his friend for ever having indulged such a character (cf. Ross 2010, 224). (By the way, I treat the Hume-Rousseau affair in Klein 2021.)

Rasmussen (56) also relates Saint-Fond's 1787 remembrances of conversing in 1784 with Smith about Rousseau. Here I say only that I think Rasmussen gives those remembrances too much weight and neglects the negative aspect of the sentence, even if perfectly accurate, about *The Social Contract* avenging Rousseau's persecutions.

I have left myself little space to treat the final two thirds of Rasmussen's book, on Smith's sympathy with and usage of Rousseau's criticism, and then Smith's responses. These chapters, too, are excellent. Rasmussen justly elaborates Smith's worries about commercial society, some shared with Rousseau.

On the parable of the poor man's son, I feel that perhaps Rasmussen does not give sufficient consideration to the reading that sees the parable as Smith's dwelling especially in what is only one view, namely the "splenetic" one. Indeed, Smith leaves us in doubt about whether he makes the splenetic view paramount—rendering ambitious projects "what they are, enormous and operose machines" (TMS 182), impelled by nature's "deception" (TMS 183)—or as merely one among multiple views, each coming and going and none clearly paramount. Even if Smith did not mean to suggest the splenetic view as paramount, however, the fact that he dwelled so much on it is testimony to Rasmussen's central contention that Smith is engaging Rousseau.

On the matter of happiness, Rasmussen nicely contrasts Smith's emphasis on avoiding misery and on improvement or betterment, with Rousseau's anguish over some sublime happiness denied (Rasmussen, 47f, 82f, 137f, 168f). Rasmussen gradually develops the contrast between Smith's pragmatism, based on sensible formulation of an issue and responsible consideration of relevant costs and benefits, and Rousseau's "naïve and utterly impracticable" antonyms (161). Rasmussen even twice zeroes in on what I've heard called the Thomas Sowell question, "Compared to what?" (161, 174), which, of course, should always be the first question. Rasmussen allows that Rousseau's ideas ultimately invoke irrelevant and impracticable comparisons, whereas Smith is rooted in meaningful comparisons (92f, 160f).

Rasmussen's treatment of Smith on the costs and benefits of commercial society, and of the liberty principle as brought to bear on policy issues (98–99), which is really the heart of the book, is rich, instructive, and, to my mind, reasonably complete. Rasmussen nicely discusses Smith's views on how commercial society raises all boats (101f), encourages ordinary virtues such as probity and punctuality (121f), and improves political institutions (136f). Especially good is his treatment of how Smith sees market forces and free competition as affording personal independence (125, 140, 147). Rasmussen explains Rousseau's denial of the desire for praiseworthiness, and Smith's rejection of that denial (114f). "For Smith, the good outweighs the bad in commercial society with respect to morality, just as it does with respect to economics, especially in comparison with previous forms of society" (129). One point which Rasmussen might have picked up on is Smith's regard for the multiplication of the species.

In all this, Rasmussen elaborates just what Smith intends, a public-spirited perspective on the industriousness of the poor man's son and commercial society generally, a perspective that can now be entered into by the son himself.

Rasmussen ends the book with a discussion of what Smith means for us today; he admirably shrugs off objections to "presentism." Some of Rasmussen's representations of Smith's policy judgments are misleading in a left-Smithian way (106–107, 110, 113, 163, 172). In relating matters to present concerns, Rasmussen, sometimes citing Samuel Fleischacker, takes Smith into some left turns that he (Smith) may not go along with (107, 156f, 163–72). Throughout the book Rasmussen disabuses us of unnamed phantoms who have Smith a doctrinaire of laissez-faire, etc. But, again, these differences are ones that readers will easily adjust for. *The Problems and Promise of Commercial Society* is a very fine book, one that makes us realize how important it is to consider Smith in relation to Rousseau and that guides us profitably in that consideration.

TMS's Appeal Has Moved with Openness to Nonfoundationalism: 35 Critics, 1765–1949

The more open people are to nonfoundationalism, the more they warm to TMS. Thus, the appeal of TMS has moved with openness to nonfoundationalism. This chapter provides evidence of that bivariate relationship—though I do not mean to suggest that openness to nonfoundationalism is the sole factor affecting TMS's appeal. The first six chapters of this book exposit and endorse nonfoundationalism.

Adam Smith became a Glasgow professor in 1751, having published nothing. He won goodwill and advancement from lecturing, collegiality, and a dignity of mind and personality. I suspect that by age 25 Smith furtively felt himself to be deeply aligned with David Hume, and that he was throughout these years discreet or even dissembling about his nonfoundationalist, non-demarcationist Humean tendencies, which, only after becoming more apparent, would come to be openly criticized.

Ed. 1 of TMS received warm and highly favorable, albeit unsigned, notices by Hume (1759), Edmund Burke (1759), and William Rose (1759). From the first, TMS contained intimations to the effect that moral approval always involves, or even *depends on*, a sympathy. That organon would in time become a major point of dissatisfaction. The critics saw it something like this: If a person, call her Anna, is to find moral authorization, only to be found in sympathy with another person, for example Anna's older sister, named Joy, then the matter of moral authorization has been shifted to whatever Joy's sensibilities happen to be. Moreover, the sympathy that Anna finds is, in one instance, with Joy, but in another with someone else, and then with yet someone else. Smith therefore fails, because he has not shown how Anna's sensibilities can rest on a firm and commonly accessible foundation for moral judgment.

In 1764, Thomas Reid took over the moral philosophy course that Smith vacated (Norton and Stewart-Robertson 1980, 382).

In 1776, *The Wealth of Nations* (WN) elevated Smith to still greater eminence.

In 1790, Ed. 6 of TMS appeared in May, and Smith died in July.

With TMS as finalized in Ed. 6, readers found more to object to, and, no longer stayed by Smith's personage, began to express criticism openly. Within a few decades a pattern of criticisms became quite common. TMS's career hit the skids. In 1899 H.C. Macpherson pronounced it "dead" (p. 40). Into the 20th century, admirers were rare indeed. One, Glenn Morrow, lamented in 1927 that it had long been consigned to "oblivion" (1927, 336). And J.N. Findlay wrote in 1950 of TMS as "the great, strangely neglected work of Adam Smith" (1950, 25n1).

TMS had been utterly eclipsed by WN—even though Smith "always considered his *Theory of Moral Sentiments* as a much superior work to his *Wealth of Nations*," according to Smith's friend Samuel Romilly (from a letter written in 1790, Romilly 1840, 404).

In the late 1970s TMS began a resurgence that continues to today. Many scholars (e.g., Griswold 1999, 165; Fleischacker 2004, 23–26; Roth-schild 2001, 231, 238; 2004, 152) note that Smith's moral philosophy was not foundationalist. That feature was not celebrated in the resurgence; but now readers stopped holding Smith's not being foundationalist against him[77] and no longer found serious fault in related features for which TMS had been forsaken by roughly seven generations.

---

77. Samuel Fleischacker concurs that TMS's return to great favor in recent decades was because people stopped holding its nonfoundationalism against it (Fleischacker 2016, listen around 9:00).

FIGURE 10.1: GOOGLE BOOKS PLOT OF FOUR NGRAMS

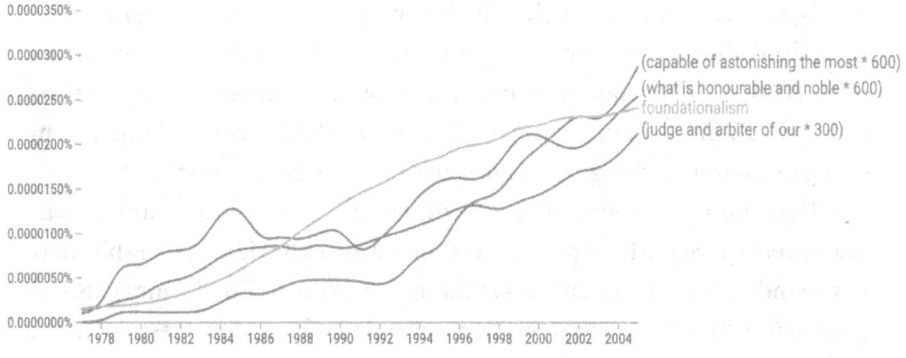

Source: Google Ngram Viewer

In Figure 10.1, the curves run from 1977 to 2005 and move together. They show a chief reason why TMS has made a great comeback since 1976—a reason besides the appearance that year of the 1976 OUP edition (eds. Raphael and Macfie). One of the curves plots (with 3-year smoothing) the percentage of all 1grams that are the 1gram "foundationalism," in millions of books. The rising use of "foundationalism" reflects discussion and criticism of foundationalism in ethics and epistemology. It reflects favor for nonfoundationalism—Wayne Booth, Richard Rorty, Deirdre McCloskey, "postmodernism," and all that. The other curves represent a famous passage in TMS, namely, the pinky-earthquake passage, which illustrates our concern with the sympathy of "the inhabitant of the breast, the man within, the great judge and arbiter of our conduct" (137.4). Each curve plots the percentage (multiplied by a scalar) of a 5-gram from that passage: "judge and arbiter of our," "what is honourable and noble," and "capable of astonishing the most." The figure emblematizes that the appeal of TMS has risen with openness to nonfoundationalism. In the past several decades, people have stopped holding TMS's nonfoundationalism against it.

If Figure 10.1 shows how the appeal of TMS rose with openness to nonfoundationalism, we may wonder whether such a relationship can help us understand other parts of TMS's career. In particular, the relationship might help us understand TMS's fall into oblivion.

It seems that initially, in 1759, TMS had great appeal, but during the decades after Smith's death in 1790, its fortunes declined precipitously. Did the decline relate to declining openness to nonfoundationalism? In other words, did it relate to a growing tendency toward foundationalism?

I think the answer is definitely yes. The period in question might be said to be 1790 to 1976. I cannot demonstrate my claim about this long period by way of a concise figure comparable to Figure 10.1. Instead, I proceed by citing numerous writings to make sense of intellectual trends.

The differences between the six editions of TMS are important. In particular, compared to the previous edition, Ed. 6 of 1790 is considerably more nonfoundationalist—or, more *openly* so. Speaking of Ed. 6, Dugald Stewart (1829, 213) observed that Smith now "laid much greater stress upon" the man within the breast. Smith now referred repeatedly to the man within the breast as a *supposed* impartial spectator and described him as a "representative of the *impartial spectator*."[78] From Ed. 5 to Ed. 6, there was a threefold increase in the number of occurrences of the expression impartial spectator. TMS became much more allegorical, and its nonfoundationalism more elaborate. Thus, in pondering Smith's rising star after 1759, bear in mind that earlier editions of TMS did not yet emanate nonfoundationalist overtones as strongly as Ed. 6.

The remainder of this paper catalogues the disrespect, dislike, disparagement, and dismissal—in a word, the dissing—of TMS up to 1949, by 35 figures. This paper derives from a much longer article in *Econ Journal Watch* in 2018. I have pared down the quotations vastly and included nine additional dissers.[79]

The set of TMS dissers featured in this paper are listed here by their native origin:

> *Scotland* (16 authors): Thomas Reid, George Ridpath, Henry Home Lord Kames, John Witherspoon (moved to New Jersey, 1768), Adam Ferguson, Dugald Stewart, Thomas Brown,

---

78. The expression "supposed impartial spectator" occurs at 131.32, 134.1, 226.22, 262.1, 262.2, 287.34—all new to Ed. 6. The man within the breast as "representative of the impartial spectator" is at 215.11—also new to Ed. 6.

79. The nine authors added since the 2018 piece are: John Witherspoon, the anonymous *Quarterly Theological Review* author, Levi Frisbie, George Payne, J. R. McCulloch, Ralph Wardlaw, Arthur Thomas Malkin, J. M. Robertson, and Jacob Viner.

James Mackintosh, Henry Brougham, Ralph Wardlaw, John Ramsay McCulloch, Alexander Bain, H. C. Macpherson, James Bonar, J. M. Robertson, and William R. Scott (born in Northern Ireland)

England (8 authors): George Payne, Arthur Thomas Malkin, Henry Thomas Buckle, Leslie Stephen, Walter Bagehot, Henry Sidgwick, J. A. Farrer, Harold Laski

France (5 authors): Sophie de Grouchy Marquise de Condorcet, Pierre Jean Georges Cabanis, Victor Cousin, Théodore Jouffroy, Henri Baudrillart

United States (5 authors): Anonymous in *Quarterly Theological Review*, Levi Frisbie, Simon Patten, Richard T. Ely, Jacob Viner

New Zealand (1 author): Arthur N. Prior

Several points of criticism are commonly made by them: TMS was said to err by relying on allegory, metaphor, and figurative language at the most crucial points in the theory; at those points it was said to invoke principles themselves vague or, even worse, circular; it was said to lack foundations; it was said to violate foundational demarcations.

I use only works written in or translated into English (and thus bypass several German critics, for example). I seize upon criticisms, not praise: Many of the quoted authors (notably Stewart, Brown, Mackintosh, Brougham, Frisbie, Farrer, Macpherson, Bonar, Scott, and Viner) also express more than token praise for TMS.[80] I included criticism only when it is clear that it is TMS that is being criticized.[81] The ordering of the authors generally follows the order of the onset of their dissing of TMS,

---

80. For my citations to English-available commentary on TMS 1790 to 1976 favorable to TMS, see above note 26, p. 75.

81. Thus, for example, I exclude Hugh Murray (1808), a work that says it "is only recently" that the science of the faculty of the human mind "has reached its *acme* of corruption, and has with difficulty found any sure ground on which to rest its foot." In the next paragraph he looks forward to the science's "establishment on a firm and permanent foundation" (120). I suspect that Murray's acme of corruption is TMS, but he never mentions Smith, though he mentions several other Scottish thinkers and writes of the four-stage theory (157f, 276f).

although the French authors are grouped together. Footnotes are omitted except when indicated otherwise. I put certain bits in **boldface**, notably criticism of TMS's metaphorical or allegorical language, the vagueness and supposed circularity of its principles, its lack of foundations, and its violation of supposedly foundational demarcations. All boldface has been added (and no italicization has been added by me).

Thomas Reid (1710–1796)

The opening paragraphs of a chapter on the "First Principles of Morals" provide a taste of Reid's thinking:

> Morals, like all other sciences, must **have first principles**, on which all moral reasoning is grounded.
>
> In every branch of knowledge where disputes have been raised, it is useful to distinguish the first principles from the superstructure. They are the **foundation** on which the whole fabric of the science leans; and whatever is not supported by this **foundation** can have no stability.
>
> In all rational belief, the thing believed is either itself a first principle, or it is by just reasoning deduced from first principles. When men differ about deductions of reasoning, the appeal must be to the rules of reasoning, which have been very unanimously fixed from the days of Aristotle. But when they differ about a first principle, the appeal is made to another tribunal; to that of common sense. (Reid 1788, 369).

In the same work, Reid writes: "A very ingenious author has resolved our moral sentiments respecting the virtues of self-government, into a regard to the opinion of men. This I think is giving a great deal too much to the love of esteem, and putting the shadow of virtue in place of the substance" (1788, 139; see also 163).

When in 1764 Glasgow was selecting a replacement for Smith, Smith received a letter from John Millar, the truest next-generation heir to Hume and Smith (Haakonssen 1996, 7, 159, 163, 180–181, 269). Millar reported that Reid had received support from influential people outside the University (Lord Kames and leading aristocrats), declared his and Joseph Black's support for another candidate (Thomas Young), and seemed confident that Smith would concur: "We earnestly beg that if you can do any thing in counterworking these extraneous operations you will exert yourself.... No body knows of my writing this but Black" (Corr. 100). Thus Millar urged Smith to help stop the appointment of Reid. The appointment went forward, and it arguably was quite fateful, as it gave Reid a secure prominence from which to propound and publish so-called common sense. There is no paper trail of Smith having weighed in, nor correspondence between Reid and Smith.

Reid scarcely alludes to Smith in his published works, but, as a Glasgow professor, Reid criticized TMS. His lecture notes, presumed reflective of 1765 to his retirement in 1780, treat Smith amply. The following is a selection of the rough text (Reid 1984), with some simplification of the editorial paraphernalia.

> The Author in this System endeavours to reduce Morals to very few original Principles, for as all Our moral Sentiments are resolved into Sympathy so even this Sympathy seems to be resolved into self love. (Reid 1984, 311)

> This Sympathy being a part of our frame implys no virtue at all.... But The Sympathy which can with any propriety be called virtuous is a fixed determination of the will.... Now this kind of Sympathy supposes a moral faculty.... Sympathy when we take it in the first of these senses is a natural affection, resulting immediately from our frame. And requires no imaginary change of persons. When we take Sympathy in the second Sense no change of persons will account for it without supposing a faculty by which perceive right and wrong. (ibid., 312)

> I observe that the word Sympathy seems not to have always the same **fixed and determinate** meaning in this System, nor to be so **accurately** defined as is necessary to make it **the foundation** of a distinct Theory of Morals. (313)

[T]his definition of Sympathy makes a moral faculty to be necessarily antecedent to our Sympathy and consequently our moral Sentiments cannot be the Effect of Sympathy[;] they must go
before it, and set bounds to it. (314)

We may observe that this Author speaks all along of the passions and the feelings of ourselves and others as being not onely the proper but the onely object of moral Approbation & Disapprobation.... Now as the whole of this System by which our
moral Sentiments are resolved into Sympathy is built upon this
foundation. That what we call Virtue and what we account the
object of Moral Approbation is a certain tone or temperament of
our feelings and passions. If that is not true the **foundation** of it
must fail. (314–315)

Yet I see no other way Agreable to this System of accounting for
our Approbation or disapprobation of our Own Actions. To Judge
of the Propriety of my own Passions and feelings, I must change
persons with the impartial Spectator and view them with his
Eyes. But how shall I know what judgment he would pass upon
them[?] (317)

[I]t is obvious that according to this System there is **no fixed
Standard of Virtue at all**[;].... It is evident that the **ultimate**
Measure & Standard of Right and Wrong in human Conduct
according to this System of Sympathy, is not any fixed Judgment
grounded upon Truth or upon the dictates of a well informed
Conscience but the variable opinions and passions of Men. (317–
318)

In 1778 Reid received a letter and enclosure from Lord Kames, who
had revised one of his works, and shared a draft of a new insertion critical
of TMS (the final version appears below). Reid approved, and wrote back:
"I have always thought Dr Smith's System of Sympathy wrong. It is indeed
only a Refinement of the selfish System" (quoted in Reeder 1997, 66).

George Ridpath (1716–1772)

George Ridpath was a parish minister, scholar, historian, and Edinburgh graduate. In his diary he wrote in 1759:

> *Thursday, October 11ᵗʰ.*—Read over a good deal more of Smith's *Theory of Moral Sentiments* and looked over the rest.... I can by no means join in the applauses I have heard bestowed on it. What is new in it is perhaps of no great moment in itself, and is **neither distinctly nor clearly established**. An extravagant turn to declaim and embellish leads him quite astray from that study of **accuracy, precision, and clearness** that is so essentially necessary to the delivering of any theory, especially a new one.... (ibid., 275)

Henry Home, Lord Kames (1696–1782)

Of our TMS dissers, Lord Kames was the first to come into the world and the first to put criticism into print—trailing TMS's first appearance by 20 years! A very prominent judge and author, he had been Smith's early patron, and later warmed to Reid. His new insertions into the third and final edition of *Essays on the Principles of Morality and Natural Religion* (1779) mark a significant early moment in the train of disparagement:

> A system that resolves every moral sensation of sentiment into sympathy, shall next be introduced. [Kames then quotes TMS.]
>
> The **foundation** here assigned for the various sentiments of morality, ought to have been very strictly examined before venturing to **erect so weighty a superstructure upon it**....
>
> ... Sympathy is but one of many principles that constitute us moral beings; and yet is held furth as the **foundation** of every moral sentiment. **Had not morality a more solid foundation in our nature**, it would give very little obstruction to vicious desires or

unjust actions. It is observed above, that, according to this system, sympathy would be rare among the lower ranks. And I now add, that if moral sentiments had no **foundation** but the imagining myself to be another, the far greater part of mankind would be destitute of any moral sentiment.

This system...may pretend to account for my sentiments regarding others; but my sentiments regarding myself are entirely left out. My distress upon losing an only son, or my gratitude for a kindly office, are sentiments that neither need to be explained by imagining myself to be another person, nor do they admit of such explanation.

The sympathetic system is a harmless conceit; but a system that resolves all morality into self-love, cannot but be dangerous among luxurious nations whose bent to selfish pleasures is already too strong. (Kames 2005/1779, 70–73)

John Witherspoon (1723-1794)

Born in Scotland and studying at Edinburgh, Witherspoon moved to America in 1768 to become president of College of New Jersey (later, Princeton). He was a signer of the Declaration of Independence and the Articles of Confederation, and in 1789 was the convening moderator of the First General Assembly of the Presbyterian Church in the United States of America. As college president, minister, teacher, and statesman, he was a major figure, and was very influential in advancing Thomas Reid's common-sense philosophy in the United States.

In the assembled text of his *Lectures on Moral Philosophy*, Witherspoon says that there are three questions about "the principle of moral action," one being "The **foundation** of virtue" (1822, 31). "When we speak of the *foundation* of virtue, we ask or answer the question,...Why is this course of action preferable to the contrary? What is its excellence?" (31; see also 171). Giving a sentence or two to a series of thinkers, he comes to

Smith: "Some of late have made sympathy the standard of virtue, particularly Smith, in his Theory of Moral Sentiments. He says we have a certain feeling, by which we *sympathize*, and as he calls it, *go along* with what appears to be right. This is but a new phraseology for the moral sense" (34).

Adam Ferguson (1723–1816)

Adam Ferguson was born four days after Adam Smith but outlived him by 26 years. Their relationship "had its ups and downs" (Ross 2010, 203).

Our first item from Ferguson is from his *Principles of Moral and Political Science* (1792). It does not mention TMS specifically, but implicates it. After remarking on Nicolas Malebranche, John Locke, and Thomas Hobbes and their "allegorical substitutions" and "metaphorical language" (1792, 75), he writes (his notes inserted in brackets):

> The author of an Enquiry into the Mind,* [*Dr Reid]...removed the mist of **hypothesis and metaphor,** with which the subject was enveloped; and, in having taught us **to state the facts, of which we are conscious,** not in figurative language, but in the terms which are proper to the subject. In this it will be our advantage to follow him; the more, that in former theories so much attention had been paid to the introduction of ideas or images, as the elements of knowledge, that the belief of any external existence or prototype has been left to be inferred from the mere idea or image; and this inference indeed is **so little founded,** that many who have come to examine its evidence have thought themselves warranted to deny it altogether* [*See the Writings of Dr [George] Berk[e]ley and Mr Hume]. And hence the scepticism of ingenious men, who not seeing a proper access to knowledge, through medium of ideas, without considering whether the road they had been directed to take was the true, or a false one, denied the possibility of **arriving at an end.** (Ferguson 1792, 75–76)

Ferguson composed a short discourse apparently sometime after 1800 (Ross 2010, 200). The discourse involves Hume, the not so tactful General

Robert Clerk, and Smith. After Clerk and Hume have conversed about morality and utility, Smith enters the room "with a smile on his Countenance and muttering somewhat to himself" (Ferguson 1960, 228). Smith is told they have been discussing a subject treated by TMS and Smith asks for Clerk's opinion of the work:

CLERK. Your Book is to me a Heap of absolute Nonsense.
Smith seemed to be stunnd and Clerk went on, You endeavour to explain away the distinction of Right and Wrong by telling us that all the difference is the Sympathy or want of Sympathy, that is, the Assent or Dissent of some two or more persons of whom some one acts & some other observes the action and agrees or does not agree in the same feeling with the actor. If the Observer agree, sympathise, go along with him, or feel that he would have done the same himself, he cannot but approve of the Action. If, on the Contrary, he does not Sympathise or agree with the Actor, he dissents & cannot but disapprove of him; and you seem to mean that where there is neither assent nor dissent there is neither Right nor wrong, and no one would ever suppose any such thing. Or if you don't deny the reality of the Distinction, you at least furnish but a very inadequate means of discovering it. How can I believe that a Person is in the right because I sympathise with him? May not I myself be in the wrong? Does the presence of any sympathy ascertain a good action, or the want, of a bad one?
    SMITH. No! I have cleared up that point. Parties concerned in any transaction may be willing each to flatter himself or both Mutually to flatter one another, But to the monitor may not fail to present himself. The well informed and impartial observer will bring to view what the Ignorant or prejudiced would overlook.
    CLERK. That is convenient, to be able to bring Virtue itself to your aid when actual Sympathy fails. You began with calling Sympathy to explain Moral Sentiment. You now call up moral sentiment to explain itself: what is a well informed & impartial observer, but a Virtuous Person whose Sympathy may be relyed on as a Test of Virtue? If he be well informed, of what is he informed? Not of Astronomy or Geography, for these would be

of little use to him in distinguishing the Chara[c]ters of men. For this purpose he must be informed of the distinction of Right, how constituted and applyed in particular Instances. And to be impartial must aim at a fair application without By [bias?] to any Side. Such a Person is not likely to misslead those who confide in him and such a Person everyone is concerned to become in himself & instead of acquiesing in Sympathy as the Test of Virtue, appeals to Virtue as the test of Just Sympathy.

Here then ends your System. After beating round **a Circle of Objections & Answers,** you **return to the point from which you set** the Phaenomena of moral distinctions, moral sentiments, to be explained. (Ferguson 1960, 228–229)82

A couple of paragraphs later, Smith resumes:

SMITH. ....a man who participates in the Passion of another cannot but approve of it. Every Passion or strong motive urging a Person to act justifies itself and, if others go along with it or Sympathise, they too approve: if they do not go along with it, they disapprove or condemn his Conduct and so he does himself if, when the occasion is past, he cannot go along with the passion which actuated him.

CLERK. The whole amount then is that what others term Conscience, you Term Sympathy or the want of Sympathy. Every body knows, that under the operation of any strong Passion men are incapable of cool reflection. This you call justifying their Passion; but when it [is] over & they come to reflect, a Crime if committed stares them in the face & they become a prey to remorse or self condemnation. I do not see that your account of the matter is any way more Intelligible than this, or that we are any way nearer **the ultimate** in the one account than in the other. Most men repose on the Fact that men are by nature endued with a Principle of Conscience. But you say the Fact commonly called Conscience is Sympathy or the want of Sympathy, and the supposed Theory is a mere change of Words or at best an attempt to con-

---

82. The bracketed insertions are those of Mossner.

found two distinct principles of Nature....

I confess I was affraid that your Sympathy might have some such Effects as this or that the difference of right & wrong might vanish into an assent or dissent of two or more Persons who may agree in the wrong as well [as] in the Right: but you relieve us at last by telling us you do not mean any assent or dissent at random but that of a well informed & impartial observer, who we would say in common language is a virtuous man or Competent Judge. And the preference due to such a Person is what no one doubts, tho it is the Phaenomenon which you sett out with a Purpose to explain in your Theory, and so have it at last as others do as a self evident Truth which needs no Explanation. (ibid., 229–230)

Ferguson left another unpublished, incomplete discourse. In its published form, its editor Ernest Mossner (1963) quotes the discourse as he, as it were, narrates the conversation to us. Ferguson himself is a participant in the discourse. The topic comes to the principle of approbation. I quote thusly directly from Mossner, where quotation marks indicate the Ferguson character speaking in the dialogue, and other text is Mossner narrating for us:

"Others in treating of this Subject confound two questions together as different as Wisdom is from folly and Candour from Partiality."

The first question is, "From what Principle may we Safely & truly decide of Action and Character?"

The second question is, "On what Principle do men actually decide or entertain Sentiments of Praise or Blame?"

Ferguson's answers are speedily forthcoming.

"To the first Question we have now endeavoured to Answer that Wisdom & Goodness, the Excellence of Intelligent Being, is the Test of moral Rectitude & Felicity and that well Informed Intelligence is competent to judge of such Merits.

"To the second Question we may admit that men frequently consult their own Interest in judging of merit in others.

"To others we may admit that what they are pleased to call

sympathy or even coincidence of Sentiment or [the] reverse is the ordinary or frequent **ground** of Estimation of praise or Censure. But we cannot admit that either is a safe **ground** of Estimation, much less the only **Ground** which Nature has laid for the distinction of Right & Wrong. And every attempt to Instruct us on the Subject without distinguishing the Questions [that is, the first and second stated previously] is not only Nugatory and Perplexing to the unwary but actually tending to **explain away** distinctions of the utmost importance to Mankind, turning Zeal for Morals into a mere selfish Interest or into a mere coincidence of sentiment which may take place among Knaves and Fools as well as among honest Men." (Ferguson, presented by Mossner 1963, 307–308)

Dugald Stewart (1753–1828)

Dugald Stewart "decisively influenced a large number of men who must all, in varying degrees, be characterized as intellectual epigoni" (Haakonssen 1996, 261). From Stewart's long years of eminence at Edinburgh, his influence was felt in their careers in opinion, publishing, reform, and politics, including leaders at *The Edinburgh Review.*

In his account of Smith's life and writings, delivered orally in 1793, Stewart politely summarized TMS, criticizing only gently: "For my own part I must confess, that it does not coincide with my notions concerning the **foundation** of Morals" (1982/1795, 290). He suggested engagement with its "author's peculiar theories" as follows: "it is easy for an attentive reader, by stripping them of **hypothetical** terms, to state them to himself with that logical **precision**, which, in such very difficult disquisitions, can alone conduct us with certainty to the truth" (1982/1795, 291).

But in Stewart's lectures his dissatisfaction is elaborated, as in The *Philosophy of the Active and Moral Powers of Man* (Collected Works edition,1829):

Mr. Smith...has been led to resolve our sense of duty into a regard to the good opinion, and a desire to obtain the *sympathy* of our fellow creatures.... [H]is theory may account for the desire which all men, both good and bad, have to *assume the appearance of virture*, it never can explain **the origin** of our notions of duty and moral obligation. (Stewart 1829, 37-38)

...Mr. Smith...has been led to attempt an explanation from this single principle [sympathy] of all the phenomena of moral perception.... [He] has mistaken a very subordinate principle in our moral constitution...for that faculty which distinguishes right from wrong, and which (by what name soever we may choose to call it) recurs on us constantly in all our ethical disquisitions, as **an ultimate fact in the nature of man.** (209-210)

[A]fter all his reasonings on the subject, the metaphysical problem concerning **the primary sources** of our moral ideas and emotions will be found involved in the same **obscurity** as before... [T]his may account for a man's assuming the appearance of virtue, and I believe that something of this sort is **the real foundation** of the rules of good breeding in polished society; but in the important concerns of life, I apprehend there is something more,—for when I have once satisfied myself with respect to the conduct which an impartial judge would approve of, I feel that this conduct is *right* for me, and that I am under a moral obligation to put it in practice. (211-212)

Smith was forced to have recourse to the supposition of "*an abstract man* within the breast, the representative of mankind and substitute of the Deity, whom nature has constituted the supreme judge of all our actions."[83] Of this very ingenious fiction he has availed himself in various passages of the *first* edition of his book; but he has laid much greater stress upon it in the *last* edition, published a short time before his death...

...It is only to be regretted, that, instead of **the metaphorical expression** of "*the man within the breast*, to whose opinions and

---

83   This passage is from Ed. 5 of TMS, and appears in the standard edition at p. 130 note r.

feelings we find it of more consequence to conform our conduct than to those of the whole world,"[84] he had not made use of the simpler and more familiar words *reason* and *conscience*. This mode of speaking was indeed suggested to him, or rather obtruded on him by the theory of sympathy, and nothing can exceed the skill and the taste with which he has availed himself of its assistance in perfecting his system; but it has the effect, with many readers, of keeping out of view the real state of the question, and (like Plato's Commonwealth of the Soul, and Council of State) to encourage among inferior writers **a figurative or allegorical style** in treating of subjects which, more than any other, **require all the simplicity, precision, and logical consistency** of which language is susceptible. (212–214)

Thomas Brown (1778–1820)

As a teenager studying at Edinburgh under Dugald Stewart, Thomas Brown pondered moral and mental experience as psychological or physiological phenomena. At age 20 he published a challenge to Erasmus Darwin's materialism. Brown studied medicine, participated in the early years of *The Edinburgh Review*, published poetry, and wrote on Hume's views of causality. Beginning in 1808 Brown assisted Stewart and then co-occupied the moral philosophy chair at Edinburgh, where he developed lectures that captivated students—and that criticized TMS—until 1820, when Brown suffered an early death at age 42. The year of his death he published several works, including his four-volume *Lectures on the Philosophy of the Human Mind*, which in its last volume criticizes TMS at length (Brown 1820, 112–145):

> [T]here is still one system [Smith's TMS] which deserves to be considered by us...as appearing to fix morality on **a basis**, that is not sufficiently firm; with the discovery of the instability of which, therefore, the virtues that are represented as supported on it, might be considered as themselves unstable; as the statue,

---

84. This does not seem to be a direct quotation of Smith, but perhaps is a paraphrase of a passage prior to Ed. 6 found in the standard edition of TMS at p. 129 note r.

though it be the image of a God, or the column, though it be a part of a sacred temple, may fall, not because it is not sufficiently cohesive and firm in itself, but because it is too massy, for the feeble **pedestal** on which it has been placed. (Brown 1820, 113; 2017/1820, 5)

The sympathy, therefore, on which the feeling of propriety is said to depend, assumes the previous belief of that very propriety.... (Brown 1820, 124; 2017/1820, 10)

If, indeed, we had *previously* any moral notions of actions as right or wrong, we might very easily judge of the propriety or impropriety of the sentiments of others, according as our own do or do not sympathize with them; and it is this *previous* feeling of propriety or impropriety which Dr Smith tacitly assumes, even in contending for the exclusive influence of the *sympathy*, as itself the **original** source of every moral sentiment. (Brown 1820, 134; 2017/1820, 15)

That his own penetrating mind should not have discovered the inconsistencies that are involved in his theory, and that these should not have readily occurred to the many philosophic readers and admirers of his work, may, in part, have arisen,—as many other seeming wonders of the kind have arisen,—from the ambiguities of language. The meaning of the important word *sympathy*, is **not sufficiently definite**, so as to present always one clear notion to the mind. (Brown 1820, 142–143; 2017/1820, 20)

James Mackintosh (1765–1832)

A pupil of Stewart, James Mackintosh was a philosopher, historian, politician, and commentator (e.g., on Burke and James Mill). In 1820 Stewart wanted Mackintosh to be his successor at Edinburgh, but Mackintosh, "something of a social and intellectual gadfly, declined to present himself, preferring to pursue his career in politics" (Reeder 1997, xviii). In 1836, Mackintosh published the *Dissertation on the Progress of Ethical Philosophy,* in an introductory volume of the new edition of the *Encyclopedia Britannica,* republished in volume I of his *Miscellaneous Works* (1846). It contains this critical section regarding TMS, listing the work's "main defects," including:

> The same error has involved him in another difficulty perhaps still more fatal. The sympathies have nothing more of an *imperative* character than any other emotions....

> It is to this representation that Smith's theory owes that unhappy appearance of rendering the rule of our conduct dependent on the notions and passions of those who surround us, of which the utmost efforts of the most refined ingenuity have not been able to divest it. This objection, or topic, is often ignorantly urged; the answers are frequently solid; but to most men they must always appear to be an **ingenious and intricate contrivance of cycles and epicycles,** which perplex the mind too much to satisfy it, and seem devised to evade difficulties which cannot be solved. All theories which treat Conscience as built up by circumstances inevitably acting on all human minds, are, indeed, liable to somewhat of the same misconception; unless they place in the strongest light (what Smith's theory excludes) the total destruction of the scaffolding, which was necessary only to the erection of the building, after the mind is adult and mature, and warn the hastiest reader, that it then rests **on its own foundation alone.**

> [T]his ingenious system **renders all morality *relative*,** by referring it to the pleasure of an agreement of our feelings with those of others,—by confining itself entirely to the question of moral approbation, and by providing no place for the consideration of that quality which distinguishes all good from all bad actions;—a defect which will appear in the sequel to be more immediately fatal to a theorist of the *sentimental,* than to one of

the *intellectual* school. Smith shrinks from considering utility in
that light, as soon as it presents itself, or very strangely ascribes
its power over our moral feelings to admiration of the mere adap-
tation of means to ends, (which might surely be as well felt for
the production of wide-spread misery, by a consistent system of
wicked conduct,)—instead of ascribing it to benevolence, with
Hutcheson and Hume, or to an extension of that very sympathy
which is his own **first principle**. (Mackintosh 1846, 151–154)

Henry Brougham (1778–1868)

Henry Brougham, a student of Dugald Stewart, was one of the founders
and heavy contributors to *The Edinburgh Review*, and a prodigious public intellectual. He became an eminent public figure, MP, and in 1830 lord
chancellor. His *Lives of Philosophers of the Time of George III* contains
lengthy treatment of Adam Smith, principally WN. The following is from
Ed. 3 of 1855:

> The "Theory of Moral Sentiments"...has not, indeed, been
> approved by the philosophical world, and it seems liable to
> insuperable objections when considered even with an ordinary
> degree of attention, objections which never could have escaped
> the acuteness of its author but for the veil so easily drawn over
> an inquirer's eyes when directed to the weak points of his own
> supposed discovery.... [E]ven if our sympathy were admitted to
> be the **foundation** of our approval, our inability to sympathise
> the **ground** of our disapproval, this in no way explains why we
> should approve because of the accord and disapprove because
> of the discord.
>
> The theory, with the utmost concession that can be made to it
> as to **the ground-work**, leaves the super-structure still defective,
> and defective in the same degree in which the 'Theory of Utili-
> ty' is defective; we are still left to seek for a reason why approval
> follows the perception of corresponding feelings in the one case,

of general utility in the other. Dr. [William] Paley is so sensible of this, that after resolving all questions of morals into questions of utility, he is obliged to call in the Divine Will as the **ground** of our doing or approving that which is found to be generally useful.... But all this...**assumes it to stand on as good a foundation** as that of 'Utility.' Now one consideration, which has in part been anticipated, shows that **such is not the case**.... [T]his appeal to others in general...can only exert any influence, or apply any correction, **upon some other hypothesis**. It appears, therefore, that in every view the theory is unsound. (Brougham 1855, 197–199)

John Ramsay McCulloch (1789-1864)

From Scotland and having studied at Edinburgh, McCulloch became a leading political economist. In 1828 he presented *The Wealth of Nations* with considerable supplementary materials written by himself, including "Sketch of the Life of Dr. Smith," in which he wrote about TMS:

> The fundamental principle maintained by Dr. Smith is, that *sympathy* forms the real **foundation** of morals.... (McCulloch 1828, xxi)

> Several, and, as it is now generally admitted, some unanswerable objections have been urged against this most ingenious theory... Dr. [Thomas] Brown...has criticised Dr. Smith's theory with his usual acuteness, and has shown that though sympathy may diffuse moral sentiments it can never **originate** them....(xxii)

McCulloch presents *The Wealth of Nations* as venerable but poorly arranged already corrected on numerous points. By the quotations just given, he indicates that TMS is a failed work. In his sketch of Smith's life, he makes no mention of the revisions made at the end of Smith's life.

George Payne (1781–1848)

Payne was born in England and graduate from Glasgow in 1807, became a Congregational minister, moved to England and in 1829 received an honorary degree from Glasgow for his *Elements of Mental and Moral Science* (Payne 1828). In that work, he wrote:

> The theory of Dr. Adam Smith is considerably different from that of Hutcheson. If, on contemplating the actions of our fellow men, we are able fully to sympathize with them, we regard the action as right, and the agent as virtuous.... Dr. Brown examines this fantastical doctrine with great minuteness, thus giving to it more importance than it deserves.... [Payne then recapitulates criticism from Brown]. There is, however, I imagine, a more important objection against the theory of Smith, than any to which Dr. Brown has adverted. It obviously founds rectitude on the arbitrary constitution of the mind. The mind is so constituted that it sympathizes with certain actions; those actions, says Dr. Smith, are right. Does he mean that the sympathy *renders* them virtuous—or *proves* them to be so? If he mean the latter merely, then the system does not exhibit the *foundation* of virtue at all.... So far, then, is the theory of Dr. Smith from exhibiting the *foundation* of virtue, that it does not furnish us with an accurate criterion of virtue. (Payne 1828, 469-471; see also 476)

Ralph Wardlaw (1779–1853)

The Glaswegian Ralph Wardlaw was a theologian and Congregational minister. In *Christian Ethic; or, Moral Philosophy on the Principles of Divine Revelation* (Wardlaw 1833), he said TMS deserves heavy "condemnation" and quotes Thomas Brown at some length, including that TMS is "manifestly false" (74, 75). "[B]ut for the well-earned celebrity of the name attached to it [TMS]," says Wardlaw, "it would hardly have been deemed deserving of serious regard" (76). He cites Payne calling TMS "fantastical," and characterizes TMS "as the *enthusiasm* of moral science" (76). Wardlaw writes:

I do not intend attempting the exposure of all the fallacies with which this system is chargeable.... If our sympathy with the actions of others, and with the emotions of the agents, only *ascertains* to us their rectitude, then it has nothing to do with the determination of the principle or **foundation** of virtue, but serves the purpose merely of a criterion or test. But even in this view, how unsatisfactory is it! (Wardlaw 1833, 78)

How uncertain a thing, alas! would virtue be, were this fellow-feeling to be its criterion! (79)

How extraordinary, too, is the oversight, that the " impartial spectator"...is a spectator of our own imagining ; to whom, of course, we will, naturally and unavoidably, transfer a portion at least, if not even the whole, of our self-partiality; so that, after all, our reflex sympathy...turns out to be nothing more than an illusory fellow-feeling with ourselves! (79-80)

Anonymous in the *Quarterly Theological Review*

A journal called the *Quarterly Theological Review* was published 1818–1819, "conducted by," according to the title page of the 1818 volume, Rev. Ezra Stiles Ely. In the journal there appeared a two-part review essay of sorts, of both TMS and two works by Thomas Cogan. The reviewer writes:

Dr. Smith's theory of moral sentiments...is reducible to one word, 'sympathy.' Disrobing his theory of gaudy dress, it stands forth naked thus: Mankind think those thoughts, feelings, volitions and actions to be *proper* in their neighbours, which they imagine would be excited in, or performed by, themselves, were they in the situation of their neighbours. Whatever they conceive they should not themselves feel, think, choose and perform, under certain given circumstances, they judge to be *improper* in their neighbours, in those circumstances. (*Quarterly Theol. Rev.* 1818, 472).

The sum of this part of his theory is, that *we judge our neigh-bours by ourselves*. Of the **foundation** of our judgments concerning our own moral or immoral conduct, and of the sense of duty, Dr. S. teaches, that we think that to be suitable and meritorious which we conceive would meet with the "sympathy" of our neighbours. (473)

[W]e cannot think, that propriety and impropriety, merit and demerit, justice and injustice, approbation and dis. approbation, are **founded** on *sympathy*. ¶ While we reject Dr. Smith's theory, however, we take delight in recurring to his many just exhibitions of human modes and principles of action. (474)

[S]ome have called *approbation* an act of the judgment, and others an act of the heart. Dr. Reid, we think, has clearly shown, that it [approbation] is neither the one nor the other, but a distinct mental act, that partakes of the nature of both. (485)

Levi Frisbie (1783-1822)

Levi Frisbie taught moral philosophy at Harvard before his death at age 39. An edition of TMS was published in Boston in 1817, occasioning a review essay in the *North-American Review*:

The **great basis** of moral sentiments, according to Dr. Smith, is sympathy. (Frisbie 1819, 374)

[D]oes it not follow, that moral approbation is not the consciousness that we can go along with the affections of another, but that it is **founded on** the moral excellence of those affections themselves [?] (379)

We enter into feelings which we disapprove, and we secretly condemn ourselves that we do so. Nor can this be explained by supposing with Dr. Smith, that in such cases, we refer to the sympathy of a more impartial judge; since the sympathies of different men cannot be compared with each other, in respect to their justness and impartiality; but by applying to them some common standard. And **that can never be an ultimate standard, which is itself to be judge by one more so.** (382)

[Smith] has, we think, through his work, denominated that sentiment moral approbation, which is properly only a consequence of it. (382)

[F]orgiveness is...sometimes received with the liveliest gratitude; but...the instance of this are not so numerous, as to furnish any general sympathy, which might be **the foundation** of the high esteem, in which we hold the virtue [i.e., forgiveness]. (386)

Many ideas [as expressed in TMS]...want that **exactness** of form, which is necessary to determine their application to other ideas, and their **precise** bearing upon the point in question. (395)

Sophie de Grouchy Marquise de Condorcet (1764–1822), Pierre Jean Georges Cabanis (1757–1808), and Henri Baudrillart (1821–1892)

Michaël Biziou is one of the composers of the 1999 French translation of TMS (Smith 1999). I crib from his essay about the French translations (Biziou 2015).

Prior to Smith's Ed. 6, two separate translations had appeared. In 1798 came the translation of Ed. 6 by Sophie de Grouchy, Marquise de Condorcet. Biziou notes that all three translations tended to interpret "Scottish moral sentimentalism through the framework of French moral rationalism" (2015, 59). Biziou explains that Grouchy regrets that TMS "does not go philosophically far enough in the explanation it gives of the foundation of morals" (Biziou 2015, 59). Grouchy published, along with her translation, a set of letters on morals and sympathy. She writes: "Smith did not go further than establishing the existence of [sympathy] and showing its principal effects. I was sorry that he had not done more, had not penetrated **its first cause**" (Grouchy, quoted and translated in Biziou 2015, 58). For Grouchy virtue comes to be defined as "actions giving to others a pleasure that is approved by reason" (Grouchy 2015, 59).

Grouchy's commentary, known as *Letters on Sympathy*,[85] are addressed to "C," presumed to be her brother-in-law Pierre Jean Georges Cabanis, physician, philosopher, and *idéologue*. In work from 1802, Cabanis writes: "Smith had made a very learned study, which was nevertheless incomplete for want of his having **linked it to physical laws**, and which Mme Condorcet, by means of simple rational considerations, knew how to remove from the **vagueness** in which it was left by the *Theory of Moral Sentiments*" (Cabanis, quoted and translated in Forget 2001, 321; see Cabanis 1867, 283–284).

Biziou writes that during the first half of the 19th century, readers of TMS in French "shared the same moral rationalism as that of its translator." He mentions Théodore Jouffroy and Victor Cousin, whose "favourite [Scottish] author…is much rather Thomas Reid" (Biziou 2015, 62). "Then," writes Biziou, from about 1850 "to the late twentieth century, in France people almost stopped reading Smith as a moral philosopher" (2015, 62). In 1860 Grouchy's translation was reissued with a new introduction by the economist Henri Baudrillart. In the following quotation, Biziou (who is open to nonfoundationalism, I think) relates and quotes Baudrillart on TMS:

> So [according to Baudrillart] sympathy, in the *Theory*, is just another name for harmony. In this [Baudrillart's] interpretation, the "impartial spectator" becomes quite an **abstruse and tortuous** concept, which Smith had had better replaced by the concept of reason: "This ideal spectator that we carry inside us… Smith should have given him right away his real name, which is reason, instead of trying to explain it as an artificial production

---

85. *See* Grouchy (2017), for an online English translation by Jonathan Bennett.

of sympathy alone." Baudrillart thus adopts the moral rationalism of the French tradition, just as Cousin and Jouffroy a few
years before.... Baudrillart is satisfied with the Marquise's translation, through which, he says, Smith's thought "is always con-
veyed with the utmost precision." (Biziou 2015, 63, including his
translations of passages from Baudrillart 1860)

Victor Cousin (1792–1867)

The Scottish philosophy of common sense was introduced into the French
university philosophy curriculum after 1814 by Pierre Paul Royer-Collard,
whose disciples Victor Cousin and Théodore Jouffroy commented at great
length on TMS (Reeder 1997, xx). A popular and prestigious professor, and
later minister of public instruction, Cousin commented at great length on
TMS in his history of modern philosophy (Cousin 1846, 192–246), but the
material is not available in English. His *Lectures on the True, the Beautiful,
and the Good* contain pertinent remarks:

> [T]here are philosophers, for example, Hutcheson, Smith, and
> others, who, mistrusting the senses and reason, give **the suprem-
> acy** to sentiment. (Cousin 1855, 347)

The philosophy which **deduces** all our ideas from the senses falls
to the ground, then, before the idea of the beautiful. It remains
to see whether this idea can be better explained by means of
sentiment, which is different from sensation, which so nearly
resembles reason that good judges have often taken it for reason, and have made it the principle of the idea of the beautiful as
well as that of the good. It is already a progress, without doubt,
to go from sensation to sentiment, and Hutcheson and Smith
are in our eyes very different philosophers from Condillac and
Helvetius; but we believe that we have sufficiently established
that, in confounding sentiment with reason, we deprive it of its
foundation and rule, that sentiment, particular and variable in

its nature, different to different men, and in each man continually changing, cannot be sufficient for itself. (Cousin 1855, 129–130)

Théodore Jouffroy (1796–1842)

Théodore Jouffroy translated Stewart and Reid, lectured, and published philosophical works, particularly expositing the ideas of others. In 1840 an English translation appeared, *Introduction to Ethics; Including a Critical Survey of Moral Systems*, discussing TMS very extensively (Jouffroy 1840, Vol. 2, 98–176).

> Let me suppose myself in the presence of a great number of persons of different ages, sexes, and professions.... Which of these kinds of sympathy shall be my rule, which shall I select as a test of the propriety or impropriety of my feeling? (132–133)

> [I]t is impossible not to see that his [Smith's] efforts are fruitless, and that his theory is wrecked upon this difficulty. (135)

> Now, who is this impartial spectator? Is it John or Peter? No! but an abstract spectator, who has neither the prejudices of the one nor the weaknesses of the other, and who sees correctly and soundly, precisely because he is abstract. It is in the presence of this abstract spectator, who is another *me*, separate from the impassioned *me*, and its judge, that, in my deepest consciousness, I deliberate, decide, and act. Not only is this spectator no particular man, but he does not even represent any portion of society—no age nor sex, no village nor city, no nation nor era; he represents humanity—he represents God. (135–136)

> [T]his...is introducing an entirely new view, into which Smith has unconsciously entered, without perceiving that he was not led into it by setting out from his own principle, and that he cannot return from it to his principle again. (136)

Now, what is it that I do, when, for the sentiments of actual spectators, I substitute those of an abstract spectator? Most evidently, gentlemen, I not only abandon the rule of sympathy, and adopt another in its place, but I even deny this rule, and pronounce it false, and condemn it; for this abstract spectator **does not exist, and never existed**; and his sentiments, therefore, have no **reality**, and are wholly **fictitious**. (136–137)

In truth, gentlemen, it is quite plain that this abstract spectator, imagined by Smith, is nothing else than reason, judging, in the name of order, and of the immutable nature of things, the mutable and blind decisions of men. It is a consciousness of the reality of this **supreme** faculty, that embarrasses Smith in the exposition of his system.... Instead of the words *conscience*, or *reason*, therefore, he makes use of the expression *abstract spectator*.... (137–138)

[T]he rules of moral appreciation...consist not in emotions of sympathy, but in conceptions of reason. (142)

A judgment is a judgment; an emotion is an emotion; but an emotion is no more a judgment than a sensation is an idea.

Our author proceeds to say, that, when I approve an emotion, I feel it to be good; to which I answer, This is not the way in which the human mind reasons; from the goodness of the act we are led to approve it, but not from our approbation to pronounce it good.... Smith reverses this order of nature, for he makes the approbation the sign and proof of the goodness....

Once possessed of the word *good*, Smith dashes on with full sails, and without difficulty arrives at the idea of obligation; for what is more evident to reason than that that which is good ought to be done, and that which is evil avoided? But what mean such words as these, in a system which preserves nothing of moral good but its name, while it destroys the reality? (145–147)

[W]hat embarrassment systematic minds must feel, and to what sophistries the loftiest genius must descend, in its attempt to endue error with a character which it cannot justly claim. (148)

And, in my view, the remarks suggested by Smith's system extend to all others which seek in instinct for the laws of morality.... (151)

[Smith's] efforts to establish the authority of the instinct of sym- pathy...led only to **evident paralogisms**. Instead of proving that the instinct of sympathy is the true moral motive, he describes the characteristics of this moral motive, and then gratuitously attributes them to the instinct of sympathy; thus proving, to be sure, that, if the instinct had these characteristics, it would be the moral motive, but forgetting altogether the evidence that it possesses them. (163)

The point to be proved is not that the instinct of sympathy acts *like* the moral motive, but that it *is* the moral motive. (166)

Smith has the art of connecting his errors with a truth, and of thus rendering them specious. (168)

Incidentally, Morrow (1923, 36) indicates that Albert Delatour (1866) was another significant French critic of TMS.

Arthur Thomas Malkin (1803-1888)

An English popular biographer and sportsman (cricket, rowing), Malkin wrote *Gallery of Portraits: with Memoirs*, treating Smith in Volume 6 (1836). He drew on McCulloch to say that according to TMS "sympathy forms the real **foundation** in morals" (Malkin 1836, 51). Malkin adds: "Dr. Brown has argued, and the objection seems fatal, that though sympathy may diffuse, it cannot **originate** moral sentiments" (51).

Interlude: Up to this point, most of the commentators may be associated with Reid-Stewart common-sense philosophy. Peaking in influence during the first half of the 19th century in Scotland, France, and America, its inculcation to college students continued in some schools in Scotland and America right to the end of the century. But by mid-century, other philosophical trends increasingly left it behind (Davie 1964, 257, 261, 272). The new trends kept TMS's career in the doldrums.

Alexander Bain (1818–1903)

A Scot and a religious skeptic, Alexander Bain studied and taught mathematics and philosophy in Scotland before moving to London in 1848 and falling in with J. S. Mill and his circle. Heavily influenced by and touted by Mill, he developed associationist theory in works on psychology and philosophy. With Mill he edited James Mill's *Analysis of the Phenomena of the Human Mind*, in which James Mill says that the love of praiseworthiness is "eloquently described, but not explained, by Adam Smith" (J. Mill 1869, 298; see also J. S. Mill's remarks on p. 309). Bain also wrote a biography of James Mill (Bain 1882).

In *Mental and Moral Science* (1868), Bain says of TMS:

> The Ethical Standard is the judgment of an impartial spectator or critic; and our own judgments are derived by reference to what this spectator would approve or disapprove.

> Probably to no one has this ever appeared a sufficient account of Right and Wrong. It provides against one defect, the self-partiality of the agent; but gives no account whatever of **the grounds** of the critic's own judgment, and makes no provision against his infallibility. (Bain 1868, 631)

> He affords little or no grounds for remarking on the connexion of Morality with Politics. Our duties as citizens are a part of Morality, and that is all.

He gives his views on the alliance of Ethics with Religion. He does not admit that we should refer to the Religious sanction on all occasions. He assumes a benevolent and all-wise Governor of the world, who will ultimately redress all inequalities, and remedy all outstanding injustice. What this Being approves, however, is to be inferred solely from the principles of benevolence....

[Smith] never pushes **home** a metaphysical analysis; so that even his favourite theme, Sympathy, is not **philosophically sifted to the bottom**. (632–633)

In treating Dugald Stewart, Bain writes:

[H]e introduces a criticism of the Ethical theory of Adam Smith; and, adverting to the inadequacy of the theory to distinguish the *right* from the *actual* judgments of mankind, he remarks on Smith's ingenious fiction 'of *an abstract man* within the breast;' and states that Smith laid much greater stress on this fiction in the last edition of the Moral Sentiments published before his death. It is not without reason that Stewart warns **against grounding theories on metaphorical expressions**, such as this of Smith, or the Platonic Commonwealth of the Soul. (642)

In treating Thomas Brown, Bain writes:

Admitting that we have the sympathetic feeling that Smith proceeds upon, [Brown] questions its adequacy to constitute the moral sentiment, on the ground that it is not a perpetual accompaniment of our actions....

But the essential error of Smith's system is, that it assumes the very moral feelings that it is meant to explain....The feelings that we sympathize with, are themselves moral feelings already; if it were not so, the reflexion of them from a thousand breasts would not give them a moral nature.

Brown thinks that Adam Smith was to some extent misled by an ambiguity in the word sympathy; a word applied not merely to the participation of other men's feelings, but to the further and distinct fact of the *approbation* of those feelings. (650)

In treating James Mackintosh, Bain writes:

[Mackintosh] objects to the theory of Adam Smith, that no allowance is made in it for the transfer of our feelings, and the disappearing of the original reference from the view. Granting that our approbation began in sympathy, as Smith says, certain it is, that the adult man approves action and dispositions as right, while he [the adult man] is distinctly aware that no process of sympathy intervenes between the approval and its object.... He [Mackintosh]...objects to Smith, that his system renders all morality relative to the pleasure of our coinciding in feeling with others, which is merely to decide on the Faculty, without considering the Standard....

He commends Smith for **grounding** Benevolence on Sympathy, whereas Butler, Hutcheson, and Hume had **grounded** Sympathy on Benevolence. (672)

Henry Thomas Buckle (1821–1862)

Henry Thomas Buckle, an Englishman, published a once-famous work, *Introduction to the History of Civilization in England*, in two volumes, 1857 and 1861. He died aged 41, in Damascus. He extolled Smith, but chiefly for WN. He said that TMS "has had no influence except on a very small class of metaphysicians," and that compared to WN "it is certainly easier to understand" (Buckle 1904, 895). He claimed that WN "assumes that selfishness is the main regulator of human affairs, just as his previous work had assumed sympathy to be so" (811). Each work proceeds deductively: "And in each work he reasons from only part of his premisses; supplying the other part in the other work. None of us are exclusively selfish, and none of us are exclusively sympathetic. But Adam Smith separates in speculation qualities which are inseparable in reality. In his *Moral Sentiments*, he ascribes our actions to sympathy; in his *Wealth of Nations*, he ascribes them to selfishness" (808). About TMS he wrote:

> Sympathy, then, is the main-spring of human conduct.... By this bold hypothesis Adam Smith, at one stroke, so narrowed the field of inquiry as to exclude from it all considerations of selfishness as a primary principle, and only to admit its great antagonist, sympathy.... [I]t did not suit the method of his philosophy to subject the principle of sympathy to such an inductive analysis as would reveal its elements. His business was **to reason from it, and not to it**. Concentrating his energy upon the deductive process, and displaying that dialectic skill which is natural to his countrymen, and of which he himself was one of the most consummate masters the world has ever seen, he constructed a system of philosophy, imperfect indeed, because **the premises** were imperfect.... [I]nasmuch as his plan involved **a deliberate suppression of preliminary and essential facts**, the results which he obtained do not strictly correspond to those which are actually observed in the world. (Buckle 1904, 810)

Walter Bagehot (1826–1877)

Walter Bagehot was an influential political commentator, economist, author, and journalist, affiliated with *The Economist*, as well as a banker. He published "Adam Smith as a Person" in the *Fortnightly Review* in 1876, reproduced in Bagehot (1915, 1–32), including:

> [H]is lectures on Moral Philosophy...formed the once celebrated *Theory of Moral Sentiments*, which, though we should now think them rather pompous, were then much praised and much read....
> The Theory of Moral Sentiments was, indeed, for many years,

exceedingly praised.... But a mere student of philosophy who cares for no sect, and wants only to know the truth, will nowadays, I think, find little to interest him in this celebrated book.... For unquestionably its arguments are very weak, and attractive to refutation.... There is a fundamental difficulty in **founding** morals on sympathy; an obvious confusion of two familiar sentiments.... Even the wisest party men more or less sympathise with the errors of their own side; they would be powerless if they did not do so; they would gain no influence if they were not of like passions with those near them. Adam Smith could not help being aware of this obvious objection; he was far too able a reasoner to elaborate a theory without foreseeing what would be said against it. But the way in which he tries to meet the objection only shows that the objection is invincible. He sets up a supplementary theory—**a little epicycle**—that the sympathy which is to test good morals must be the sympathy of an 'impartial spectator.' But, then, who is to watch the watchman? Who is to say when the spectator is impartial, and when he is not? If he sympathises with one side, the other will always say that he is partial... He is a fiction of inconsistent halves; if he sympathises he is not impartial, and if he is impartial he does not sympathise. **The radical vice of the theory is shown by its requiring this accessory invention of a being both hot and cold,** because the essence of the theory is to identify the passion which loves with the sentiment which approves. (Bagehot 1915, 11–13)

If it had not been for this odd consequence of *The Theory of Moral Sentiments* [viz., the Buccleuch engagement], he might have passed all his life in Scotland, delivering similar lectures and clothing very questionable theories in rather pompous words.... [T]he mere removal from his professorship was to him a gain of the first magnitude. It was of cardinal importance to him to be delivered from the production of incessant words and to be brought into contact with facts and the world. (15–16)

[A]lmost everybody will probably now think, in spite of Dr. Carlyle, that the style [in WN] is very much better than that of the

Moral Sentiments. There is about the latter a certain showiness and an 'air of the professor trying to be fascinating,' which are not very agreeable; and, after all, there is a ponderous weight in the words which seems to bear down the rather flimsy matter. (23–24)

Leslie Stephen (1832–1904)

Leslie Stephen was an author, literary critic, and first editor of the *Dictionary of National Biography. His History of English Thought in the Eighteenth Century* (1876) had a large and lasting influence, and in it he addresses TMS:

Smith's ingenuity in tracing the working of the mechanism of human nature is so marked and so delightful to himself that he almost forgets to enquire into **the primary forces** which set it in action.... Smith, in fact, is a thorough representative of that optimistic Deism which we have seen illustrated by Shaftesbury and Hutcheson.... (Stephen 1876, 70–71)

We must consider A's sympathy for B, and then B's sympathy with A's sympathy, and then A's own sympathy with B's sympathy with A's sympathy for B, and we are finally rather puzzled to discover **the ultimate basis** of the sympathy. From some points the doctrine seems to resolve itself into a regard for public opinion as embodied in the hypothetical 'impartial spectators.' But which sympathies are right and which wrong? Where is **the ultimate** criterion?... Smith avoids all reference to supernatural revelation, and we must assume that the decisions of this final and absolute tribunal are to be sought in nature. But **on what principle they are to be discovered is nowhere apparent**. Smith asserts that, beyond the standard of conduct which is formed from the ordinary opinions of the world, there is a higher standard, slowly framed by the 'demigod,' and approximating indef-

initely to the 'archetype of perfection' framed by the Divine artist—but we seek in vain for any **definite** account of its nature.
The appeal is ultimately made to an inaccessible tribunal, or, in
other words, **the standard of absolute morality seems to be
hopelessly uncertain**....

The general laws of morality, then, are merely formulae expres-
sive of the mode in which sympathy habitually acts, and are convenient standards of reference, but not **the ultimate foundation of morality**. Utility, again, occupies a strictly subordinate
position. Smith rejects Hume's explanation of our sentiments as
founded upon it, because we praise a man for other reasons than
those which lead us to praise 'a chest of drawers ;' and because
the usefulness of any disposition is not the 'first ground of our
approbation.'

I think that the respect [due to Smith] is due chiefly to his eco-
nomical labours.... [I]t is impossible to resist the impression,
whilst we read his fluent rhetoric, and observe his easy accep-
tance of theological principles already exposed by his master
Hume, that we are not listening to a thinker really grappling with
a difficult problem, so much as to an ambitious professor who has
found an excellent opportunity for displaying his command of
language, and making brilliant lectures. The whole tone savours
of that complacent optimism of the time which retained theological phrases to round a paragraph, and to save the trouble of genuine thought. Smith's main proposition was hardly original,...and
it is rather **calculated to lead us dexterously round difficult
questions than to supply us with a genuine answer**. (73–77)

Stephen turns to political economy, and says:

[W]hat is the true nature of the blind struggle which rag-
es around us? and what are the ultimate barriers by which its
issues are confined? we get a rather cursory and perfunctory

answer. The difficulty is analogous to that which meets us in the 'Moral Sentiments.' We there follow the play of sympathy till we are perplexed by the intricacy of the results, but **we do not perceive what is the ultimate ground which determines the limits and the efficacy of sympathy**. And here, after tracing hither and thither the complex actions and reactions of supply and demand, we somehow feel that we have gone over all the ropes and pulleys by which force is transmitted, but have not fairly come in sight of the weights **by which the force is originated**. (325–326)

Henry Sidgwick (1838–1900)

Henry Sidgwick was an ethical philosopher and economist, a self-described utilitarian, who studied at Cambridge University, became professor there, and wrote several major books on ethics, political philosophy, political economy, and philosophy of science.

Adam Smith, like Hume, regards sympathy as the **ultimate** element into which moral sentiments may be analysed.... (Sidgwick 1896, 213)

Again, the report of the 'man within the breast' is liable to be perverted from truth by the internal influence of passion and self-regard, as well as by the opinions of the 'man without.' But against such self-deceit a valuable remedy has been provided by Nature in the 'general rules of morality'... [Smith] further takes care to assure us that the general rules of morality are 'justly to be regarded as the laws of the Deity,' and that the voice of 'the man within the breast, the supposed impartial spectator,' if we listen to it with 'diligent and reverential attention,' will 'never deceive us': but it can hardly be said that his theory affords **any cogent arguments** for these conclusions.

The theories of Hume and Adam Smith taken together antici-
pate, to an important extent, the explanations of the origin of
moral sentiments which have been more recently current in the
utilitarian school. But both of them err in underrating the complexity of the moral sentiments, and in not recognising that,
however these sentiments may have originated, they are now, as
introspectively examined, different from mere sympathy with
the feelings and impulses of others; they are compounds that
cannot be directly analysed into the simple element of sympathy, however complicated and combined. In these respects both
Hume's and Adam Smith's methods of explanation compare
unfavourably with that of [David] Hartley, whose *Observations
on Man* (1749) come in time before Hume's *Inquiry*. (217–218)

Adam Smith's work...passes from psychological analysis to ethical **construction**. It would seem that the intellectual energy of
this period of English ethical thought had a general tendency to
take a psychological rather than a **strictly ethical** turn. (223)

James Anson Farrer (1849–1925)

Barrister and writer James Anson Farrer published a too-forgotten book
on TMS (Farrer 1881), for a series on English philosophers. He presents
background and many of the main ideas in TMS, quoting amply. The final
chapter "Review of the Principal Criticisms of Adam Smith's Theory" runs
to 30 pages in length. He draws from Stewart, Mackintosh and especially Jouffroy and Brown, interlacing the criticisms with suggestions on how
Smith might have responded. At the end, he signals a turn to his own voice
and judgment, from which I quote:

It is difficult to read Adam Smith's account of the identification
of sympathy and approbation, without feeling that throughout
his argument there is an unconscious play upon words, and that
an equivocal use of the word "sympathy" lends all its specious-

ness to the theory he expounds.... In the one case a mere state of feeling is intended, in the other a judgment of reason.... To say that we approve of another person's sentiments when we sympathize with them is, therefore, nothing more than saying that we approve of them when we approve of them—**a purely tautological proposition**. (Farrer 1881, 196–197.)

The feeling of moral approbation is therefore much more complex than it is in Adam Smith's theory. Above all things it **is one and indivisible**, and it is impossible to distinguish our moral judgments of ourselves from our judgments of others. There is an obvious inconsistency in saying that we can only judge of other people's sentiments and actions by reference to our own power to sympathize with them, and yet that we can only judge of our own by reference to the same power in them. The moral standard cannot primarily exist in ourselves, and yet, at the same time, be only derivable from without. If by the hypothesis moral feelings relating to ourselves only exist by prior reference to the feelings of others, how can we at the same time form any moral judgment of the feelings of others by reference to any feelings of our own? (200)

Hector C. Macpherson (1851–1924)

A Scot, H. C. Macpherson was a Spencerian and a prolific writer and journalist. His little book on Smith is instructive and affectionate, apart from some remarks about TMS:

Smith set himself to show the complex phenomena of the moral life is reducible to Sympathy. Sympathy, with him, is the **ultimate** root of ethical judgments.

Detailed criticism of the Theory of Moral Sentiments would carry us too far afield. As a literary production it holds a high place, but its philosophic value is slight. Little reflection is needed to see that Sympathy, **upon which Smith rests his whole ethical system**, has not the oneness and simplicity he imagined.... Smith's mistake in imagining Sympathy was a simple instead of a complex feeling, and had universality enough and coercive power enough **to be the basis** of morality, rose out of a conception of human nature peculiar to all the eighteenth-century thinkers. It was assumed that man was everywhere the same, that at all times and in all countries he possessed nearly the same general ideas, and was regulated by much the same class of motives.... *The Theory of Moral Sentiments* is dead, because it was the representative of a metaphysical method, which in result was almost as sterile as the scholasticism which it displaced. (Macpherson 1899, 38–40)

Simon Patten (1852–1922)

Simon Patten was a professor at the Wharton School of the University of Pennsylvania from 1888 until 1917, when his anti-war views precipitated his retirement. A strong protectionist and the founder of the American Economic Association and the American Academy of Political and Social Science, he was associated with the social gospel movement, eugenics, progressivism, and the German historical school of economics (Leonard 2016, 118–119; Coats 2008).

To-day we see more clearly than Smith did that unguided sympathy is often immoral. Modern charity furnishes a good example of how sympathy may promote more evils than it checks. A feeling that needs the intellect to guide it aright cannot of itself be **the force** which gives an intellectual process its sanction. We must, therefore, seek the sanction of morality in an older and more fundamental feeling. Pain gives rise to two kinds of feeling. Either a desire to approach and destroy the cause of pain which is called wrath, or else a shrinking from it which is called fear. The first of these feelings is **the source of morality**. (Patten 1899, 268–269)

James Bonar (1852–1941)

James Bonar, a Scot, though employed as examiner in the Scottish civil service, was a philosophical economist, historian of thought (especially on Malthus), prodigious contributor to Palgrave's *Dictionary of Political Economy* and reviewer for *Economic Journal*, important player in what became the Royal Economic Society, and cataloguer of Adam Smith's library (Shirras 1941). He inclined toward Immanuel Kant and Thomas Hill Green. His book *Moral Sense* (1930) treats TMS at length.

> He [Smith] **did not show warrant for all he put in**. This may help to explain why, with its striking merits, his *Moral Senti-ments* made no new beginning in moral philosophy. In Econom-ics we have been sometimes told to go 'back to Adam Smith'; the cry has not been raised in Ethics.... [Jeremy] Bentham's system was as destitute as Adam Smith's of a **metaphysical basis** such as Kant's. (Bonar 1930, 228)[86]

> A theory drawn up in all seriousness by Adam Smith and found adequate by Edmund Burke cannot be treated lightly as obvious-ly futile. Times, men, and philosophies, however, have changed much; they were changing then; and there are features in the theory of which the weakness is more evident to plain folk now than to the acutest critics in those days. (231–232)

In another work, *The Tables Turned* (Bonar 1931), Bonar offers a dia-logue between a "Victorian," resembling himself, and Adam Smith. I repro-duce the concluding lines, laid out as there:

> *Victorian*
> You mean, Sir, that a fine style is of no account in the eye of
> pure reason, *sub specie æternitatis*. For all that, it is a great
> comfort to us here in the Wilderness, and we are glad to have it
> in your *Moral Sentiments*.

---

86. For more from Bonar on Kant, and in relation to Smith, see Bonar 1930, 246–257.

Adam Smith

Observe that there is less of it in the *Wealth of Nations*, to the
latter's advantage, if a man can judge his own books.

Victorian

That same test of Reason, Sir, would hold not only for your
compositions, which stand the test well, but for all your library,
parts of which would stand it indifferently. The books in your
library, say the minor French classics or no classics, would not
all appeal to our reason now. When some soul of reason lay in
them, you were the man discerningly to distil it out.

Adam Smith

What I have read I have read, including much that both worlds
will quite willingly let die. I add again: what I have written I
have written, with same saving clause. (Bonar 1931, 50–51)

Here Bonar seems to suggest that Smith himself regarded WN as a
superior work to TMS. Such suggestion directly contradicts the testimony of Romilly.

Richard T. Ely (1854–1943)

Richard T. Ely was a progressive economist and founder and first secretary of the American Economic Association, and also a founder and first secretary of the Christian Social Union. He was professor at the University of Wisconsin from 1892 to 1925 and then at Northwestern until 1933. He was prolific as an economist and popularizer. For an anthology that reproduced some text from Smith, Ely contributed a short essay on Smith, from which I draw the following:

The 'Theory of Moral Sentiments,' it has been maintained, would
have achieved renown for its author, and a place for him in literature, had it been presented to the world simply as a collection
of essays on the topics with which it deals; viz., the 'Propriety

and Impropriety of Actions,' their 'Merit and Demerit,' 'Virtue,' 'Justice,' 'Duty,' etc. The essays are finely written, full of subtle analysis and truthful illustration. The book is least significant, however, as philosophy, because it **lacks any profound examination of the foundation** upon which the author's views rest. (Ely 1902, 13521)

J. M. Robertson (1856–1933)

J. M. Robertson was a prolific Scottish writer and a Liberal MP 1906 to 1918. In *A Short History of Morals* (1920), he says repeatedly that Smith strings together ideas and claims that do not cohere (326–337). He suggests that underneath the farrago is a system "founded in self-regard." After quoting Smith, Robertson remarks: "It would be difficult to reduce sympathy more plainly to a **self-regarding foundation**, after a parade of a priori altruism" (332). Figuring that the charitable way to read Smith is to try to ascribe some kind of ethical foundation to his work, he ascribes a "self-regarding" foundation. Robertson writes: "Again and again he [Smith] shows how contracted, how conventional, how often merely customary, is the ethic of sympathy which he is formulating" (333). Robertson suggests that Smith might have simplified his teaching by treating sympathy as "the *purification* of the current nationalized and racialized moral codes" (335).

William R. Scott (1868–1940)

William R. Scott taught at St. Andrews from 1896 to 1915, published a study of Francis Hutcheson (Scott 1900), and moved to Glasgow to become the Adam Smith Professor of Political Economy, 1915–1940, publishing an important work on Smith's life (Scott 1937). The following is from a 1923 address on Smith to the British Academy:

Certainly when he [Smith] came to write his *Theory of Moral Sentiments* he displayed no deep philosophical acumen. That book has its own place in the development of British Ethics, and it shows the kindly heart of the man, but its greatest importance consists in aiding us to understand some obscure parts of Smith's growth as an Economist. (Scott 1923, 438–439)

It was the weakness of Smith's Ethics that he attributed to others the high degree of imaginative power which he himself possessed. (444)

Harold Laski (1893–1950)

Harold Laski, a Fabian socialist, was a prolific economist, political theorist, author, and lecturer, and professor at the London School of Economics from 1926 to 1950. He served as chairman of the British Labour Party. In *Political Thought in England: From Locke to Bentham*, he wrote that TMS was "written with sufficient power of style to obscure its inner poverty of thought" (Laski 1920, 291).

Jacob Viner (1892–1970)

The economist Jacob Viner authored a famous paper "Adam Smith and Laissez-Faire" (1927). He offered remarks on the evolution of Smith's thought:

I will endeavor to show that the *Wealth of Nations* was a better book because of its partial breach with the *Theory of Moral Sentiments*, and that it could not have remained, as it has, a living book were it not that in its methods of analysis, its basic assumptions, and its conclusions it abandoned the absolutism, the rigidity, the romanticism which characterize the earlier book. (Viner 1927, 201)

Viner says that TMS reasons "from notions masquerading as self-evident verities" (216). Viner's narrative faces an obvious problem in the fact that Smith greatly revised TMS in Ed. 6. Viner says Smith was "elderly and unwell" and "had lost the capacity to make drastic changes in his philosophy" but not the "capacity to overlook" problems in it (217).

Arthur N. Prior (1914–1969)

Arthur Prior grew up in New Zealand and there studied under John N. Findlay. He went on to be professor in New Zealand and England and write works on logic, ethics, time, and language. The following comes from his first book *Logic and the Basis of Ethics* (1949), in which at the outset he expresses his especially high regard for G.E. Moore, a chapter of Reid (1788), and the reason-slave-to-the-passions section and the *is/ought* section of Hume's *Treatise* (Prior 1949, x).

> Smith...distinguishes not only between 'what are' and 'what, upon a certain condition, would be' the judgement of others (the 'condition' being perfect knowledge of our motives and circumstances), but also between the latter and 'what, we imagine, ought to be the judgment of others.' 'What, we imagine, ought to be the judgment of others' is, of course, simply what ours would be if we were in their place. Every man is endowed 'not only with a desire of being approved of, but with a desire of being what ought to be approved; *or of being what he himself approves of in other men*' (italics mine [Prior's]).

> Smith's final word, even here, thus directs us to **his undisguisedly subjective notion** of 'propriety'.... (Prior 1949, 91)

Concluding Remark

If you feel little love for TMS, you might tend toward foundationalism in ethics and epistemology. If you love TMS, you might tend toward nonfoundationalism.

In any case, I have provided evidence that the career of TMS has waned and waxed with openness to nonfoundationalism.

Circa 1800

R
are is the individual who lives through two turns of a century. Many do not live through one.

The turning of a century is focal for thinking about shifts in man's moral condition. The year 1900 was a time of developments worthy of the word *momentous*. But a contemplation of 1800 pertains to TMS's time in the tomb; it also helps us understand 1900. And 2026.

Arthur Prior (1949) noted one aspect of circa 1800 when he wrote that William Paley's *Moral and Political Philosophy* (1785) "crystallized the theological Utilitarianism of the preceding period, while Bentham's secular Utilitarianism caught the ear of the age which followed it" (Prior 1949, 103–104).

Again, it is remarkable that a book by a thinker of the age and thought by him his best work (Romilly 1840, 404) would fall into oblivion. For generations after 1790 the number of exponents of TMS was precisely zero. TMS dwelled in oblivion for some 180 years. Thus, the explanandum: A great thinker's great work quickly falling out of favor and being forsaken for so long. Do we have an explanation?

To supply an explanation, we would need to interpret human experience back to at least 1759, but think about the 30 years centered on 1800, that is, 1785–1815. Events ramify with a lag. Consider publications by Paley or Smith or Bentham and political events, like American independence, the Constitution of the United States, and the French Revolution. After 1800 we see ramifications in society and culture, as well as more events. We see broad cultural shifts.

What broad shifts occurred circa 1800?

Here I string together some materials, like beads on string. Some of the beads are heady and shown without much explanation from me. Nor do I try to relate the beads to one another. The string of beads is meant to convey that a set of major and related changes occurred circa 1800.

Before commencing, let me say: Our discourse always is meant for the present and future. We do not persuade the past. I talk now of things that went wrong circa 1800 in culture and thought to make our futures brighter. Remember that, in the fortunes of TMS over time, there is a happy fact about our present and future: Since 1976 TMS has risen from the tomb— even soared. Any pessimistic overtone may be deterred further by realizing that the circa-1800 changes touched upon here are about spiritual leadership, not life and justice on the whole. In many ways, since 1800 life has improved and injustices have lessened. The string of beads is not meant to paint a full picture and it is not a prognosis. In some ways, today is looking up, and tomorrow is another day.

To commence, consider two meaty quotations from J.G.A. Pocock's *Virtue, Commerce, and History: Essays on Political Thought and History, Chiefly in the Eighteenth Century* (1985). He writes:

But the defense of commercial society, no less than the vindication of classical virtue, was carried out with the weapons of
humanism. The eighteenth century presents us with a legal
humanism, or humanist jurisprudence, whose roots were in
[Donald R.] Kelley's 'civil science of the Renaissance,' being
employed against the civic humanism of the classical republi-
cans in a way hard to parallel in the sixteenth century. The effect
was to construct a liberalism which made the state's authority
guarantee the liberty of the individual's social behavior, but had
no intention whatever of impoverishing that behavior by confin-
ing it to the rigorous assertion of ego-centered individual rights.
On the contrary, down at least to the end of the 1780s, it was the
world of ancient politics which could be made to seem rigid and
austere, impoverished because underspecialized; and the new
world of the social and sentimental, the commercial and cultural,
was made to proliferate with alternatives to ancient *virtus* and
libertas, largely in consequence of the jurists' fascination with
the universe of *res*. Now, at last, a right to things became a way
to the practice of virtue, so long as virtue could be defined as the
practice and refinement of manners. *A commercial humanism*

had been not unsuccessfully constructed.

About 1789, a wedge was driven through this burgeoning universe, and rather suddenly we begin to hear denunciations of commerce as found upon soullessly rational calculation and the cold, mechanical philosophy of Bacon, Hobbes, Locke, and Newton. How this reversal of strategies came about is not at present well understood. It may have to do with the rise of an administrative ideology, in which Condorcet, Hartley, and Bentham *tried to erect a science of legislation on a foundation of highly reductionist assumptions.* But that is another chapter in the history of both jurisprudence and humanism.... (Pocock 1985, 50; italics added)

In the same work, Pocock writes:

I suggest that we cannot understand the vindication of commercial society unless we understand the grounds on which it was assailed and acknowledge the attack's continuous validity. This obliges us to take a route which leads through Mandeville and Hume to Ferguson and Smith, and to encounter classical economics at the end of it, after long debate between virtue and commerce, virtue and corruption, virtue and passion.... But if classical economics emerged in this way, if the last of the civic humanists was the first of the Scottish economists, if the quarrel of the ancients and moderns furnished the context in which the developing understanding of market relations took on problematic meaning, then the classical economics seem rapidly to have hardened into a paradigm which *operated to deny the ambivalent historicism of late Whig culture.* Bentham and the elder Mill, as well as McCulloch and Ricardo, would seem to have much to do with this, and we are left trying to see how their thought emerged in history. *The space from Smith to Ricardo is replete with problems and possibilities.* (Pocock 1985, 123; italics added)

Pocock seems to suggest that Smith was the apogee among those moralists who "not unsuccessfully constructed" a "commercial humanism," but, then, thinkers and culture turned away from that culmination quite promptly. Deirdre McCloskey (2008) suggests that Smith was the last moralist to approach ethics in terms of virtues (at least until some in the 20th century returned to doing so).

Maybe the commercial humanism was rapidly overwhelmed by the myth and mentality of democracy, "the public," and "public opinion," aided by expanding literacy and vernacular print culture? Maybe an accomplice is the notion, which a paradoxical paragraph in the first chapter of WN (21–22) abets, that moral philosophy can be divided and subdivided into distinct and separate sciences, which, led by an invisible hand, conduce to the good of the whole by trading with one another? Eugene F. Miller, the modern editor of Hume's *Essays*, wrote wistfully of the attempt to recover "the unity and comprehensiveness of human knowledge that was lost after Hume's time, with the division of learning into departments or disciplines" (Editor's Note of EMPL, xxvii).

Two particular intellectual changes (in the Anglosphere) circa 1800 should be noted. One is the discontinuation[87] of natural jurisprudence or, if you will, jural theory, in which the place and status of commutative justice (by whatever name) is recognized as a fundamental set of nonconflicting rules (Klein 2023b, ch. 9), a set that, in fact, preconditions legal rules (Beever 2013). The other is a receding of political theory, by which I mean understandings of government's authority and the grounds for a legitimacy in, and a qualified allegiance to, the government's institutionalizations of initiations of coercion—that is, theorizing how government is not just an elaborate syndicate of organized crime, which is the way it looks when one first learns to see commutative justice.[88]

Speaking of organized crime, now consider Arthur Melzer's *Philosophy*

---

87. After 1810, natural jurisprudence was scarcely taught in the Scottish universities; see Moore (2006, 314–316) and Haakonssen (1996, 248–260), both implicating Dugald Stewart.

88. I lament that Hume, in reworking ideas of the *Treatise* before disavowing it at the end of his life, did not reprise more of the *Treatise*'s conventionalist theorizing, notably his exposition of the obligations of commutative justice and the obligations of political authority, of the sources of those obligations, and of how those sources are "not of the nature of a *promise*" (T 3.2.2.10).

Between the Lines: The Lost History of Esoteric Writing (2014). Melzer maintains the following three historical claims: (1) up to some time in the 18th century it was common knowledge that most great writers wrote esoterically, (2) in the 18th century there was much lively discourse *about* esotericism, and (3) from about 1790 esotericism declined sharply as a practice, and, moreover, people would soon neglect or forget how much it had been practiced. To illustrate, Melzer says that Johann Wolfgang von Goethe wrote in an 1811 letter "of an act of forgetting taking place before his eyes" (Melzer 2014, xii). Goethe writes: "I have always considered it an evil, indeed a disaster which, in the second half of the previous century, gained more and more ground that one no longer drew a distinction between exoteric and esoteric."[89] Melzer elaborates on changes circa 1800:

> [Esotericism] *became* unknown in the course of the nineteenth
> century (as Goethe was reporting). But how does a whole culture
> suddenly lose awareness of a practice that was, until relatively
> recently, so widespread, so openly discussed, so long enduring,
> so crucially important, and so thoroughly documented in the his-
> torical record? It is not easy to think of a comparable episode of
> philosophical forgetting, of intellectual expungement. Mustn't
> powerful cultural forces of some kind be at work here? (Melzer
> 2014, 96)

After 1800, as political contenders addressed "the public mind" and as experts spoon-fed pupils in distinct and separate sciences, the discourse needed to sound univocal. There was a flattening. Esotericism was driven from the conscious part of the mind.

The flattening also impaired understandings of irony. In *A Rhetoric of Irony* (1974a), Wayne Booth wrote that "The way irony works in uniting (or dividing) authors and readers has been relatively neglected since the latter part of the eighteenth century" (ix). And:

---

89. Melzer (2014, vii) cites Goethe's correspondence (1988, 3, 168) and credits Werner J. Dannhauser for the translation of the quoted passage.

It was not until well along into the eighteenth century that the-
orists were forced, by explosive developments in the use of irony
itself, to begin thinking about ironic effects as somehow self-suf-
ficient literary ends. And then of course irony burst its bonds so
effectively that men finally dismissed merely functional ironies
as not even ironic, or as self-evidently less artistic. (Booth 1974a,
139–140)

Booth extols what he calls stable irony, a play of perspectives or interpretations, each evoking sentiments, a play that is stable in the sense that
it endeavors to make our sentiments and reasoning, together, sounder,
juster, more worthy. Booth suggests that the stable irony which marked
the 18th century was not subsequently sustained or venerated. In *Modern
Dogma and the Rhetoric of Assent* (1974b), Booth speaks of a disjunction
between sentiment and worthy reasoning, a disjunction guarded by unwor-
thy demarcationist dogmas ("value" vs. "fact," "normative" vs. "positive,"
"emotion" vs. "logic," etc.). The foolish disjunction maintained "the help-
lessness of reason in dealing with any values but the calculation of means
to ends" (1974b, 15).

The dogmas had been debunked by good arguments, suggests Booth
(1974b, 15). Those arguments persuaded many people, including myself.
But the debunking did not bring forth, instead, the healthy play of nonfoundational yet stable dialectics. Such healthy dialectics is something that
depends on a sort of friendship. Rather, the dogmas, though undefended
and indefensible, trudge on, like zombies. If you if wish to challenge them,
type your query into the Zoom chat and the TA will bring it to the instructor's attention; you may also find an answer by asking ChatGPT at the link
below. That's all there is.

Friendship is one of the titular four loves in C.S. Lewis's *The Four Loves*
(1960). He expounds on friendship "in the sense I give to the word" (82) as
a shared estimation or appreciation of objects that are significant to the
friends—a concurrence in interpretation and judgment regarding things
they care about and pursue. Lewis writes: "Some forms of democratic sentiment are naturally hostile to it because it is selective and an affair of the
few. To say 'These are my friends' implies 'Those are not'" (76).

"To the Ancients, Friendship seemed the happiest and most fully human of all loves; the crown of life and the school of virtue" (Lewis 1960, 73). As Melzer indicates a circa-1800 loss of esotericism and Booth a loss of stable irony, Lewis indicates a circa-1800 loss of his sense of friendship—he says the modern world ignores friendship (73) and speaks of "the modern disparagement of friendship" (96). Here are more snippets:

> [Friendship] was exalted in ancient and medieval times and has come to be made light of in our own.... But then came Romanticism.... For all these reasons if a man believes (as I do) that the old estimate of Friendship was the correct one, he can hardly write a chapter on it except as a rehabilitation.... We, not they, are out of step. (Lewis 1960, 75–80)

That Lewis perceived the big shifts to have come circa 1800 is confirmed by his lecture inaugurating his professorship at Cambridge University in 1954. The title "De Descriptione Temporum" translates as "On the Description of Times." (It appears in Lewis 1962.)

Our times are very different than earlier times, he says. He offers circa 1800 as "the greatest of all divisions in the history of the West," "that which divides the present [1954] from, say, the age of Jane Austen and [Walter] Scott" (17). The chasm runs, he says, "somewhere...between us and *Persuasion*." Lewis also speaks of "Gibbon's time" (12) and of potent beginnings well before 1800 but suggests, as we have, that it takes time for things to ramify. Here are some of the major circa-1800 changes suggested by Lewis (the headings are by me):

Scientism and specialization (Lewis 1954):

- "In our time something which was once the possession of all educated men has shrunk to being the technical accomplishment of a few specialists" (13).
- "[I]f one were looking for a man who could not read Virgil though his father could, he might be found more easily in the twentieth century than in the fifth" (13).

- "All through the eighteenth century the tone of the common mind remained ethical, rhetorical, juristic, rather than scientific.... Science was not the business of Man because Man had not yet become the business of science" (16).

The birth of the machines (Lewis 1954):

- "Between Jane Austen and us...comes the birth of the machines.... This is on a level with the change from...a pastoral to an agricultural economy. It alters Man's place in nature. The theme has been celebrated till we are all sick of it, so I will here say nothing about its economic and social consequences, immeasurable though they are. What concerns us more is its psychological effect. How has it come about that we use the highly emotive word 'stagnation,' with all its malodorous and malarial overtones, for what other ages would have called 'permanence'? Why does the word at once suggest to us clumsiness, inefficiency, barbarity? When our ancestors talked of the primitive church or the primitive purity of our constitution they meant nothing of that sort.... Why does 'latest' in advertisements mean 'best'?... I submit that what has imposed this climate of opinion so firmly on the human mind is a new archetypal image. It is the image of old machines being superseded by new and better ones. For in the world of machines the new most often really is better and the primitive really is the clumsy. And this image, potent in all our minds, reigns almost without rival in the minds of the uneducated. For to them, after their marriage and the births of their children, the very milestones of life are technical advances. From the old push-bike to the motor-bike and thence to the little car; from gramophone to radio and from radio to television; from the range to the stove; these are the very stages of their pilgrimage. But whether from this cause or from some other, assuredly that approach to life which has left these footprints on our language is the thing that separates us most sharply from our ancestors and whose absence would strike us as most alien if we could return to their world. Conversely, our assumption that everything is provisional and soon to be superseded, that the attainment of goods we have never yet had, rather than the defence and conservation of those we have already, is the cardinal business of life, would most shock and bewilder them if they could visit ours" (20–22)

Lewis's remarks on changing attitudes about what is new prompted me to reflect on the word *news*. If you look at today's dictionaries, you find emphasized accounts *of recent events*; yet in Johnson's 1755 dictionary, the first definition is "Fresh account *of any thing*" (italics added), even if not new, and the second is "Something not heard before." Thus, the gospel was news ("good news") to those who had not heard it before. But what was learned was not new. Thus, *news* denoted someone's recently becoming a knower or believer of some notion. Only Johnson's third and final definition moves toward the present dominant meaning: "Papers which give an account of the transactions of the present times." Those papers sell narratives, but the narrative insinuated by them and supposed by many of their readers is that our presently becoming believers of important notions comes from reading those papers. That narrative is now crumbling. The rise of "news" since 1800 may be seen at Google's Ngram Viewer.

Politics (Lewis 1954):

- "The change...extends to all nations, those we call democracies as well as dictatorships. If I wished to satirise the present political order I should borrow for it the name which *Punch* invented during the first German War: *Govertisement*. This is a portmanteau word and means 'government by advertisement'" (17).

- "In all previous ages that I can think of the principal aim of rulers, except at rare and short intervals, was to keep their subjects quiet, to forestall or extinguish widespread excitement and persuade people to attend quietly to their several occupations. And on the whole their subjects agreed with them. They even prayed (in words that sound curiously

old-fashioned) to be able to live 'a peaceable life in all god-
liness and honesty' and 'pass their time in rest and quiet-
ness.' But now the organisation of mass excitement seems
to be almost the normal organ of political power. We live in
an age of...'campaigns'" (17–18).

- "[Y]ou notice that I am guilty of a slight archaism in calling them 'rulers.' 'Leaders' is the modem word.... [T]his is a
deeply significant change of vocabulary. Our demand upon
them has changed no less than theirs on us. For of a ruler
one asks justice, incorruption, diligence, perhaps clemen-
cy; of a leader, dash, initiative, and (I suppose) what people
call 'magnetism' or 'personality'" (18).

The Beholder denied (Lewis 1954):

- "[W]hereas all history was for our ancestors divided into
two periods, the pre-Christian and the Christian, and two
only, for us it falls into three—the pre-Christian, the Christian, and what may reasonably be called the post-Christian.... [I]t appears to me that the second change is even
more radical than the first. Christians and Pagans had much
more in common with each other than either has with a
post-Christian. The gap between those who worship different gods is not so wide as that between those who worship
and those who do not" (13–14).

- "It is hard to have patience with those Jeremiahs, in Press
or pulpit, who warn us that we are 'relapsing into Pagan-
ism'.... A post-Christian man is not a Pagan; you might as well
think that a married woman recovers her virginity by divorce.
The post-Christian is cut off from the Christian past and therefore doubly from the Pagan past" (20).

- "[T]here were lots of sceptics in Jane Austen's time and long
before, as there are lots of Christians now. But the presumption has changed. In her days some kind and degree of religious belief and practice were the norm: now...they are the
exception" (19–20).

Conclusion to the chapter and the book

As noted in our previous chapter, Lord Kames, in 1778, before inserting criticism of TMS into a new edition of one of his works, shared the insertion with Smith. In reply, Smith assured Kames that "Nothing can be more perfectly friendly and polite." Smith added:

> I am no doubt extremely sorry to find myself of a different opinion both from so able a judge of the subject and from so old and so good a friend. But differences of this kind are unavoidable; and besides, *partium contentionibus respublica crescit*. (Corr. 234)

A Latin instructor advised me to understand *partium contentionibus respublica crescit* as: *"The republic grows by the struggles of factions."* Smith is acknowledging to Kames, his former patron, who by then had taken considerably to Thomas Reid's way of thought, that afoot was the forming of intellectual parties divided over the issues treated in our previous chapter and jostling over university curricula, appointments, and favorable opinion (see the Millar letter quoted on page 243 above).

The materials in this chapter began with Pocock, who said that in Smith's times a commercial humanism had been not unsuccessfully constructed. That construction soon hit hard times. It seems to me that unfortunate circa-1800 developments paved the way for circa-1900 developments and circa-2000 developments. Nonetheless, each of us today may work our way back to the commercial humanism of Smith's times, by befriending authors like Booth, Lewis, and Smith.

It is likely that Smith saw that his way in moral theorizing was losing ground. But nonetheless, with Ed. 6, he only took it to new depths. In describing the unceasing work of "[t]he wise and virtuous man," Smith said that that man aims high, "But he imitates the work of a divine artist" (247.25). Virtue, therefore, is an unceasing art and an art that imitates something divine, but, moreover, an art that imitates *an artist*. The wise and virtuous man imitates an imitator. Imitation depends on ostension, which means exemplars; the virtuous exemplar, who has imitated others and now is imitated by others, "acts suitably to his divine extraction" (131. 32). "Follow me as I follow."

It would take a long time for Smith's way to once again have more than sparse appeal. Since 1976 and continuing today, a growing number of readers do not hold TMS's not being foundationalist/demarcationist against it. Today, the magnitude of the influence of thinkers like Jordan Peterson and Iain McGilchrist signals a potential return to a more natural and wholesome orientation to life and society, an orientation that is deeply spiritual by virtue of its natural embrace of a deep relationship with spirits like the man within the breast and a beholder like God/Joy.

TMS continues its rise from the tomb. By pondering circa-1800 shifts, we may reconsider elements of the cultures we have belonged to.

References

Ashraf, Nava, Colin F. Camerer, and George Loewenstein. 2005. Adam Smith, Behavioral Economist. *Journal of Economic Perspectives* 19(3): 131–145.

Aydinonat, N. Emrah. 2008. *The Invisible Hand in Economics: How Economists Explain Unintended Social Consequences*. Routledge.

Bagehot, Walter. 1915 [1876]. Adam Smith as a Person. In *The Works and Life of Walter Bagehot*, vol. 7, ed. Emilie Isabel Barrington: 1–32. Longmans, Green and Co.

Baier, Annette. 1991. *A Progress of Sentiments: Reflections on Hume's Treatise*. Harvard University Press.

Bain, Alexander. 1868. *Mental and Moral Science*. Longmans, Green and Co.

Bain, Alexander. 1882. *James Mill: A Biography*. Longmans, Green, and Co.

Barry, Norman. 1982. The Tradition of Spontaneous Order. *Literature of Liberty* 2(2), Summer, 7–58.

Bateson, Melissa, Daniel Nettle, and Gilbert Roberts. 2006. Cues of Being Watched Enhance Cooperation in a Real-world Setting. *Biology Letters* 2(3): 412–414.

Baudrillart, Henri. 1860. Introduction to *Théorie des Sentiments Moraux by Adam Smith*. Guillaumin et Compagnie.

Beauchamp, Tom L. 2000. Introduction to David Hume's *An Enquiry Concerning Human Understanding: A Critical Edition*, ed. T. L. Beauchamp: xi–ciii. Oxford University Press.

Beccaria, Cesare. 1963 [1764]. Dei Delitti e delle Pene. English translation by H. Paolucci: *On Crimes and Punishments*. Bobbs-Merrill.

Beever, Allan. 2013. *Forgotten Law: The Forms of Justice in the History of Legal and Political Theory*. Oxford University Press.

Bentham, Jeremy. [1830]. Jeremy Bentham to His Fellow-Citizens of France, on Houses of Peers and Senates. In *The Works of Jeremy Bentham*, ed. J. Bowring, vol. 4: 419–450. William Tait.

Bentham, Jeremy. 1843. *The Works of Jeremy Bentham*, ed. J. Bowring. William Tait.

Bentham, Jeremy. 1954. *Jeremy Bentham's Economic Writings*, vol. 3, ed. W. Stark. Allen & Unwin.

Bentham, Jeremy. 2008. Gulphs in Mankind's Career of Prosperity: A Critique of Adam Smith on Interest Rate Restrictions [A selection of Bentham's *Defence of Usury*]. *Econ Journal Watch* 5(1): 66–77.

Bitterman, Henry J. 1940a. Adam Smith's Empiricism and the Law of Nature: I. *Journal of Political Economy* 48(4): 487–520.

Bitterman, Henry J. 1940b. Adam Smith's Empiricism and the Law of Nature: II. *Journal of Political Economy* 48(5): 703–734.

Biziou, Michaël. 2015. French Translations and Re-translations of Smith's "Theory of Moral Sentiments." *Adam Smith Review* 8: 53–80.

Blackburn, Simon. 2008. *How to Read Hume*. Granta Publications.

Bonar, James. 1930. *Moral Sense*. Allen & Unwin.

Bonar, James. 1931. *The Tables Turned*. Macmillan.

Booth, Wayne C. 1974a. *A Rhetoric of Irony*. University of Chicago Press.

Booth, Wayne C. 1974b. *Modern Dogma and the Rhetoric of Assent*. University of Chicago Press.

Bowring, John. 1834. History of the Greatest-Happiness Principle. In Jeremy Bentham, *Deontology, or the Science of Morality*, ed. John Bowring, vol. 1: 287–331. 2 vols. Longman.

Brougham, Henry. 1855. *Lives of Philosophers of the Time of George III*, 3rd ed., Richard Griffin and Co.

Brown, Thomas. 1820. *Lectures on the Philosophy of the Human Mind*, vol. 4. James Ballantyne and Co. for W. and C. Tait.

Brown, Thomas. 2017 [1820]. Examination of Dr Smith's System. *Econ Journal Watch* 14(1): 2–21.

Brown, Vivienne. 1994. *Adam Smith's Discourse: Canonicity, Commerce, and Conscience*. Routledge.

Bryce, J. C. 1980. Introduction to the Contributions to *The Edinburgh Review*. In Adam Smith's *Essay on Philosophical Subjects*, ed. W. P. D. Wightman, J. C. Bryce, and I. S. Ross: 229–31. Oxford University Press.

Buchanan, James M. 1969. *Cost and Choice: An Inquiry into Economic Theory*. University of Chicago Press.

Buckle, Henry T. 1904 [1861]. *Introduction to the History of Civilization in England*, ed. J. M. Robertson. George Routledge & Sons.

Burke, Edmund [unsigned]. 1759. *Review of The Theory of Moral Sentiments, by Adam Smith*. Annual Register 2: 484–489.

Burke, Edmund. 1957. *A Note-Book of Edmund Burke: Poems, Characters, Essays and Other Sketches in the Hands of Edmund and William Burke*, ed. H.V. F. Somerset. Cambridge at the University Press.

Burke, Edmund. 1990. *A Philosophical Enquiry into the Origin of our Ideas of the Sublime and Beautiful*, ed. A. Phillips. Oxford University Press.

Burke, Edmund. 1999 [1790]. *Reflections on the Revolution in France*. In vol. 2 of Selected Works of Edmund Burke, a new imprint of the Payne Edition. Foreword by Francis Canavan. Liberty Fund.

Burns, J. H. 2005. Happiness and Utility: Jeremy Bentham's Equation. *Utilitas* 17(1): 46–61.

Butler, Joseph. 1736. *Analogy of Religion, Natural and Revealed to the Constitution and Course of Nature to Which Are Added, Two Brief Dissertations*. Christian Classics Ethereal Library, http://www.ccel.org/ccel/butler/analogy.toc.html.

Cabanis, Pierre Jean Georges. 1867. *Rapports du Physique et du Moral de l'Homme*. Paris: Victor Masson et fils.

Campbell, Lewis and William Garnett. 1882. *The Life of James Clerk Maxwell, With Selections from his Correspondence and Occasional Writings*. Macmillan.

Campbell, R. H., and A. S. Skinner. 1976. General Introduction to Adam Smith's *An Inquiry into the Nature and Causes of the Wealth of Nations* [1776]. Eds. R. H. Campbell and A. S. Skinner. Oxford University Press. Reprint: Liberty Fund, 1981.

Campbell, T. D. 1971. *Adam Smith's Science of Morals*. George Allen & Unwin.

Cannan, Edwin. 1928. Adam Smith as an Economist: The Gospel of Mutual Services. In Cannan's *An Economist's Protest*: 417–430. Adelphi. The chapter is reprinted from *Economica* 17

(June 1926):123–134, but the subtitle is new to the 1928 appearance.

Chappell, Vere C., ed. 1966. *Hume: A Collection of Critical Essays*. Anchor Books.

Chesterton, Gilbert K. 1933. *St. Thomas Aquinas*. Sheed &Ward, Inc.

Coase, Ronald. 1960. The Problem of Social Cost. *Journal of Law and Economics* 3(October): 1–44.

Coase, Ronald H. 1976. Adam Smith's View of Man. *Journal of Law & Economics* 19(3): 529–546.

Coats, A. W. 2008. Patten, Simon Nelson (1852–1922). In *The New Palgrave Dictionary of Economics*, 2nd ed., eds. Steven N. Durlauf and Lawrence E. Blume. Palgrave Macmillan.

Collins. 2018. Free Online Dictionary. https://www.collinsdictionary.com/.

Cousin, Victor. 1846. *Cours d'Histoire de la Philosophie Morale au XVIIIe Siècle*, vol. 4. Paris: Ladrange.

Cousin, Victor. 1855. *Lectures on the True, the Beautiful, and the Good*, trans. O. W. Wright. D. Appleton.

Cranston, Maurice. 1984. Introduction to Rousseau's *A Discourse on Inequality*: 9–53. Penguin.

Cropsey, Joseph. 2001. *Polity and Economy: Further Thoughts on the Principles of Adam Smith*. St. Augustine Press.

Davie, George. 1964. *The Democratic Intellectual*: Scotland and Her Universities in the Nineteenth Century, 2nd ed. Edinburgh University Press.

Dear, Keith, Kevin Dutton, and Elaine Fox. 2019. Do 'Watching Eyes' Influence Antisocial Behavior? A Systematic Review and Meta-analysis. *Evolution and Human Behavior* 40(3): 269–280.

Delatour, Albert. 1866. *Adam Smith: Sa Vie, Ses Travaux, Ses Doctrines*. Paris: Guillaumin.

DelliSanti, Dylan. 2023. Moral Innovation and Man within the Breast. *Adam Smith Review* 13: 327–346.

DeLong, J. Bradford. 2009. As If the Invisible Hand Had Played a Losing Card... Brad DeLong's Weblog. May 14.

Den Uyl, Douglas J. 2016. Impartial Spectating and the Price Analogy. *Econ Journal Watch* 13 (2): 264–72.

Duncan, Elmer H., and Robert M. Baird. 1977. Thomas Reid's Criticisms of Adam Smith's 'Theory of Moral Sentiments.' *Journal of the History of Ideas* 38(3): 509–522.

Durkheim, Emile. 1915. *The Elementary Forms of Religious Life*. Trans. J.W. Swain. George Allen & Unwin.

Ely, Richard T. 1902. Adam Smith. In *Library of the World's Best Literature*, Ancient and Modern, vol. 34, ed. C. D. Warner:13519–13523. J. A. Hill.

Emmett, Ross B. 2011. Man and Society in Adam Smith's Natural Morality: The Impartial Spectator, the Man of System and the Invisible Hand. *Adam Smith as Theologian*, ed. P. Oslington: 125–132. Routledge.

Etzioni, Amitai. 2016. Happiness Is the Wrong Metric. *Society* 53: 246–257.

Evensky, Jerry. 1987. The Two Voices of Adam Smith: Moral Philosopher and Social Critic. *History of Political Economy* 19(3): 447–468.

Farrer, James Anson. 1881. *Adam Smith*. G. P. Putnam's Sons.

Ferguson, Adam. 1792. *Principles of Moral and Political Science*, vol. 1. Strahan and Cadell.

Fieser, James, ed. 2005. *Early Responses to Hume's Moral, Literary and Political Writings*, 2 vols. Bristol: Thoemmes Press.

Findlay, John N. 1950. Values in Speaking. *Philosophy* 25(92): 20–39.

Firth, Roderick. 1952. Ethical Absolutism and the Ideal Observer. *Philosophy and Phenomenological Research* 12(3): 317–345.

Fleischacker, Samuel. 2004. *On Adam Smith's Wealth of Nations*. Princeton University Press.

Fleischacker, Samuel. 2016a. Adam Smith's Impartial Spectator: Symposium Remarks. *Econ Journal Watch* 13(2): 273–83.

Fleischacker, Samuel. 2016b. Samuel Fleischacker on Adam Smith's Impartial Spectator. Podcast, interviewed by Daniel Klein. *Econ Journal Watch* May: https://econjwatch.org/podcast/samuel-fleischacker-on-adam-smith-s-impartial-spectator.

Force, Pierre. 2003. *Self-Interest before Adam Smith: A Genealogy of Economic Science*. Cambridge University Press.

Forget, Evelyn L. 2001. Cultivating Sympathy: Sophie Condorcet's Letters on Sympathy. *Journal of the History of Economic Thought* 23(3): 319–337.

Forman-Barzilai, Fonna. 2010. *Adam Smith and the Circles of Sympathy: Cosmopolitanism and Moral Theory*. Cambridge University Press.

Friedman, David D. 1994. A Positive Account of Property Rights. *Social Philosophy and Policy* 11(2):1–16.

Friedman, Milton. 1953. *Essays in Positive Economics*. University of Chicago Press.

Frisbie, Levi. 1819. Review essay of The Theory of Moral Sentiments. *North-American Review* 8(23): 371–396. (And reproduced in a collection of Frisbie's writings in 1823.)

Glaze, Simon. 2017. Adam Smith and William James on the Psychological Basis of Progress. *Cambridge Journal of Economics* 41(2): 349–365.

Griswold, Charles L. 1999. *Adam Smith and the Virtues of Enlightenment*. Cambridge University Press.

Griswold, Charles L. 2006. On the Incompleteness of Adam Smith's System. *Adam Smith Review* 2: 181–186.

Grouchy, Sophie de. 2017 [1798]. *Letters on Sympathy*, trans. Jonathan Bennett. EarlyModernTexts.com.

Haakonssen, Knud. 1981. *The Science of a Legislator: The Natural Jurisprudence of David Hume and Adam Smith*. Cambridge University Press.

Haakonssen, Knud. 1996. *Natural Law and Moral Philosophy: From Grotius to the Scottish Enlightenment*. Cambridge University Press.

Hamowy, Ronald. 2005. *The Political Sociology of Freedom: Adam Ferguson and F.A. Hayek*. Edward Elgar.

Hanley, Ryan Patrick. 2009. *Adam Smith and the Character of Virtue*. Cambridge University Press.

Hanley, Ryan. 2019. *Our Great Purpose: Adam Smith on Living a Better Life*. Princeton University Press.

Hayek, Friedrich A. 1967a [1963]. The Legal and Political Philosophy of David Hume. In *Studies in Philosophy, Politics, and Economics*, 106–121. University of Chicago Press.

Hayek, Friedrich A. 1967b. Rules, Perception, and Intelligibility. In *Studies in Philosophy, Politics, and Economics*: 43–65. University of Chicago Press.

Hayek, Friedrich A. 1976. *Law, Legislation and Liberty*, vol. 2: *The Mirage of Social Justice*. University of Chicago Press.

Hayek, Friedrich A. 1978a. Competition as a Discovery Procedure. In *New Studies in Philosophy, Politics, Economics and the History of Ideas*: 179–190. University of Chicago Press.

Hayek, Friedrich A. 1978b. The Atavism of Social Justice. In *New Studies in Philosophy, Politics, Economics and the History of Ideas*: 57–68. University of Chicago Press.

Hayek, Friedrich A. 1979. The Three Sources of Human Values. In *Law, Legislation and Liberty* vol. 3, *The Political Order of a Free People*: 153–176. University of Chicago Press.

Hayek, Friedrich A. 1988. *The Fatal Conceit: The Errors of Socialism*. University of Chicago Press.

Hayek, Friedrich A. 1989. The Pretence of Knowledge. *American Economic Review* 79(6): 3–7.

Heineccius, Johann Gottlieb. 2008. *A Methodical System of Universal Law: Or, the Laws of Nature and Nations*, with Supplements and a Discourse by George Turnbull. Translated from the Latin by George Turnbull, edited with an Introduction by Thomas Albert and Peter Schröder. Liberty Fund.

Henderson, Willie. 2004. A Very Cautious, or Very Polite, Dr. Smith? Hedging in the *Wealth of Nations*. *Adam Smith Review* 1: 60–81.

Hirst, Francis W. 1904. *Adam Smith*. Macmillan.

Höffding, Harald. 1900. *A History of Modern Philosophy*, 2 vols., trans. B. E. Meyer. Macmillan.

Hume, David [unsigned]. 1759. Review of *The Theory of Moral Sentiments*, by Adam Smith. *Critical Review, or, Annals of Literature* 7(May): 383–399.

Hume, David. 1777. *Essays and Treatises on Several Subjects*. Vol. 2. Cadell.

Hume, David. 1932. *The Letters of David Hume*. Ed. J. Y. T. Greig. Oxford University Press.

Hume, David. 1983. *The History of England*, six vols. Liberty Fund.

Hume, David. 1987. *Essays: Moral, Political, and Literary*. Ed. E. F. Miller. Liberty Fund.

Hume, David. 1998. *An Enquiry Concerning the Principles of Morals*. Ed. T. L. Beauchamp. Clarendon Press.

Hume, David. 2000. *An Enquiry Concerning Human Understanding*. Ed. by T. L. Beauchamp. Clarendon Press.

Hume, David. 2007. *A Treatise of Human Nature: A Critical Edition*. Eds. David F. Norton and Mary J. Norton. Clarendon Press.

Hundert, E.G. 1994. *The Enlightenment's Fable: Bernard Mandeville and the Discovery of Society*. Cambridge University Press.

Hunter, Geoffrey. 1962. Hume on Is and Ought. *Philosophy* 37(140): 148–152.

Hunter, Geoffrey. 1963. Reply to Professor Flew. *Philosophy* 38(144): 182–184. Reprinted in Chappell 1966: 287–294.

Hutcheson, Francis. 2008. *An Inquiry into the Original of Our Ideas of Beauty and Virtue in Two Treatises*. ed. Wolfgang Leidhold. Natural Law and Enlightenment Classics. Liberty Fund.

Johnson, Samuel. 1755. *A Dictionary of the English Language*. Strahan. http://johnsonsdictionaryonline.com/.

Jouffroy, Théodore Simon. 1840. *Introduction to Ethics; Including a Critical Survey of Moral Systems*, trans. W. H. Channing. Boston: James Munroe and Co.

Jouffroy, Théodore. 1840/1997. [From] Introduction to Ethics, Including a Critical Survey of Moral Systems. In *On Moral Sentiments: Contemporary Responses to Adam Smith*, ed. John Reeder: 167–216. Bristol: Thoemmes Press.

Kahneman, Daniel. 2013. *Thinking Fast and Slow*. Farrar, Straus and Giroux.

Kames, Henry Home, Lord. 2005 [1779]. *Essays on the Principles of Morality and Natural Religion*, ed. Mary Catherine Moran. Liberty Fund.

Kennedy, Gavin. 2009a. Adam Smith and the Invisible Hand: From Metaphor to Myth. *Econ Journal Watch* 6(2): 239–262.

Kennedy, Gavin. 2009b. A Reply to Daniel Klein on Adam Smith and the Invisible Hand. *Econ Journal Watch* 6(3): 374–88.

Keynes, John Neville. 1904. *The Scope and Method of Political Economy*. Third ed. Macmillan.

Kierkegaard, Søren. 1948 [1847]. *Purity of Heart Is to Will One Thing*, trans. D. V. Steere. Harper & Row.

Kierkegaard, Søren. 1989. *The Sickness unto Death*. Trans. A. Hannay. Penguin.

Klein, Daniel B. 2009. In Adam Smith's Invisible Hands: Comment on Gavin Kennedy. *Econ Journal Watch* 6(3): 264–279.

Klein, Daniel B. 2012. *Knowledge and Coordination: A Liberal Interpretation*. Oxford University Press.

Klein, Daniel B. 2018. Hume as Non-foundationalist. *Liberty Matters*, January 19.

Klein, Daniel B. 2021. To Tolerant England and a Pension from the King: Did Hume Subconsciously Aim to Subvert Rousseau's Legacy? *Econ Journal Watch* 18(2): 327–350.

Klein, Daniel B. 2023a. *Smithian Morals*. CL Press/Fraser Institute.

Klein, Daniel B. 2023b. *Central Notions of Smithian Liberalism*. CL Press/Fraser Institute.

Klein, Daniel B., and Erik W. Matson. 2015. David Hume on Reason as a Passion. *GMU Working Paper in Economics*: 15–13. George Mason University.

La Rochefoucauld. 1959. *The Maxims of La Rochefoucauld*, trans. Louis Kronenberger. Random House.

Laski, Harold J. 1920. *Political Thought in England: From Locke to Bentham*. Henry Holt and Company.

Leechman, William. 1755. Account of the Life, Writings, and Character of Francis Hutcheson. A Preface: i–xlviii. In: *Francis Hutcheson. A System of Moral Philosophy* (his son F. Hutcheson, ed.), 2 vols. A. Millar.

Leonard, Thomas C. 2016. *Illiberal Reformers: Race, Eugenics, and American Economics in the Progressive Era*. Princeton University Press.

Leslie, T.E. Cliffe. 1888. *Essays in Political Economy*. Longmans, Green, & Co.

Lewis, C. S. 1962 [1954] 1962. De Descriptione Temporum. In *They Asked for a Paper: Papers and Addresses*: 9–25. Geoffrey Bles.

Lewis, C. S. 1960. *The Four Loves*. Harcourt Brace.

Lewis, C. S. 2002. *The Signature Classics*. Harper One.

Lindgren, J. Ralph. 1969. Adam Smith's Theory of Inquiry. *Journal of Political Economy* 77(6): 897–915.

Lindgren, J. Ralph. 1973. *The Social Philosophy of Adam Smith*. Martinus Nijhoff.

Liu, Glory, and Barry Weingast. 2021. Deriving "General Principles" in Adam Smith: The Ubiquity of Equilibrium and Comparative Statics Analysis throughout His Works. *Adam Smith Review* 12:134–165.

Livingston, Donald. 1984. *David Hume's Philosophy of Common Life*. University of Chicago Press.

Lucas, Brandon. 2010. Adam Smith's Congruence with the Hayekian Narrative. A chapter of the author's Ph.D. dissertation, The Influence of Adam Smith: The Invisible Hand, Hayekian Narrative, and Honest Profit. Department of Economics, George Mason University.

Lund, Nelson. 2022. Adam Smith on Rousseau and the Origin of Languages. *Interpretation: A Journal of Political Philosophy* 48(2): 209–238.

Luther, Martin. 1999. *Luther's Works*, vol. 32: Career of the Reformer II, eds. Jaroslav Jan Pelikan, Hilton C. Oswald, and Helmut T. Lehmann. Fortress Press.

Macfie, A.L. 1967. *The Individual in Society: Papers on Adam Smith*. London: Allen and Unwin.

Macfie. Alec. 1971. The Invisible Hand of Jupiter. *Journal of the History of Ideas* 32(4): 595–599.

Mackintosh, James. 1818. Preface to the 1818 reprint of *The Edinburgh Review for the Year 1755*. Reprinted by Kessinger Publishing's Legacy Reprints.

Mackintosh, James. 1846. *Miscellaneous Works of the Right Honorable Sir James Mackintosh*, vol. 1. Longman.

Macpherson, Hector C. 1899. *Adam Smith*. Oliphant, Anderson, and Ferrier.

Malkin, Arthur Thomas. 1836. *The Gallery of Portraits: with Memoirs*, vol. 6. Charles Knight.

Martin, Marie. 1990. Utility and Morality: Adam Smith's Critique of Hume. *Hume Studies* 16(2): 107–120.

Matson, Erik W. 2017a. The Sympathetic Formation of Reason and the Limits of Science. *Society* 54(3): 246–252.

Matson, Erik W. 2017b. The Dual Account of Reason and the Spirit of Philosophy in Hume's Treatise. *Hume Studies* 43(2): 29–56.

Matson, Erik W. 2022. God, Commerce, and Adam Smith through the Editions of *Theory of Moral Sentiments*. *Journal of Markets and Morality* 24(2): 269–288.

Matson, Erik W. 2022. The Edifying Discourses of Adam Smith: Focalism, Commerce, and Serving the Common Good. *Journal of the History of Economic Thought* 45(2): 298–320.

Matson, Erik W., and Colin Doran. 2017. The Elevated Imagination: Contemplation and Action in David Hume and Adam Smith. *Journal of Scottish Philosophy* 15(1):27–45.

McCloskey, Deirdre N. 1985. *The Rhetoric of Economics*. University of Wisconsin Press.

McCloskey, Deirdre N. 2008. Adam Smith, the Last of the Former Virtue Ethicists. *History of Political Economy* 40(1): 43–71.

McCloskey, Deirdre N. 1995. Some News That at Least Will Not Bore You. *Eastern Economic Journal* 21(4): 551–553.

McCulloch, John Ramsay. 1828. Sketch of the Life of Dr. Smith. In *Wealth of Nations*, by Adam Smith, ed. McCulloch: i–xiii. Black and Tait and Longman.

Melzer, Arthur M. 2001. Anti-anti-Foundationalism: Is a Theory of Moral Sentiments Possible? *Perspectives on Political Science* 30(3): 151–155.

Melzer, Arthur M. 2014. Philosophy between the Lines: *The Lost Art of Esoteric Writing*. University of Chicago Press.

Menand, Louis. 2001. *The Metaphysical Club: A Story of Ideas in America*. Farrar, Straus and Giroux.

Mill, James. 1869. *Analysis of the Phenomena of the Human Mind*, new ed., vol. 2, eds. Alexander Bain, Andrew Findlater, George Grote, and John Stuart Mill. Longmans, Green, Reader and Dyer.

Mill, John Stuart. 1909. *Principles of Political Economy*. Ed. W.J. Ashley. Longman, Green, and Co.

Minowitz, Peter. 1993. *Profits, Priests, and Princes: Adam Smith's Emancipation of Economics from Politics and Religion*. Stanford University Press.

Minowitz, Peter. 2004. Adam Smith's Invisible Hands. *Econ Journal Watch* 1(3): 381–12.

Minowitz, Peter. 2009. *Straussophobia: Defending Leo Strauss and Straussians against Shadia Drury and Other Accusers*. Lexington Books.

Mises, Ludwig von. 1966. *Human Action*. Henry Regnery.

Montagu, Richard. 1642. Acts and Monuments of the Church. London.

Moore, James. 2006. Natural Rights in the Scottish Enlightenment. In *Cambridge History of Eighteenth-Century Political Thought*, eds. M. Goldie and R. Wokler: 291–316. Cambridge University Press.

Morrow, Glenn R. 1923. *The Ethical and Economic Theories of Adam Smith*. Longmans.

Morrow, Glenn R. 1927. Adam Smith: Moralist and Philosopher. *Journal of Political Economy* 35(3): 321–342.

Mossner, Ernest Campbell. 1960. 'Of the Principle of Moral Estimation: A Discourse between David Hume, Robert Clerk, and Adam Smith': An Unpublished MS by Adam Ferguson. *Journal of the History of Ideas* 21(2): 222–232.

Mossner, Ernest Campbell. 1963. Adam Ferguson's 'Dialogue on a Highland Jaunt' with Robert Adam, William Cleghorn, David Hume, and William Wilkie. *In Restoration & Eighteenth-Century Literature: Essays in Honor of Alan Dugald McKillop*, ed. Carroll Camden: 297–308. University of Chicago Press.

Mossner, Ernest Campbell. 2001. *The Life of David Hume*. Oxford University Press.

Mueller, Paul D. 2016. Adam Smith's Impartial Spectator. *Econ Journal Watch* 13(2): 312–318.

Mueller, Paul D. 2021. Adam Smith on Moral Judgment: Why People Tend to Make Better Judgments within Liberal Institutions. *Journal of Economic Behavior and Organization* 184: 813–825.

Murray, Hugh. 1808. *Enquiries Historical and Moral, Respecting the Character of Nations, and the Progress of Society*. Longman.

Norton, David Fate, and J. C. Stewart-Robertson. 1980. Thomas Reid on Adam Smith's Theory of Morals. *Journal of the History of Ideas* 41(3): 381–398.

Norton, David Fate. 2007. Historical Account of *A Treatise of Human Nature* from Its Beginnings to the Time of Hume's Death. In vol. 2 of Hume 2007: 433–588.

Old Radio World. Undated. The Shadow. http://www.oldradioworld.com/shows/The_Shadow.php.

Oslington, Paul. 2012. God and the Market: Adam Smith's Invisible Hands. *Journal of Business Ethics* 108(4): 429–438.

Otteson, James. 2002. *Adam Smith's Marketplace of Life*. Cambridge University Press.

Otteson, James. 2011. How High Does the Impartial Spectator Go? In *Adam Smith as Theologian*, ed. Paul Oslington. Routledge.

Pack, Spencer and Eric Schliesser. 2006. Smith's Humean Criticism of Hume's Account of the Origins of Justice. *Journal of the History of Philosophy* 44(1): 47–63.

Paine, Thomas. 1795. *The Age of Reason, Part II*. Paris: Barrios.

Paley, William. 2002 [1785]. *The Principles of Moral and Political Philosophy*. Liberty Fund.

Patten, Simon N. 1899. *The Development of English Thought: A Study in the Economic Interpretation of History*. Macmillan.

Payne, George. 1828. *Elements of Mental and Moral Science*. Holdsworth.

Peart, Sandra J., and David M. Levy. 2005. *The 'Vanity of the Philosopher': From Equality to Hierarchy in Post-Classical Economics*. University of Michigan Press.

Phillipson, Nicholas. 1973. Towards a Definition of the Scottish Enlightenment. In *City & Society in the 18th Century*. Eds P. Fritz and D. Williams: 125–147. Toronto: Hakkert.

Phillipson, Nicholas. 2010. *Adam Smith: An Enlightened Life*. Yale University Press.

Polanyi, Karl. 1944. *The Great Transformation: The Political and Economic Origins of Our Time*. Reprint: Rinehart & Co.

Polanyi, Michael. 1963. *The Study of Man*. University of Chicago Press.

Polanyi, Michael. 1966. *The Tacit Dimension*. Doubleday & Co.

Prasch, Robert, and Thierry Warin. 2009. Il Est Encore Plus Important de Bien Faire Que de Bien Dire: A Translation and Analysis of Dupont de Nemours' 1788 letter to Adam Smith. *History of Economics Review* 49(1): 67–75.

Prior, Arthur N. 1949. *Logic and the Basis of Ethics*. Clarendon.

Pufendorf, Samuel. 2003. *The Whole Duty of Man, According to the Law of Nature*. Eds. Ian Hunter and David Saunders. Trans. Andrew Tooke (and anonymous editors). Liberty Fund.

Quarterly Theological Review. 1818. Conducted by Rev. Ezra Stiles Ely. Vol. 1. Anthony Finley.

Quine, Willard Van Orman. 1961. *From a Logical Point of View*. 2nd edition. Harvard University Press.

Rae, John. 1895. *Life of Adam Smith*. Macmillan.

Raphael, D. D. 2007. *The Impartial Spectator: Adam Smith's Moral Philosophy*. Clarendon Press.

Raphael, David D. and Alec L. Macfie. 1976. Introduction to Adam Smith's *The Theory of Moral Sentiments*, eds. D. D. Raphael and A.L. Macfie: 1–52. Oxford University Press. Reprint: Liberty Fund, 1982.

Rasmussen, Dennis C. 2008. *The Problems and Promise of Commercial Society: Adam Smith's Response to Rousseau*. Pennsylvania State University Press.

Rasmussen, Dennis C. 2017. *The Infidel and the Professor: David Hume, Adam Smith, and the Friendship that Shaped the Modern World*. Princeton University Press.

Raynor, David R. 1984. Hume's Abstract of Adam Smith's *Theory of Moral Sentiments*. *Journal of the History of Philosophy* 22(1): 51–79.

Reeder, John, ed. 1997. *On Moral Sentiments: Contemporary Responses to Adam Smith*. Bristol: Thoemmes Press.

Reid, Thomas. 1788. *Essay on the Active Powers of Man*. John Bell.

Ridge, Michael. 2003. Epistemology Moralized: David Hume's Practical Epistemology. *Hume Studies* 29(2): 165–204.

Ridpath, George. 1922. *Diary of George Ridpath, Minister of Stitchel, 1755–1761*, ed. James Balfour Paul. Constable.

Robertson, J.M. 1920. *A Short History of Morals*. Watts & Co.

Romilly, Samuel. 1840. *Memoirs of the Life of Sir Samuel Romilly, with a Selection from His Correspondence*, vol. 1. John Murray.

Rose, David C. 2011. *The Moral Foundation of Economic Behavior*. Oxford University Press.

Rose, David. 2019. *Why Culture Matters Most*. Oxford University Press.

Rose, William [unsigned]. 1759. Review of *The Theory of Moral Sentiments*, by Adam Smith. *Monthly Review, or, Literary Journal* 21(July): 1–18.

Ross, Ian Simpson. 2010. *The Life of Adam Smith*, 2nd ed. Oxford University Press.

Rothschild, Emma. 1994. Adam Smith and the Invisible Hand. *American Economic Review*, Papers and Proceedings 84(2): 319–322.

Rothschild, Emma. 2001. *Economic Sentiments: Adam Smith, Condorcet, and the Enlightenment*. Harvard University Press.

Rothschild, Emma. 2004. Dignity or Meanness. *Adam Smith Review* 1: 150–162.

Schelling, Thomas C. 1960. *The Strategy of Conflict*. Harvard University Press.

Schottenstein Edition 1992. *Talmud Bavli: Tractate Kiddushin*, vol 1. Mesorah Publishers.

Scott, William R. 1900. *Francis Hutcheson: His Life, Teaching and Position in the History of Philosophy.* Cambridge University Press.

Scott, William R. 1923. Adam Smith. In *Proceedings of the British Academy,* vol. 10, 435–453. Oxford University Press.

Scott, William R. 1937. *Adam Smith as Student and Professor.* Jackson.

Searle, John R. 1964. How to Derive 'Ought' from 'Is.' *Philosophical Review* 7(1): 43–58.

Searle, John R. 1969. *Speech Acts: An Essay in the Philosophy of Language.* Cambridge University Press.

Shaftesbury, Anthony Ashley Cooper, Earl of. 2001 [1732]. *Characteristicks of Men, Manners, Opinions, Times.* Liberty Fund.

Shakespeare, William. 1623. *Merry Wives of Windsor.*

Shera, Marcus. 2022. William James' Pragmatism and Adam Smith's Moral Sentiments. Adam Smith Works (Liberty Fund), August 24.

G. Findlay. 1941. Obituary: James Bonar (1852–1941). *Economic Journal* 51(201): 145–156.

Shouse, J. B. 1952. David Hume and William James: A Comparison. *Journal of the History of Ideas* 13(4): 514–527.

Sidgwick, Henry. 1896. *Outlines of the History of Ethics for English Readers,* 4th ed. Macmillan.

Siedentop, Larry. 2014. *Inventing the Individual: The Origins of Western Liberalism.* Allen Lane.

Small, Albion W. 1907. *Adam Smith and Modern Sociology.* University of Chicago Press.

Smith, Adam. 1976 [1776] (WN). *An Inquiry into the Nature and Causes of the Wealth of Nations.* eds. R.H. Campbell and A.S. Skinner. Oxford University Press. Reprint: Liberty Fund, 1981.

Smith, Adam. 1976 [1790] (TMS). *The Theory of Moral Sentiments,* eds. D. D. Raphael and A. L. Macfie. Oxford University Press. Reprint: Liberty Fund, 1985.

Smith, Adam. 1978 (LJ). *Lectures on Jurisprudence,* eds. R. L. Meek, D. D. Raphael, and P. G. Stein. Oxford University Press. Reprint: Liberty Fund, 1982.

Smith, Adam. 1980 (EPS). *Essays on Philosophical Subjects,* eds. W. P. D. Wightman and J. C. Bryce. Oxford University Press. Reprint: Liberty Fund, 1982.

Smith, Adam. 1983 [1761]. Considerations Concerning the First Formation of Languages. Reproduced in Smith's *Lectures on Rhetoric and Belles Lettres,* ed. J.C. Bryce: 203–226. Oxford University Press. Reprint: Liberty Fund, 1985.

Smith, Adam. 1983 [1762–1764]. (LRBL). *Lectures on Rhetoric and Belles Lettres,* ed. J. C. Bryce. Oxford: Clarendon Press.

Smith, Adam. 1999. *Théorie des Sentiments Moraux,* trans. Michaël Biziou, Claude Gautier, and Jean-François Pradeau. Paris: PUF.

Smith, Craig. 2006. *Adam Smith's Political Philosophy: The Invisible Hand and Spontaneous Order.* Routledge.

Smith, Craig. 2016. Peer Review and the Development of the Impartial Spectator. *Econ Journal Watch* 13(2): 324–29.

Smith, Norman Kemp. 1941. *The Philosophy of David Hume.* Macmillan Press.

Stein, Solomon M. 2014. Coordination: Descriptive or Normative?: A Response to Daniel B. Klein's *Knowledge and Coordination. Studies in Emergent Order* 7: 41–55.

Stephen, Leslie. 1876. *History of English Thought in the Eighteenth Century,* vol. 2. Smith, Elder & Co.

Stewart, Dugald. 1829. *The Philosophy of the Active and Moral Powers of Man* (*The Works of Dugald Stewart*, vol. 5). Cambridge, UK: Hilliard and Brown.

Stewart, Dugald. 1982 [1795]. *An Account of the Life and Writings of Adam Smith, LL.D.* Ed. Ian Simpson Ross. *In Essays on Philosophical Subjects*, by Adam Smith: 269–351. Oxford University Press.

Stewart-Robertson, J. C., and David Fate Norton. 1984. Thomas Reid on Adam Smith's Theory of Morals. *Journal of the History of Ideas* 45(2): 309–321.

Strauss, Leo. 1952. *Persecution and the Art of Writing*. University of Chicago Press.

Taylor, Overton H. 1960. *A History of Economic Thought: Social Ideals and Economic Theories from Quesnay to Keynes*. McGraw-Hill.

Turner, Daniel. 1729. *The Art of Surgery*, vol 2. C. Rivington.

Turner, Daniel. 1731. *De Morbis Cutaneis: A Treatise of Diseases Incident to the Skin*. J. Walthoe.

Tytler, A. F., Lord Woodhouselee. 1814. *Memoirs of the Life and Writings of the Honourable Henry Home of Kames*, 3 vols., 2nd ed. T. Cadell and W. Davies.

Vaughn, Karen I. 1983. Invisible Hand. In *The New Palgrave* 2:997–99. Macmillan.

Viner, Jacob. 1927. Adam Smith and Laissez-Faire. *Journal of Political Economy* 35(2): 198–232.

Voltaire. 1755. Letter to Jean-Jacques Rousseau. English translation online at: https://courses.washington.edu/hsteu302/Voltaire%20Letter%20to%20Rousseau.htm.

Wardlaw, Ralph. 1833. *Christian Ethic; or, Moral Philosophy on the Principles of Divine Revelation*. Jackson and Walford.

Weinstein, Jack Russell. 2016. My Understanding of Adam Smith's Impartial Spectator. *Econ Journal Watch* 13(2): 351–58.

West, E. G. 1976. *Adam Smith: The Man and His Works*. Liberty Fund.

Westermarck, Edward. 2023. Edward Westermarck's Lectures on Adam Smith. Translation of 1914 lectures and Foreword by Otto Pipatti. *Econ Journal Watch* 20(1): 139–158.

Wierzbicka, Anna. 2006. English: Meaning and Culture. Oxford University Press.

Wilson, Matthew. 2023. Five Hidden Symbols in Vermeer's Paintings. BBC, February 20.

Windelband, Wilhelm. 1901. *A History of Philosophy*, trans. J. H. Tufts. Macmillan.

Winters, Barbara. 1979. Hume on Reason. *Hume Studies* 5(1): 20–35.

Witherspoon, John. 1822. *Lectures on Moral Philosophy*. Philadelphia: W. W. Woodward.

Young, Jeffrey T. 1992. Natural Morality and the Ideal Impartial Spectator in Adam Smith. *International Journal of Social Economics* 19(10/11/12): 71–82.

Zemach, E. M. 1971. Ought, Is, and a Game Called 'Promise.' *Philosophical Quarterly* 21(82): 61–63.

Zuckert, Michael P. 1994. *Natural Rights and the New Republicanism*. Princeton University Press.

Index

CL Press

A Fraser Institute Project

https://clpress.net/

Professor Daniel Klein (George Mason University, Economics and Mercatus Center) and Dr. Erik Matson (Mercatus Center), directors of the Adam Smith Program at George Mason University, are the editors and directors of CL Press. CL stands at once for classical liberal and conservative liberal.

CL Press is a project of the Fraser Institute (Vancouver, Canada).

People:

Dan Klein and **Erik Matson** are the co-editors and executives of the imprint.

Jane Shaw Stroup is Editorial Advisor, doing especially copy-editing and text preparation.

Zachary Yost is Production Manager of CL Reprints.

Advisory Board:

Marc Sidwell, *New Culture Forum*

Craig Smith, *Univ. of Glasgow*

Emily Skarbek, *Brown Univ.*

David Walsh, *Catholic Univ. of America*

Richard Whatmore, *Univ. of St. Andrews*

Barry Weingast, *Stanford Univ.*

Lawrence H. White, *George Mason Univ.*

Amy Willis, *Liberty Fund*

Bart Wilson, *Chapman Univ.*

Todd Zywicki, *George Mason Univ.*

Why start CL Press?

CL Press publishes good, low-priced work in intellectual history, political theory, political economy, and moral philosophy. More specifically, CL Press explores and advance discourse in the following areas:

- The intellectual history and meaning of liberalism.

- The relationship between liberalism and conservatism.

- The role of religion in disseminating liberal understandings and institutions including: humankind's ethical universalism, the moral equality of souls, the rule of law, religious liberty, the meaning and virtues of economic life.

- The relationship between religion and economic philosophy.

- The political, social, and economic philosophy of the Scottish Enlightenment, especially Adam Smith.

- The state of classically liberal ideas and policies across the world today.

www.ingramcontent.com/pod-product-compliance
Lightning Source LLC
Chambersburg PA
CBHW011219120626
46545CB00010B/3071